First World War
and Army of Occupation
War Diary
France, Belgium and Germany

15 DIVISION
44 Infantry Brigade
Queen's Own Cameron Highlanders
7th Battalion
4 July 1915 - 14 August 1918

WO95/1941/1

The Naval & Military Press Ltd
www.nmarchive.com
Published in association with The National Archives

Published by

The Naval & Military Press Ltd

Unit 10 Ridgewood Industrial Park,

Uckfield, East Sussex,

TN22 5QE England

Tel: +44 (0) 1825 749494

www.naval-military-press.com

www.nmarchive.com

This diary has been reprinted in facsimile from the original. Any imperfections are inevitably reproduced and the quality may fall short of modern type and cartographic standards.

© **Crown Copyright**
Images reproduced by permission of The National Archives, London, England, 2015.

Contents

Document type	Place/Title	Date From	Date To
Heading	WO95/1941/1 1915 Jul-1918 Ag 7 Battalion Cameron Highlanders 15 Div 44 Inf Brig		
Heading	15th Division 44th Infy Bde 7th Bn Cameron Hdrs Jly 1915 Aug 1918 Disbanded 14 8.18		
Heading	44/15th Division 7th Cameron Highlanders: Vol. I-31.7.15 7th Cameron July 1915 Aug 18 1s1/ 6250		
Heading	Confidential War Diary of Seventh (S) Battalion Queen Own Cameron Highlanders From 3rd July 1915 To 31st July 1915		
War Diary	Park House Tidworth	04/07/1915	04/07/1915
War Diary	Tidworth Stn.	07/07/1915	08/07/1915
War Diary	Southampton	08/07/1915	08/07/1915
War Diary	Boulogne	09/07/1915	09/07/1915
War Diary	Havre	09/07/1915	09/07/1915
War Diary	Boulogne	10/07/1915	10/07/1915
War Diary	Pont Des Briques (Boulogne)	10/07/1915	10/07/1915
War Diary	Watten	10/07/1915	10/07/1915
War Diary	Houlle	10/07/1915	15/07/1915
War Diary	Hazebrouck.	15/07/1915	16/07/1915
War Diary	Gonnehem	16/07/1915	17/07/1915
War Diary	Houchin	18/07/1915	18/07/1915
War Diary	Les Brebis	18/07/1915	24/07/1915
War Diary	Houchin	25/07/1915	31/07/1915
Heading	15th Division 7th Cameron Highlanders Vol.II August 15 7th Cameron August 1915 121/6754		
War Diary	Houchin	01/08/1915	02/08/1915
War Diary	In Trenches Sub Sector W.I.	02/08/1915	02/08/1915
War Diary	In Trenches W.I.	02/08/1915	02/08/1915
War Diary	In Trenches	10/08/1915	10/08/1915
War Diary	Mazingarbe	11/08/1915	18/08/1915
War Diary	In Trenches	19/08/1915	26/08/1915
War Diary	Mazingarbe	27/08/1915	28/08/1915
War Diary	Noeux Les Mines	30/08/1915	31/08/1915
Heading	44th Inf. Bde. 15th Div. War Diary 7th Battn. The Cameron Highlanders. September 1915.		
Heading	War Diary.		
War Diary	Noeux Les Mines	01/09/1915	07/09/1915
War Diary	In Trenches	07/09/1915	12/09/1915
War Diary	Verquin	12/09/1915	21/09/1915
War Diary	Grenay. Vermelles Line	22/09/1915	29/09/1915
Miscellaneous	Report On Operations 25th/26th September.		
Miscellaneous	Headquarters, 44th Infantry Brigade.	28/09/1915	28/09/1915
Miscellaneous	Battalion Operation Orders.		
Miscellaneous	Battalion Orders By Lt-Colonel J.W. Sandilands, D.S.O., commanding 7th (Service) Battalion Cameron Highlanders.	12/09/1915	12/09/1915
Operation(al) Order(s)	Operation Order No. 1 By Lt-Colonel J.W. Sandilands, D.S.O., Commanding 7th (Service) Battalion Cameron Highlanders.	19/09/1915	19/09/1915

Operation(al) Order(s)	Operation Order No. 2. By Lieut-Colonel J.W. Sandilands. Commanding 7th Battalion Cameron Highlanders.	20/09/1915	20/09/1915
Heading	Notes On Attack.		
Miscellaneous	7th Battalion Cameron Highlanders. Notes On Attack. War Diary		
Heading	15th Division 7th Cameron Highrs Oct.I Vol IV October 1915		
War Diary	Houchin	01/10/1915	02/10/1915
War Diary	Lillers	03/10/1915	12/10/1915
War Diary	Nceux Les Morice	13/10/1915	31/10/1915
Heading	15th Division 7th Cameron Highrs Vol.5 7th Cameron November 1915 Vol 15		
War Diary	Trenches	01/11/1915	06/11/1915
War Diary	Nceux-Les Mories	09/11/1915	12/11/1915
War Diary	Trenches D.1.	13/11/1915	16/11/1915
War Diary	Trenches	16/11/1915	24/11/1915
War Diary	Naux	24/11/1915	25/11/1915
War Diary	Sailly La Bourse	26/11/1915	30/11/1915
Heading	7th Camerons December 1915 7th Cameron Highrs Vol. 6 5th Div 44th Bde		
War Diary	Trenches C.I.	01/12/1915	08/12/1915
War Diary	Trenches	09/12/1915	14/12/1915
War Diary	Allouagne	15/12/1915	31/12/1915
Heading	7th Cameron Highrs Vol.7		
War Diary	Allouagne	01/01/1916	05/01/1916
War Diary	Rely	06/01/1916	07/01/1916
War Diary	Allouagne	08/01/1916	13/01/1916
War Diary	Trenches Loos.	14/01/1916	14/01/1916
War Diary	Trenches Loos. Hill 70. Section 14. Bis	15/01/1916	25/01/1916
War Diary	Philosophe	26/01/1916	26/01/1916
War Diary	Noeux Les Mines	27/01/1916	31/01/1916
Heading	7th Bn Cameron Highlanders February 1916		
War Diary	Hulluch Section.	01/02/1916	03/02/1916
War Diary	Philosophe	04/02/1916	06/02/1916
War Diary	Hulluch Section	07/02/1916	12/02/1916
War Diary	Noeux-Les-Mines	13/02/1916	18/02/1916
War Diary	14 Bis Section.	19/02/1916	29/02/1916
Heading	7th Bn Cameron Highlanders March 1916		
Heading	7 Camerons Vol 9 XV 44		
War Diary	14 Bis Section	01/03/1916	01/03/1916
War Diary	Mazingarbe	02/03/1916	07/03/1916
War Diary	Hulluch Section	08/03/1916	13/03/1916
War Diary	Philosophe	14/03/1916	16/03/1916
War Diary	Hulluch Section	17/03/1916	19/03/1916
War Diary	Noeux-Les Mines	20/03/1916	24/03/1916
War Diary	Allouagne	25/03/1916	31/03/1916
Heading	7th Bn Cameron Highlander April 1916		
War Diary	Allouagne	01/04/1916	26/04/1916
War Diary	Trenches Left Sub-Section Germany Sector	26/04/1916	30/04/1916
Heading	7th Bn Cameron Highlanders May 1916		
War Diary	Noyelles & Vermelles	01/05/1916	03/05/1916
War Diary	Left Sub-Section Luarry Section	04/05/1916	11/05/1916
War Diary	Labourse	11/05/1916	14/05/1916
War Diary	Noyelles	14/05/1916	19/05/1916
War Diary	Left Sub-Section Nohngallern Section	19/05/1916	23/05/1916

War Diary	Brigade Support Hohenzollern Section		23/05/1916	26/05/1916
War Diary	Right Sub-Section Hohenzollern Section		27/05/1916	31/05/1916
Heading	7th Bn Cameron Highlanders June 1916			
War Diary	Right Sub Section Hohenzollern Section		01/06/1916	03/06/1916
War Diary	Bethune		04/06/1916	11/06/1916
War Diary	Brigade Support Hulluch Section		12/06/1916	15/06/1916
War Diary	Right Sub Section Hulluch Section		16/06/1916	29/06/1916
War Diary	Bethune & Verquineul		29/06/1916	30/06/1916
Heading	7th Bn Cameron Highlanders July 1916			
Heading	War Diary of Seventh (S) Battalion Cameron Highlanders From 1st July 1916 To 31st July. 1916 15 July 7 Cameron Vol 12			
War Diary	Bethune & Verquineul		01/07/1916	05/07/1916
War Diary	Left Sub-Section Hohenzollern Section.		06/07/1916	10/07/1916
War Diary	Brigade Support Hohenzollern Section		11/07/1916	13/07/1916
War Diary	Right Sub. Section. Hohenzollern Section		14/07/1916	21/07/1916
War Diary	Houchin		22/07/1916	22/07/1916
War Diary	Dieval		23/07/1916	25/07/1916
War Diary	Gouy-en-Ternois		26/07/1916	26/07/1916
War Diary	Occoches		27/07/1916	27/07/1916
War Diary	Autheux		28/07/1916	30/07/1916
War Diary	Naours		31/07/1916	31/07/1916
Heading	44th Brigade. 15th Division. 1/7th Battalion Highlanders August 1916			
War Diary	Naours		01/08/1916	03/08/1916
War Diary	Mirvaux		04/08/1916	04/08/1916
War Diary	Lahoussoye		05/08/1916	07/08/1916
War Diary	Albert		08/08/1916	11/08/1916
War Diary	E.5.b.7.6		12/08/1916	13/08/1916
War Diary	X22.a. (Peakewood)		14/08/1916	15/08/1916
War Diary	B. Area The Cutting		16/08/1916	16/08/1916
War Diary	A Area (Front Line)		17/08/1916	17/08/1916
War Diary	C Area		18/08/1916	19/08/1916
War Diary	B. Area		20/08/1916	21/08/1916
War Diary	A Area		22/08/1916	23/08/1916
War Diary	Scotts Redoubt		24/08/1916	25/08/1916
War Diary	C Area		26/08/1916	27/08/1916
War Diary	B. Area		28/08/1916	29/08/1916
War Diary	Bivouac OB. Trench X.26.d.		30/08/1916	31/08/1916
War Diary	A Area		17/08/1916	17/08/1916
War Diary	Appendix H3 Attack By 7th Cameron Highlanders On Switch Line		19/08/1916	19/08/1916
Heading	War Diary of 7th (Service) Battalion Cameron Highlanders For Month Of September 1916 Pages 114 To 125 Inclusive Vol 15 44/15			
War Diary	Bivouac. B 1 X.26.d		01/09/1916	04/09/1916
War Diary	Front Line Right Bde Area		05/09/1916	06/09/1916
War Diary	O.G.1 Between S.7.c.2.1 And S.1n.a.3.6		07/09/1916	09/09/1916
War Diary	B. Area		10/09/1916	10/09/1916
War Diary	Front Line		11/09/1916	11/09/1916
War Diary	Sanderson Trench		11/09/1916	11/09/1916
War Diary	Front Line		11/09/1916	12/09/1916
War Diary	Bivouac E.7. Central		13/09/1916	13/09/1916
War Diary	Shelter Wood Birch Wood Round Wood		14/09/1916	15/09/1916
War Diary	Shelter Wood Koyli Trenches		16/09/1916	18/09/1916
War Diary	Bivouac E.b.5. And Lavieville		19/09/1916	19/09/1916

War Diary	Franvillers	20/09/1916	30/09/1916
Heading	War Diary of 7th (Service) Battalion Cameron Highlanders For October 1916 Pages 126 To 138 Inclusive Vol 16 Original		
War Diary	Franvillers	01/10/1916	05/10/1916
War Diary	Becourt Wood	06/10/1916	07/10/1916
War Diary	Crescent Alley	08/10/1916	10/10/1916
War Diary	Front Line	11/10/1916	12/10/1916
War Diary	Crescent Alley	13/10/1916	13/10/1916
War Diary	Contalmaison Cuttins	14/10/1916	18/10/1916
War Diary	Right Sect Front Area	19/10/1916	20/10/1916
War Diary	Area Front Line	21/10/1916	22/10/1916
War Diary	B. Area	23/10/1916	23/10/1916
War Diary	Contalmaison Cutting	24/10/1916	26/10/1916
War Diary	C Area Starfish Line	27/10/1916	29/10/1916
War Diary	Front Line	30/10/1916	30/10/1916
Miscellaneous			
Heading	7th Bn Cameron Highlanders Nov 1916		
Heading	7th (Service) Battalion Cameron Highlanders. War Diary For Period 1st To 30th November Inclusive Pp. 139 To 144 Ind.		
War Diary	D Area Reserve Becourt Hill.	01/11/1916	04/11/1916
War Diary	Bresle	05/11/1916	30/11/1916
Miscellaneous	7th (Service) Battalion Cameron Highlanders. Programme Of Work Reference In War Diary 1st To 30th 1916	07/11/1916	07/11/1916
Miscellaneous	7th (Service) Battalion Cameron Highlanders.	12/11/1916	12/11/1916
Miscellaneous	7th (Service) Battalion Cameron Highlanders. Training Programme For Week Commencing 19th November 1916.	19/11/1916	19/11/1916
Miscellaneous	7th (Service) Battalion Cameron Highlanders. Training Programme For Week Commencing 26th November 1916.	26/11/1916	26/11/1916
Heading	7th Bn Cameron Highlanders December 1916		
Heading	Confidential War Diary of 7th (S)Battalion Cameron Highlanders. From 1st To 31st December 1916 Pp 145 To 153 Lied Vol 18		
War Diary	Albert	01/12/1916	06/12/1916
War Diary	Camp X 23 Centre	07/12/1916	15/12/1916
War Diary	Shelter Wood Scots Redoubt North	16/12/1916	18/12/1916
War Diary	C I D Drop South	19/12/1916	20/12/1916
War Diary	Front Line 26th Avenue	21/12/1916	24/12/1916
War Diary	Acid Drop Campso	25/12/1916	25/12/1916
War Diary	Shelter Wood South	26/12/1916	30/12/1916
War Diary	?	31/12/1916	31/12/1916
Heading	7th (S) Battn. The Cameron Highlanders January, 1917		
Heading	War Diary of 7th (Service) Battalion Cameron Highlanders Period From 1st To 31st January (Inclusive)1917 Pp 155 To 162 Vol 19 44th Bde 15 Div		
War Diary	Front Line Right Section	01/01/1917	03/01/1917
War Diary	Support Area	04/01/1917	06/01/1917
War Diary	Pioneer Camp	07/01/1917	07/01/1917
War Diary	Scots Redoubt North	08/01/1917	11/01/1917
War Diary	Villa Camp	12/01/1917	13/01/1917
War Diary	Acid Drop Copse	14/01/1917	15/01/1917
War Diary	Front Line	16/01/1917	17/01/1917

War Diary	Right Battn Left Sub Sector	18/01/1917	19/01/1917
War Diary	Scotts Redoubt North Camp	20/01/1917	23/01/1917
War Diary	Front Line	24/01/1917	27/01/1917
War Diary	Support Line	28/01/1917	28/01/1917
War Diary	Support Line 7 Elms.	29/01/1917	29/01/1917
War Diary	Reserve Pioneer Camp	30/01/1917	30/01/1917
War Diary	Pioneer Camp	31/01/1917	31/01/1917
Heading	7th (S) Battn. The Cameron Highlanders February, 1917		
Heading	Confidential. War Diary of 7th (Service) Battalion Cameron Highrs From 1st To 28th February 1917 Issued Pp.163 To 168 Mid Vol 20		
War Diary	Pioneer Camp	01/02/1917	01/02/1917
War Diary	Becourt Camp	02/02/1917	03/02/1917
War Diary	Contay	04/02/1917	13/02/1917
War Diary	Beauval	14/02/1917	14/02/1917
War Diary	Gazaincourt	15/02/1917	15/02/1917
War Diary	Bouquemaison	16/02/1917	16/02/1917
War Diary	Croisette	17/02/1917	17/02/1917
War Diary	Moncheaux	18/02/1917	24/02/1917
War Diary	Maisieres	24/02/1917	28/02/1917
Miscellaneous	7th (Service) Battalion Cameron Highlanders. Training Programme For Week Commencing 4th February 1917. Appendix No.1	04/02/1917	04/02/1917
Miscellaneous	7th (Service) Battalion Cameron Highlanders Training Programme For Week Commencing 18 February 1917. Appendix No.2	18/02/1917	18/02/1917
Miscellaneous			
Miscellaneous	Training Programme For Week Ending 3rd March 1917 7th Battalion Cameron Highlanders. Appendix No.3	03/03/1917	03/03/1917
Heading	Subject 7th Cameron Highlanders March 1917		
Heading	Original War Diary of 7th (Service) Battalion Cameron Highlanders For Month Of March, 1917 Pages 169 To 182 Inclusive Appendixes 1 To 4. Vol 21		
War Diary	Maisieres	01/03/1917	10/03/1917
War Diary	Arras	11/03/1917	19/03/1917
War Diary	Harbarq	20/03/1917	25/03/1917
War Diary	Arras	26/03/1917	31/03/1917
Miscellaneous	Appendix		
Miscellaneous	7th (Service) Battalion Cameron Highlanders. Orders For Tactical Exercise At Trenches At Lignereuil, On Wednesday, 7th March 1917.	07/03/1917	07/03/1917
Miscellaneous	7th (Service) Bn Cameron Highlanders. Orders For Tactical Exercise At Trenches At Lignereuil, On Friday, 9th March 1917	09/03/1917	09/03/1917
Miscellaneous	44th Infantry Brigade Tactical Exercise To Be Held On 9th March 1917	09/03/1917	09/03/1917
Miscellaneous	7th (Service) Battalion Cameron Highlanders Training Programme For Week Ending 10.3.17	10/03/1917	10/03/1917
Miscellaneous	44th Infantry Brigade Operation Report On Raid Carried Out By The 7th Cameron Hrs. On The 18th March, 1917.	18/03/1917	18/03/1917
Miscellaneous	7th (Service) Battalion Cameron Highlanders Order For Tactical Exercise at Trenches at Lignereuil on Monday 5th March 1917.	05/03/1917	05/03/1917

Miscellaneous	Unit:- 7th (Service) Battalion Cameron Highlanders Programme Of Training For Week Ending 31st March 1917.	31/03/1917	31/03/1917
Heading	Subject 7th Cameron Highlanders. April 1917 Q 20 44/15		
Heading	War Diary of 7th (Service) Battalion Cameron Highlanders Month Of April 1917 Pages 182 To 199 Vol 22		
War Diary	Arras	01/04/1917	09/04/1917
War Diary	Front Line	09/04/1917	11/04/1917
War Diary	Arras Front	11/04/1917	11/04/1917
War Diary	Arras	12/04/1917	22/04/1917
War Diary	Arras Front Line	23/04/1917	23/04/1917
War Diary	Arras	23/04/1917	28/04/1917
War Diary	Simincourt	29/04/1917	30/04/1917
Miscellaneous	7th (Service) Battalion Queens Own Cameron Highlanders, Notes On Operations. 22nd/28th April 1917.	22/04/1917	22/04/1917
Heading	Subject. 7th Cameron Highlanders May 1917 Q21 44/15		
Heading	Original War Diary of 7th (Service) Battalion Cameron Highlanders, Pages 199 To 206 Inclusive For Month Of May 1917 Vol 23		
War Diary	Simincourt	01/05/1917	07/05/1917
War Diary	Grand Rullecourt	08/05/1917	20/05/1917
War Diary	Vacqueril Le Boucq	21/05/1917	21/05/1917
War Diary	St. Georges	22/05/1917	31/05/1917
Heading	Subject. 7th Cameron Highlanders. June 1917		
Heading	War Diary of 7th (Service) Battalion Cameron Highrs For Month Of June 1917 Pages 207 To 219 Inclusive Vol 24 Original		
War Diary	St. Georges.	01/06/1917	20/06/1917
War Diary	Croix	21/06/1917	21/06/1917
War Diary	Pernes	22/06/1917	22/06/1917
War Diary	Bourecq	23/06/1917	24/06/1917
War Diary	Steenbecque	25/06/1917	25/06/1917
War Diary	St. Sylvestre Cappel	26/06/1917	26/06/1917
War Diary	Vlamertinghe	27/06/1917	30/06/1917
Heading	Subject. 7th Cameron Highlanders July 1917 44/15 Q23		
Heading	War Diary of 7th (Service) Battalion Cameron Highlanders For July, 1917 Pages 215 To 225 Inclusive Original Vol 25		
War Diary	Vlamertinghe Eerie Camp.	01/07/1917	01/07/1917
War Diary	In Support E. Of Ypres Menin Road.	02/07/1917	02/07/1917
War Diary	In Support Menin Road	03/07/1917	04/07/1917
War Diary	Front Line Dragoons Farm	05/07/1917	05/07/1917
War Diary	Dragoon Farm	05/07/1917	08/07/1917
War Diary	Vlamertinghe Eerie Camp	09/07/1917	09/07/1917
War Diary	Rubrouck Training Area	10/07/1917	16/07/1917
War Diary	Winnezeele Billeting Area.	17/07/1917	17/07/1917
War Diary	Toronto Camp Brandhoek	18/07/1917	20/07/1917
War Diary	Camp At H.16.a.5.8.	21/07/1917	22/07/1917
War Diary	Front Line Railway Dagant At South Lane	23/07/1917	28/07/1917
War Diary	Camp At H.16.d.5.8	29/07/1917	30/07/1917
War Diary	I 10.d.5.5 South Lane	31/07/1917	31/07/1917
Miscellaneous	War Diary.	02/08/1917	02/08/1917

Heading	Subject. 7th Cameron Highlanders. August 1917 Q 24 44/15		
Heading	War Diary of 7th (Service) Battalion Cameron Highrs For Month Of August 1917 Pages 227 To 237 Inclusive Original Vol 26		
War Diary	German Reserve Line	01/08/1917	01/08/1917
War Diary	Front Line.	02/08/1917	02/08/1917
War Diary	Camp H. 16.	03/08/1917	04/08/1917
War Diary	Winnizeele. In Camp.	05/08/1917	05/08/1917
War Diary	In Camp.	06/08/1917	17/08/1917
War Diary	Brandhoek Camp.	18/08/1917	19/08/1917
War Diary	Bivouac Camp. 8.17.A.1.9.	20/08/1917	20/08/1917
War Diary	Pommern Castle	21/08/1917	24/08/1917
War Diary	Erie Camp	25/08/1917	30/08/1917
War Diary	No. 2 Area Watou	31/08/1917	31/08/1917
Heading	Subject. 7th Cameron Highlanders. September 1917 Q25		
Heading	7th (Service) Battalion Cameron Highlanders War Diary For Above Unit Pages 238 To 243 Inclusive Month Of September, 1917 Original Copy Vol 27		
War Diary	Watou No. 2 Area.	01/09/1917	01/09/1917
War Diary	Montenescourt.	02/09/1917	07/09/1917
War Diary	Blangy Park.	08/09/1917	14/09/1917
War Diary	In Trenches.	15/09/1917	22/09/1917
War Diary	Middlesex Camp.	23/09/1917	30/09/1917
Heading	Subject. 7th Cameron Highlanders October 1917 Q26		
Heading	War Diary of 7th (Service) Battalion Cameron Highlanders From 1st October 1917 To 31st October 1917 Pages 244 To 248 Vol 28		
War Diary	Middlesex Camp	01/10/1917	01/10/1917
War Diary	Barrosa Camp	02/10/1917	09/10/1917
War Diary	And In The Trenches.	09/10/1917	09/10/1917
War Diary	In The Trenches.	09/10/1917	17/10/1917
War Diary	Rifle Camp	18/10/1917	25/10/1917
War Diary	Oil Works Arras	26/10/1917	31/10/1917
Heading	Subject 7th Cameron Highlanders. November 1917 Q 27		
Heading	Confidential War Diary of 7th (S) Bn Cameron Highrs For The Month Of November 1917 Vol 29		
War Diary	Oil Works. Arras.	01/11/1917	02/11/1917
War Diary	In The Trenches	03/11/1917	10/11/1917
War Diary	Rifle Camp.	11/11/1917	14/11/1917
War Diary	Near Fampoux. In Trenches	14/11/1917	18/11/1917
War Diary	Oil Works Arras.	19/11/1917	26/11/1917
War Diary	Wilderness Camp	27/11/1917	28/11/1917
War Diary	Oil Works Arras	29/11/1917	30/11/1917
Heading	Subject. 7th Cameron Highlanders. December 1917 Q 28		
Heading	War Diary 7th (Service) Battalion Cameron Highlanders 1/12/17 To 31/12/17 Pages 253 To 256 Vol 30		
War Diary	Oil Works Arras.	01/12/1917	01/12/1917
War Diary	In The Trenches.	08/12/1917	15/12/1917
War Diary	In The Trenches Support Battn	17/12/1917	18/12/1917
War Diary	Ecole Des Jeunes Filles. Arras.	19/12/1917	23/12/1917
War Diary	In The Trenches.	27/12/1917	31/12/1917
Heading	7th Bn Cameron Highlanders Jan-Feb 1918		

Heading	War Diary 7th (Service) Battalion Cameron Highlanders From 1st January 1918 To 31st January 1918 Volume 31 Pages 257 To 260.		
War Diary	In The Trenches	01/01/1918	02/01/1918
War Diary	Ecole Des Jeunes Filles.	03/01/1918	31/01/1918
War Diary	War Diary of 7th (Service) Battalion Cameron Highlanders. Pages Nos 261, 262, 263, For Month Of February 1918 Vol 32		
War Diary	Ecole Des Jeunes Filles.	01/02/1918	05/02/1918
War Diary	In The Trenches	08/02/1918	08/02/1918
War Diary	Bois Des Boeufs Camp	10/02/1918	11/02/1918
War Diary	In The Trenches	17/02/1918	23/02/1918
War Diary	Bois Des Boeufs Camp	25/02/1918	28/02/1918
Heading	44th Brigade. 15th Division 7th Battalion Cameron Highlanders March 1918		
Heading	War Diary of 7th (S) Bn. Cameron Highrs For The Month Of March 1918 Vol 33 Pages 264 To 267		
War Diary	Bois Des Boeufs.	01/03/1918	01/03/1918
War Diary	In Support. In The Trenches	07/03/1918	09/03/1918
War Diary	In Reserve Bois Des Boeufs.	13/03/1918	14/03/1918
War Diary	Bois Des Boeufs.	15/03/1918	19/03/1918
War Diary	In The Trenches.	20/03/1918	29/03/1918
War Diary	Wanquetin.	30/03/1918	30/03/1918
War Diary	Arras.	31/03/1918	31/03/1918
War Diary	Les Fosses Farm	22/03/1918	23/03/1918
War Diary	Army Line	23/03/1918	23/03/1918
War Diary	Old Support Line	23/03/1918	23/03/1918
War Diary	Support Area.	23/03/1918	24/03/1918
War Diary	Front Line	25/03/1918	28/03/1918
War Diary	Front Line	28/03/1916	29/03/1916
Map	Appendix 1.		
Map	France Appendix 2.		
Miscellaneous	Copy Memo 2/ Lt S.R. Smith A Coy 6th Cam Hrs to Lt Col N Macleod 7 Camerons Hrs Appendix 3		
Miscellaneous	Evidence Of 10495 L/Reg. A M Innes		
Miscellaneous			
Miscellaneous	The Masonic Club, Alexandria Egypt	06/01/1921	06/01/1921
Miscellaneous			
Miscellaneous	Extract From A Paper. (Date And Paper Unknown.) Scottish Gallantry.		
Map	J. Corps. T.S. No. 87 (b) Issued 23.10.17		
Map	H.L. Parker Masonie Club Alexandria Egypt		
Heading	15th Div. 44th Bde. War Diary 7th Battalion The Cameron Highlanders April 1918		
Heading	7th (S) Bn Cameron Highlanders. War Diary Pages 268 To 272 From 1st April 1918 To 30th April 1918 Vol. 34		
War Diary	Arras	01/04/1918	01/04/1918
War Diary	In Reserve In The Trenches.	02/04/1918	02/04/1918
War Diary	In The Trenches Arras.	03/04/1918	03/04/1918
War Diary	Arras.	04/04/1918	08/04/1918
War Diary	In The Trenches Arras.	09/04/1918	13/04/1918
War Diary	Arras.	13/04/1918	18/04/1918
War Diary	In The Trenches.	20/04/1918	24/04/1918
War Diary	Berneville.	24/04/1918	25/04/1918
War Diary	Auchel.	26/04/1918	30/04/1918

Type	Description	Start	End
Heading	7th Bn Cameron Highlanders May-Aug 1918		
Heading	War Diary of 7th (Service) Battalion Cameron Highlanders Pages 273 To 275 From 1st May 1918 To 31st May 1918 Vol 35		
War Diary	Auchel.	01/05/1918	04/05/1918
War Diary	Y. Huts Etrun.	05/05/1918	06/05/1918
War Diary	Support Area Arras-Lens Rd.	08/05/1918	10/05/1918
War Diary	In The Trenches.	10/05/1918	17/05/1918
War Diary	In Support Area Stirling Camp.	17/05/1918	25/05/1918
War Diary	Brigade In Divisional Reserve	25/05/1918	31/05/1918
Miscellaneous	Honours Awarded To The 7th Battalion Queen Own Cameron Highlanders		
Heading	Training Cadre 39th Division 118th Infy. Bde. 7th Bn. Q.O. Cameron Hdrs Jun-Aug 1918		
Heading	War Diary of 7th Battalion The Queen's Own Cameron Highlanders Training Staff From 1/6/18 To 30/6/18 Pages 276-280 (Both Inclusive) Vol 36 118/39 With 118 Bde 39 Div 10.6.18		
War Diary	Portsmouth Camp 8: Near Roclincourt	01/06/1918	07/06/1918
War Diary	Arras.	10/06/1918	10/06/1918
War Diary	Lens 11. 1/100,000. Maroeuil. Lens 3.I.5.9. & Hazebrouck. 5A. 1/100,000	10/06/1918	11/06/1918
War Diary	Calais 13. 1/100000	12/06/1918	15/06/1918
War Diary	Ref. Map Calais 13. 1/100,000 Rodelinghem.	16/06/1918	17/06/1918
War Diary	3.F.86.75	18/06/1918	21/06/1918
War Diary	Ref. Map Calais. 13. 1/100,000.	22/06/1918	22/06/1918
War Diary	3.F.86.75	23/06/1918	30/06/1918
Operation(al) Order(s)	Operation Order No.1 By Captain A.F.P. Christison M.C Commanding To Common Highdrs	11/06/1918	11/06/1918
Operation(al) Order(s)	Operation Order No. 2 By Capt. A.F.P. Christison Commanding 7th Cameron Highlanders Training Battalion	16/06/1918	16/06/1918
Miscellaneous	7th Cameron Hrs J S-D/L/17-5/8/18 118th Infantry Brigade	05/08/1918	05/08/1918
Heading	Confidential War Diary of The Battn The Queen Own Cameron Highlanders Training Staff From 1st July 1918 To 31st July 1918 Vol 37		
War Diary	Ref. Map. Calais. 5A. Veuse. 3.F.7480	01/07/1918	25/07/1918
War Diary	Hazebrouk. 1/100000 Listergaux 2A.7.3.	26/07/1918	28/07/1918
War Diary	Ref. Map. Hazebrouck 1/100000 Watten 2.C.58.00	29/07/1918	30/07/1918
War Diary	Arneke 3.E.90.99	31/07/1918	31/07/1918
Operation(al) Order(s)	Operation Order No.3. By Captain A.F.P. Christison M.C. Commanding 7th Battalion The Queen's Own Cameron Highlanders Training Staff.	25/07/1918	25/07/1918
Operation(al) Order(s)	Operation Order No. 4. By Captain A.F.P. Christison, M.C. Commanding 7th Battalion Queens Own Cameron Highlanders Battalion Training Staff.	28/07/1918	28/07/1918
Operation(al) Order(s)	Operation Order No. 5. By Captain A.F.P. Christison. M.C. Commanding 7th. Battalion Queens Own Cameron Highlanders Battalion Training Staff.	29/07/1918	29/07/1918
Operation(al) Order(s)	Operation Order No. 6. By Captain A.F.P. Christison, M.C. Commanding XIX Corps Reinforcement Battalion.	30/07/1918	30/07/1918
Miscellaneous	D.A.G., 3rd Echelon, G.H.Q.	28/08/1918	28/08/1918
Heading	Confidential War Diary of 7th Bn Cameron Highlanders Training Staff From 1/8/18 To 14/8/18 Vol 38		

War Diary	Ref. Map Sheet 27. 1/40,000 K.27.d.56.50	01/08/1918	01/08/1918
War Diary	Sheet. 28.1/4000 G.24.c.66. & Sheet.27.1/40000 L.33.c	02/08/1918	02/08/1918
War Diary	Sheet 28. 1/40,000 G.14.A.05.70 27/L.33.c.	03/08/1918	07/08/1918
War Diary	Ref. Map Hazebrouck 1/100,000	07/08/1918	07/08/1918
War Diary	Hazebrouck 1/100,000 Lacloche 2E 90.59	08/08/1918	12/08/1918
War Diary	Ref. Map. Hazebrouck 1/100,000 Listergaux 2.A. 70.31.	13/08/1918	14/08/1918

WO 95
1941/1

1915 Jul - 1918 Aug

7 Battalion Cameron Highlanders

15 DIV
44 INF BRIG

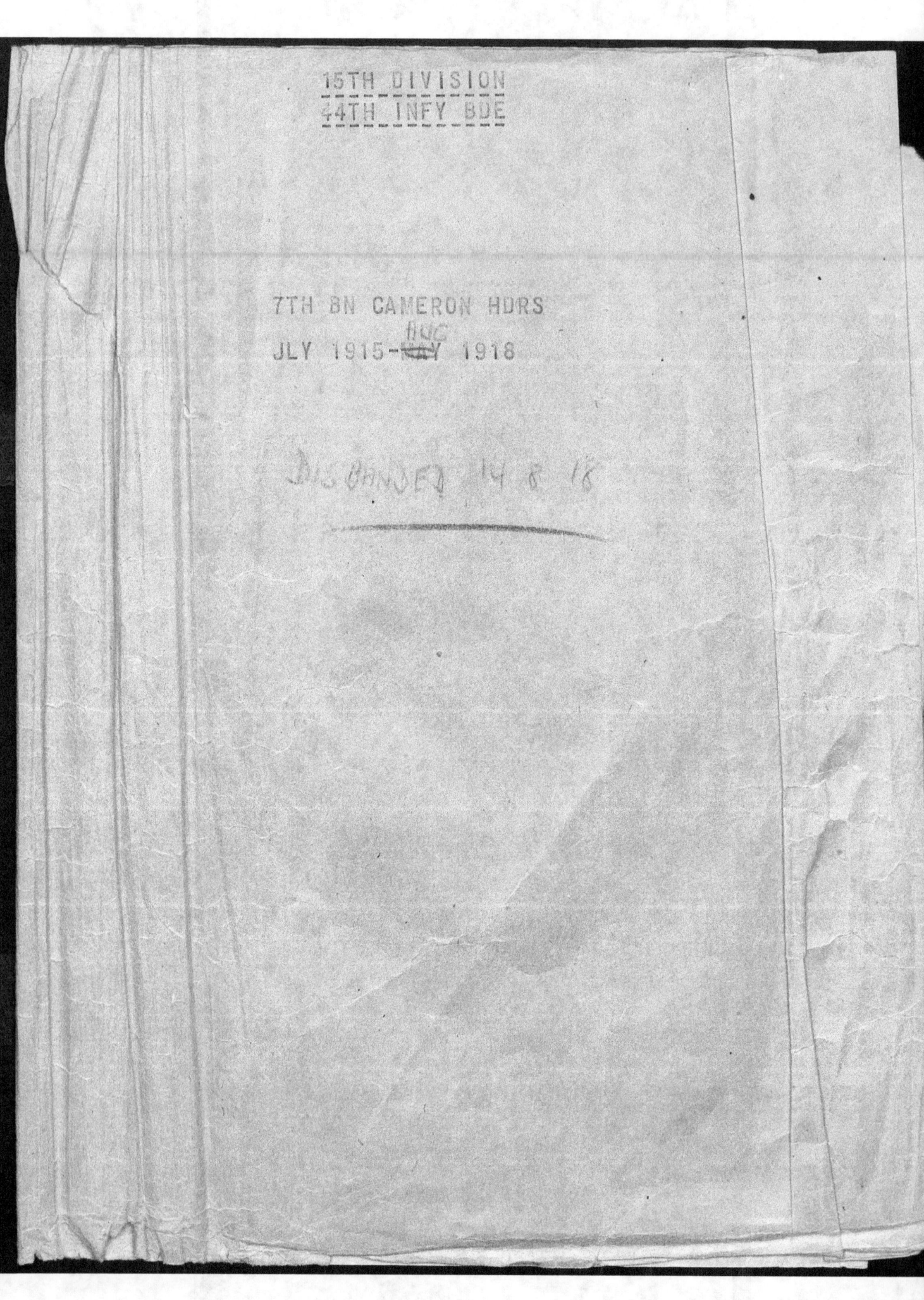

15TH DIVISION
44TH INFY BDE

7TH BN CAMERON HDRS
JLY 1915 - AUG 1918

DISBANDED 14 8 18

Q.1

7th Cameron's

July 1915.

May '18

137/6250

44/15th Division.

7th Cameron Highlanders.
Vol. I 3 — 31.7.15

CONFIDENTIAL.

WAR DIARY

of

Seventh (S) Battalion Queens Own
CAMERON HIGHLANDERS

From 3rd July 1915 to 31st July 1915

Army Form C. 2118.

WAR DIARY
INTELLIGENCE SUMMARY.
(Erase heading not required.)

Instructions regarding War Diaries and Intelligence Summaries are contained in F. S. Regs., Part II. and the Staff Manual respectively. Title pages will be prepared in manuscript.

Place	Date	Hour	Summary of Events and Information	Remarks and references to Appendices
PARK HOUSE	4/7/15	10:30 A.M.	The Battn. received orders to prepare to embark for France	7th (S) Bn. Cameron H'rs, 44th Inf. Bde. 15th Division
TIDWORTH			Major N. MACLEOD left for BOULOGNE to act as landing officer for the XVth DIVISION	
TIDWORTH STN.	7/7/15	10:55 a.m.	Advance party, under Major J. BARRON, of 3 officers + 112 other ranks, 9B (transport + machine gun Section + Details) left entrained for SOUTHAMPTON, embarked on S.S. INVENTOR at SOUTHAMPTON for HAVRE, but no escort being available the vessel did not leave till the following afternoon	yB wy
TIDWORTH STN.	8/7/15	5 pm	The Battalion, under Lt Col J. W. SANDILANDS, D.S.O., entrained for FOLKESTONE, embarked there at 11.50 p.m. on S.S. ARUNDEL	yB wy
SOUTHAMPTON	8/7/15	5.30 pm	advanced party left SOUTHAMPTON	yB wy
BOULOGNE	9/7/15	1.35 am	The Battalion disembarked + proceeded to Rest Camp	yB wy
HAVRE	9/7/15	7 am	advanced party began landing horses + vehicles	yB wy
		6.31 pm	advanced party entrained at HAVRE	yB wy
BOULOGNE	10/7/15		Battalion left in morning + marched to PONT DES BRIQUES	yB wy

WAR DIARY
INTELLIGENCE SUMMARY
(Erase heading not required.)

Army Form C. 2118.

Place	Date	Hour	Summary of Events and Information	Remarks and references to Appendices
PONT DES BRIQUES (BOULOGNE)	10/7/15	9.45 am	Page 2 — 7th Cameronians. Advanced Party arrived and was joined by remainder of Battalion here, where Baths proceeding to WATTEN.	
WATTEN	10-7-15	Noon	Battalion arrived & detrained	
HOULLE	10-7-15	2 pm	Battalion went into Billets	
HOULLE	11-7-15		Field-Marshal Sir J. FRENCH visited the Battalion Hqrs. Roll Some conversation with the Officer Commanding & conveyed to the Battalion his good wishes for the best of luck. "C" Coy (Capt KIRKLAND) passed Sir J FRENCH in Column of route.	
HOULLE	14-7-15		Orders received for a move to BETHUNE district.	
HOULLE	15-7-15	6.30 am	Battalion left with remainder of 44th Inf Bde at 6.30 a.m. Marched to HAZEBROUCK – 18 miles – and went into billets for the night – Major N. MACLEOD acts as Billeting Officer.	
HAZE-BROUCK	15-7-15	8.43 pm	Arrived HAZEBROUCK	
"	16-7-15	8 am	Left HAZEBROUCK at 8 a.m. for GONNEHEM. Route via ST VENANT and BUSNES – Marched 12 miles. MAJOR J. BARRON	
"	16-7-15			

Army Form C. 2118.

WAR DIARY
INTELLIGENCE SUMMARY.
(Erase heading not required.)

Instructions regarding War Diaries and Intelligence Summaries are contained in F. S. Regs., Part II. and the Staff Manual respectively. Title pages will be prepared in manuscript.

Page 3

Place	Date	Hour	Summary of Events and Information of the Camerons	Remarks and references to Appendices
GONNEHEM	16.7.15	—	Billeting Officers went into Billets for night.	9/3 maj
"	17.7.15	3-30	Left for HOUCHIN via CHOQUES, L'EPERLECQUES and	9/3 maj
		9 p.m.	VAUDRICOURT. - 8 miles. - Major J. BARRON leading Guides.	9/3 maj
HOUCHIN	18.7.15	12-15 a.m.	Arrived HOUCHIN. My night march on village is only about 6 miles from firing line. Yeares & Roubats seem all along the front. HOUCHIN is a somewhat dirty village, accommodation very limited. Six hundred inhabitants expected to provide shelter for whole Brigade. 9th Black Watch, 8th Seaforths found accommodation. 10th GORDONS had to bivouac about 500 men, 7th CAMERONS had about 400 men sleeping out for first time. Much of the accommodation of the village was taken up by the men & horses of two heavy batteries of French artillery. The Battalion has not taken in hand the sweeping of the streets etc. in the areas allotted to it in billets & various cleans up as a matter of routine.	

1577 Wt.W10791/1773 500,000 1/15 D.D.&L. A.D.S.S./Forms/C. 2118.

Army Form C. 2118.

WAR DIARY
or
INTELLIGENCE SUMMARY.
(Erase heading not required.)

Instructions regarding War Diaries and Intelligence Summaries are contained in F. S. Regs., Part II. and the Staff Manual respectively. Title pages will be prepared in manuscript.

Page 4

Place	Date	Hour	Summary of Events and Information	Remarks and references to Appendices
HOUCHIN (Cont'd)	18/7/16	2 pm	Received orders that wishes of remaining with the 47th Inf. Bde at HOUCHIN for the next week or fortnight with the object of going to the trenches in small parties the Battalion was to travel that night & report to the C.R.E. 2nd Indian Cavalry division at Le BREBIS. Major N. MACLEOD sent on a Meeting Officers.	7th Camerons
HOUCHIN	"	9 pm	Battalion — less party of sick & details left under Capt CUNNINGHAM left for LES BREBIS — 7 miles - LES BREBIS close to firing lines at NOEUX-LES-MINES. proceeded in small parties — platoon — not intervals via MAZINGARBE & LES BREBIS South of which is the direction of LIEVIN a heavy artillery duel was in progress. fires were numerous & incessant & guns of all calibres were apparently in action. The firing died down about midnight. The Battalion arrived at LES BREBIS & is therefore the	
LES BREBIS	"	mid night		

1577 Wt.W10791/1773 500,000 1/15 D. D. & L. A.D.S.S./Forms/C. 2118.

Army Form C. 2118.

WAR DIARY
or
INTELLIGENCE SUMMARY.
(Erase heading not required.)

Instructions regarding War Diaries and Intelligence Summaries are contained in F. S. Regs., Part II. and the Staff Manual respectively. Title pages will be prepared in manuscript.

Place	Date	Hour	Summary of Events and Information	Remarks and references to Appendices
		Page 5	4th Camerons	
LES BREBIS	19/9/15		first unit of the Second NEW ARMY to come into the fighting line. BETHUNE reported shelled this morning. Railway damaged. Received orders for the work to be carried out tonight. A Coy & D Coy find 300 men as working parties from 8 pm to midnight & B & C Coy the same work from midnight to 4 am.	A.S.C. Rations NB key.
			A Battery in the neighbourhood keeps firing all the forenoon. Shell & Shrapnel come over to the town from the other side. A Ceiling about 500 yds from our billets, or a trench Battery conceals the same distance away & to the South of Seven. About wherever enlarlement being the object Ceiling & the Pit heads were injured at the Ceiling etc so damaged they found any work is machinery etc so damaged to repair it. Many fragments of the shells fell amongst the Battalion billets but no man of the Battn was	} G3 key. } } G3 key. } } G3 key. NB.

WAR DIARY
INTELLIGENCE SUMMARY.

Place	Date	Hour	Summary of Events and Information	Remarks and references to Appendices
LES BREBIS (contd)	19/7/15 contd		Page 6 7th Camerons R.E. 150 men from A & 150 Men from D Coy marched out after dark — at 9 pm — to assist in digging a new line of trenches about one mile east of the town. There was a living party communicating along the front of a second position which was running along the front at some distance behind the front line of trenches. The party under Major J. BARRON worked on a section 350 yards long laid out by the R.E. & it was released at midnight by a similar party from B & C Companies under Major N MACLEOD which returned at 2-30 am. The Parties have to march out after dark & return before daylight to avoid observation. Heavy shelling with high explosive began at 9 am, & continued till about 11 am. Some 150 shells being dropped in a small area. The objective as on the previous day, was a coal mine near the railway	7/B Camerons

WAR DIARY
INTELLIGENCE SUMMARY

Place	Date	Hour	Summary of Events and Information	Remarks and references to Appendices
LES BREBIS (cont)	10/7/15 (cont)		Page 7 — 7th Cameron's

Station. The first shell burst near the Coy. Officer & his Sgr. Major, demolishing a smaller time & burying the overcoats. The range was then shortened & the Colliery works steadily bombarded. Fragments fell in the Hqr billets & officers all forenoon. The shells on both noops appear to be 8 or 9 midstory make a hole in the ground about 4 feet deep. One N.C.O. was talking to a native Indian U.C.O. when the latter was struck by a fragment of shell & badly wounded.

About 11 civilians & two or three Indian Soldiers were killed & about 20 others, civilians & sepoys, wounded.

A local calling himself Director states that with the possibility of a shortage of coal in Britain through the Welsh miners strike, the known shortage |
J.S. hay

J.S. hay |

WAR DIARY of INTELLIGENCE SUMMARY.

(Erase heading not required.)

Army Form C. 2118.

Place	Date	Hour	Summary of Events and Information	Remarks and references to Appendices
LES BREBIS (Cont'd)	10/7/-15 (Cont'd)		Page 8	

officers in house the Germans are daily giving their attention to the collieries within long range by demolishing pit-head works, to protect sheds, fodder the supply of coal - five days bombardment in turn to one colliery. A week's work is required to repair the damage done to the colliery on ten days to put it in working order again. The construction of dug-out was begun. Orders were received as to the arrangement for sending Officers NCOs & companies into the trenches for a tour day time for Companies at a four day for tour day Senior Officers & specialist Officers & Selected N.C.O.S.

Working parties practically completed New Section of the new fire trenches at night. Jist Party B & C Coys. Major BARRON. Second Party A & D Coys. Major MACLEOD.

7th Cameron

7th Coy

7th Coy

A.D.S.S./Forms/C. 2118.

WAR DIARY
INTELLIGENCE SUMMARY
(Erase heading not required.)

Army Form C. 2118.

Place	Date	Hour	Summary of Events and Information	Remarks and references to Appendices
LES BREBIS	21/7/15		Page 9 4th Cameron A few shells fell near the billets this morning. Shelling apparently to heavy French battery south of the Railway. Working parties marched to trenches at 9 pm & 11.30 pm in same order etc as on 19-7-15. Half a dozen H.V. shells passed our party evidently searching road on right near weighly transport. Timed 44 secs from flash of gun to explosion. Shells burst about 1½ - 2 secs before German shells burst a little distance from them. Trench guns observing fires supplying gun to explosion. Report to R.E. through motor cyclist nearly 4th Inf Bde that Lt Col the Hon MACDOUGALL comdg 10TH (S) Bn GORDON HIGHRS has been killed to date in trenches in front where he & his Adjutant had gone for instruction previous to Battn going into trenches. Reference notes on shelling on 20-7-15 the Casualties	GOC log GOC log M3 log
LES BREBIS	22/7/15			GOC log

Place	Date	Hour	Summary of Events and Information	Remarks and references to Appendices
LES BREBIS (contd)	22/7/15 (contd)		Page 10 7th Canadians to Indian troops are sent to be 4 men killed, 4 wounded principally of JODPHUR HORSE. Their curiosity has been greater than their discretion. About one dozen shells fell in the neighbourhood of one of the collieries this morning. The first man of the Battn to be wounded was No 14176 Pte V.A. TELFER who was struck by a fragment of shell sustaining slight fracture of the skull. Report of Lt Col MACDOUGALL's death confirmed. Working parties were at trenches at same times + under same arrangements as on 20-7-15. Very heavy continuous rain. Heavy firing, guns + rifle from direction of SOUCHEZ from about 8.30 to 9.30 p.m. No shells fired.	JR3 bay JR3 bay JR3 bay JR3 bay
LES BREBIS	23/7/15			

WAR DIARY
INTELLIGENCE SUMMARY

4th Camerons

Page 11

Place	Date	Hour	Summary of Events and Information	Remarks and references to Appendices
Les Brebis	24/7/15		Battalion marched back to Houchin; being relieved by 10th Gurkhas. Head of Battalion passed starting point 9 p.m. Road between Mazingarbe & Noeux les Mines very congested with hospl & transport; good deal of shelling.	J.P.
Houchin	25/7/15		Major Baron Liutnts Suttie & Chapman & 6 N.C.O.s proceeded to trenches for 4 days course Instruction & were attached 2 days 2nd Inf Bde & 2 days 142nd Inf Bde. Normal work in billets, letting of trenches.	J.P.
	26/7/15			
	27/7/15			
Houchin	28/7/15		Lieut W. Saunders & Lieut & Adjt Buchanan, Sergeant Major Andrew & 4 N.C.Os proceeded to trenches of 4 days "A" & "B" Coy proceeded to trenches attached to 142nd Brigade for two days to recon instruction in trench warfare.	J.P.

Army Form C. 2118.

WAR DIARY
INTELLIGENCE SUMMARY.
(Erase heading not required.)

Page 12 — 7th Camerons

Place	Date	Hour	Summary of Events and Information	Remarks and references to Appendices
HOUCHIN	29/7/15		In Billets	
HOUCHIN	30/7/15		C & D Coys proceeded to trenches & attached to 142nd Bde for two days instruction in trench warfare. Parade starting point 4-40 pm	
"	31/7/15		A & B Coys returned from trenches about 1 am. Instructions received as to portion of trenches to be taken over by Battn on night of 2/3 August.	

121/6754

Miss B.

Q.2

7th Camerons.

August 1915.

7th Cameron 15/7/15
Vol. II

August 1. 15.

15th K Warn

WAR DIARY
or
INTELLIGENCE SUMMARY.
(Erase heading not required.)

Army Form C. 2118.

Place	Date	Hour	Summary of Events and Information	Remarks and references to Appendices
			Page 13	4th Camerons
HOUCHIN	1/8/15		In Billets. Very heavy artillery firing heard to South during night of 31st July - 1st Aug. Reports this morning that Germans had shelled morning range boxes south of LENS.	JMB Maj
"	2/8/15	8 p.m.	A & B Coys with headquarters left HOUCHIN at 8 p.m. to join the other Coys in Subsection W1 of Section W of our line S.E. of LES BREBIS. The half Battalion began to enter the trenches at 11 p.m. Transport accompanying the Battn was held up by orders of A.P.M. at NOEUX LES MINES from 8.30 to 9.30 p.m. reason unknown. Searchlight in Germans lines E of VERMELLES was seen travelling continually east of road from NOEUX LES MINES to MAZINGARBE, the light however could not sweep this road.	J.S. Maj
IN TRENCHES Sub Sectr W.1.	2/8/15	11 p.m.	Subsector W1 which the Battalion holds is on the extreme right of the BRITISH LINE to the right of the	

WAR DIARY
INTELLIGENCE SUMMARY

(Erase heading not required.)

Army Form C. 2118.

Place	Date	Hour	Summary of Events and Information	Remarks and references to Appendices
IN TRENCHES W.I Cont'd		Page 14	The right front company (D Coy) touches the left of the Naval Div: while runs down in the direction of NOTRE DAME DE LORETTE + SOUCHEZ. Front line — Right, D Coy. " " Left, C Coy. Support " B Coy. " " A Coy. Reserve — Keeps A + B Coys. Trenches require much improvement. All patterns of trench are to be found in this Sub-Sector. Parapets require strengthening. Paradoses needs revetting. Communication trenches need to be deepened, dug out, kept deep and under parapet, requiring much more labour. Keeps are only partially constructed. From the top of a trifling mound some of our trenches are under observation, particularly portions of the communication trenches	4th Camerons

Army Form C. 2118.

WAR DIARY
or
INTELLIGENCE SUMMARY.
(Erase heading not required.)

Place	Date	Hour	Summary of Events and Information	Remarks and references to Appendices
In TRENCHES Coy D	pg 1/15		y M Cameron	
	3/8/15		and any movement or work by day provokes artillery or trench mortar fire.	JB hej
			Lt MacDONNEL located a rifle showing in either hi[s] windows at him + the disappeared into court was informed + two shelled. Artillery was informed + two shelled. In the absence of balloons this town is the only good observation point but is in front of subsector W.I.	JB hej
		8.30pm	Reported from 10th GORDONS that their listening Patrol hear sounds of mining in front. A Coy reported that some of their men being relieved heard the sound of a pick being used directly beneath them. Battalion Hqrs are in SOUTH MAROC which has not suffered very much from shell fire. The initialled however have been removed. ?ministers ? ?most of their furniture + the billets are comfortable night passed quietly.	JB hej JB hej JB hej

Army Form C. 2118.

WAR DIARY
or
INTELLIGENCE SUMMARY.
(Erase heading not required.)

4th Cameron

Place	Date	Hour	Summary of Events and Information	Remarks and references to Appendices
IN TRENCHES	4/8/15		Page 16	
			Further report from men overheard to mining that sound of underground work were heard on the left front of Section W1.	GS hq
		6-8pm	Heavy shelling of our lines in vicinity of billets - fragments of shells dropping in billets, batteries in vicinity also shelled - Direction of shelling 2 hours. Many bullets fly about at & after dusk. Some of them appear to be spent bullets from aviators or German strays. Others appear to come from a point 400- 500 yards distant - Snipers in some empty building suspected - Our artillery inactive.	YS hq GS hq
			Cy. reports what appeared to be shelling by lamp from SOUTH MAROC towards THE GERMAN lines signal being followed by a couple of shells. Direction of centre of signals towards northern end of line of houses bearing S.E.	GS hq

WAR DIARY or INTELLIGENCE SUMMARY

Army Form C. 2118.

Place	Date	Hour	Summary of Events and Information 7th Cameron Hrs	Remarks and references to Appendices
IN TRENCHES (contd)	4/8/15		Page 14 Work in trenches consists of improving parapets, completing dug outs, deepening communication trenches, constructing steps & strengthening splinter proofs	
"	5/8/15		Further reports of mining operations in front of our trenches. At 9 am our artillery bombarded the German trenches, both in trenches contained unusual hunt for snipers. Suspicious characters reported in MAROC but not detained. Instructions given for any one seen to be searched when seen.	
		9.30 p.m	Party sent to search for traces of sapping at midnight. No success	
	night 5/6 6/8 2 am		Alarm received at 2 am that attack was being made on left of Section W. Battalion stood to, but no firing heard. Afterwards reported that BLACK WATCH working party coming in was at first suspected to be	

Army Form C. 2118.

WAR DIARY
or
INTELLIGENCE SUMMARY.
(Erase heading not required.)

Instructions regarding War Diaries and Intelligence Summaries are contained in F. S. Regs., Part II. and the Staff Manual respectively. Title pages will be prepared in manuscript.

Place	Date	Hour	Summary of Events and Information	Remarks and references to Appendices
IN TRENCHES	6/8/15		The enemy R.E. officer reported at Battn Hqrs this morning to investigate report as to mining in front of our trenches & to arrange for sinking a counter-mine. Major SWINBURNE of SEAFORTHS late Chief Inspector of mines in the TRANSVAAL accompanied him. General McCRACKEN, G.O.C., XV. Div. visited the trenches this afternoon.	4th Coy army
"			The Battalion was relieved in the Schwaben W.I. by the 8th SEAFORTH HIGHRS, the relief commencing about 9 p.m. The Battn took over the SEAFORTH billets in SOUTH MAROC. Relief completed & Coys in billets by midnight.	
"	7/8/15		Conference was held at 4th Bde B.Hqrs at 11 a.m. on the report of mines being driven by the GERMANS & our front line. Recommended plans of mines & intervened with officers of the BETHUNE Coleseum. — had at	

Army Form C. 2118.

WAR DIARY
or
INTELLIGENCE SUMMARY.
(Erase heading not required.)

Place	Date	Hour	Summary of Events and Information	Remarks and references to Appendices
In TRENCHES (contd)	7/6/15	10.15 19	LES BREBIS — The mine workings are about 500 metres deep & there is no physical connection between the mining behind the GERMAN lines, which belong to the LENS Concession. The sounds of mining heard at our pit trenches could not therefore arise from men working in the mines; They could only be caused for by the GERMANS running out mining towards our front line. Work on the hearings for our counter mines therefore ordered to be pushed on at one Canada mine near C.T. 6 in trench W.1. & one in W.2. —	7th Cameron 9/3 hey
	9pm		Working parties sent out — 1 officer 50 men A Coy to Sap 7, W.2. 1 officer 100 men from B Coy for C.T. Sap 4 W.2. 1 officer 150 men from C Coy for C.T. Sap 5-6 1st A.W.2. 1 " 150 " " A Coy for C.T. Support trench from C.T. 26 to road, W.3. —	9B hey

Place	Date	Hour	Summary of Events and Information	Remarks and references to Appendices
TRENCHES on	7/8/15		The mine S.W. of Chor to the trenches of S. MAROC is daily shelled the being FRENCH & BRITISH batteries in the neighbourhood. Heavy & light shells drop & the splinters fall close to our billets. Our batteries are very active and more ammunition being expended than was the case a week ago. They are now mining the GERMANS more than what, what is a change - our batteries holding their fire won the throwing over 36 shells in succession in about a minute & kept up a slow fire afterwards - They are nightly & the trenches are patrols were sent out to search the empty houses in S. MAROC, Snipers being suspected - whether there were snipers or not, the fact remains that practically no bullets came over - Previously between the hours of 7 & 10 the Germans Seem over from different directions -	7th Cameronians 9/3 wdj

Place	Date	Hour	Summary of Events and Information	Remarks and references to Appendices
IN TRENCHES (contd)			This morning has been quiet. Patrolling began, artillery also opened. Reports that the 10th GORDONS caught a substance belonging to their Coy's going into a dreine which smokes from their position away to the GERMANS. Three Jocks being shut the knows w. of railway cutting were on 6th stopped, brought to Battn HQrs & interrogated. They produced cards bearing stamp of 4th Army Coy R.E. Labour Corps, & so they to report to the Mine manager at FOSSE the post fortnight & had to report at the SAILLY LA BOURSE trenches & that afternoon. Their parents, they said, had lived at MAROC & they had this morning been taking away some of their property - graves whenever they came into the area to report to Battn HQrs	9/3 mg. 9/3 mg. 9/3.

WAR DIARY
or
INTELLIGENCE SUMMARY.
(Erase heading not required.)

Army Form C. 2118.

Place	Date	Hour	Summary of Events and Information	Remarks and references to Appendices
In TRENCHES	7/9/15		The mine S.W. of the dunes of S. MAROC is daily shelled the living FRENCH & BRITISH batteries in the neighbourhood. Heavy & light shell burst & the splinters fall close to our billets. Our listeners are very active & must more ammunition being expended. The last week a week ago. They are now giving the GERMANS more than we get, what is a change — one battery believes we divine the German trenches & threw up 36 shell in succession in about 4 minute & put up a slow fire afterwards. Twenty two night & the previous one patrols were sent out to search the empty houses in S. MAROC, enquiries being suspects. Whether there were snipers or not, the last rumours that practically no bullets came over — previous between the hours of 7 & 10 pm or or various streams came over from different directions.	7 Cambrin g.3 log.

1577 Wt. W10791/1773 500,000 1/15 D. D. & L. A.D.S.S./Forms/C. 2118.

WAR DIARY
or
INTELLIGENCE SUMMARY.

Army Form C. 2118.

Place	Date	Hour	Summary of Events and Information	Remarks and references to Appendices
IN TRENCHES (Contd)		P21	4th Cameron's	
			This minimum has since patrolling began, entirely disappeared.	No. u.g
			Reports that the 10th GORDONS caught a strange figure in the Keep, coming into a dug-out whilst Smoke Bombs from their positions were thrown at the GERMANS.	No. u.u.g
			Three further point shots to houses w. of railway cutting were stopped, brought to Battn. Hqrs & interrogated. They produced cards bearing stamp of 4th Army Corps R.E. Labour Corps, & said they had been employed for the past fortnight at the SAILLY LA BOURSE trenches & had to report to the Mine manager at FOSSE number 5 - that afternoon. Their pass-port they said was lined at MAROC & they had this morning been taking away some of their property - graves whenever they came into the area to report to Battn Hqrs	No.

Army Form C. 2118.

WAR DIARY
or
INTELLIGENCE SUMMARY.
(Erase heading not required.)

Instructions regarding War Diaries and Intelligence Summaries are contained in F. S. Regs., Part II. and the Staff Manual respectively. Title pages will be prepared in manuscript.

Place	Date	Hour	Summary of Events and Information	Remarks and references to Appendices
In Trenches	8/8/15	am	7th Cameron's Morning Quiet. No artillery fire on either sector. Major N MACLEOD appointed Camp Commandant at HOUCHIN & left to take up duties. Working parties — total number 600 — went out at night to improve trenches etc in Sector W. Considerable rifle firing an hour before dawn a large proportion of bullets falling in our billets. Morning quiet.	M.O. sig 9/8 army M.O. M.O. M.O. M.O.
	9/8/15 (Mon)	3pm	2 small shells burst - in roof of dwelling used by 8th Seaforth. Hymn an orderly room. Heavy shelling commenced just outside houses from billets our reports - to 10th GORDONS in W2 that man has been seen climbing winding from ruins nos 6 & 7 his disappears into roof - at 4-15 pm. Later it was ascertained he was observer for 70th Bty R.F.A. but not before shell had been fired at the top of the tower	

1577 Wt. W10791/1773 500,000 1/15 D. D. & L.   A.D.S.S./Forms/C. 2118.

WAR DIARY

Army Form C. 2118.

Place	Date	Hour	Summary of Events and Information	Remarks and references to Appendices
			Page 23	4th Cameronians
In TRENCHES	10/8/15	8pm	Left SOUTH MAROC (on being relieved by 4th Bn Black Watch) & moved west of SAILLY O.S.R.] at MAZINGARBE. Men all in billets by 10 p.m. Machine Gun Section left in KEEPS A & B.	9/3
MAZING-ARBE	11/8/15		In Billets.	9/3
	12/8/15		In Billets. One working party of 50 men were kept at CUNNINGHAM KEEP. Began new front trench in X.	9/3
"	13/8/15		In Billets. Question of organization of Machine Guns has been causing some discussion. Guns have been under direction of Brigade M.G. Officer & therefore a division of control between Brigade & Regimental commanders arises which has not been satisfactory. Finally decided that machine guns shall except for certain tactical operations, be entirely under control of C.O.s Battalions.	

Army Form C. 2118.

WAR DIARY
or
INTELLIGENCE SUMMARY.
(Erase heading not required.)

Instructions regarding War Diaries and Intelligence Summaries are contained in F. S. Regs., Part II. and the Staff Manual respectively. Title pages will be prepared in manuscript.

Place	Date	Hour	Summary of Events and Information	Remarks and references to Appendices
MAZIN-GARBE	13/8/15	Pagny	Machine Guns are now allocated to each brigade in the trenches, the 4 or so to Brigade establishment which is 16, being found from Battalions of the Brigade in Reserve	903.
"	14/8/15		Rilcts - Working Party of 300 men Capt JOHNSTONE at work on trenches in Sector X at night. Capt E.K. Cameron admitted to hospital last night on Rilcts. Service - Presbyterian - in Presence of Chaplain at 11 am. 6 pm Presbyterian Communion in France - dulund Roth Stevens & O'Brien 40 men present	903.
"	15/8/15			903
"	16/8/15		New Scheme for billeting & Baths visited & two in MAZINGARBE worked out for XV Div by Major J. BARRON with assistance of Adjutant 8th SEAFORTHS. Object is to billet in MAZINGARBE the two Battalions in Brigade reserve at PHILOSOPHÉ in	903

1577 Wt. W10791/1773 500,000 1/15 D. D. & L. A.D.S.S./Forms/C. 2118.

Army Form C. 2118.

WAR DIARY
or
INTELLIGENCE SUMMARY.
(Erase heading not required.)

Place	Date	Hour	Summary of Events and Information	Remarks and references to Appendices
MAZIN-GARBE (cont.)	16/8/15		Pop 25 / 7th Cameron's. Sector X as there had been more casualties in reserve billets in PHILOSOPHE than in the trenches, working party of 300 men were sent Capt. CUNNINGHAM details for improvement of trenches tonight. Orders received for next tour of duty in trenches - 16 days in Sector X for Bn Brigade.	f/13 f/13 f/13
"	17/8/15		In Billets. Billets in MAZINGARBE unsafe, report submitted by Division (from plans submitted) into three areas, the portions West & E of the LOOS–MAZINGARBE RD being abandoned	f/13
"	18/8/15 5.30 pm		Relieved in Billets by 9th R. SCOTS FUSILIERS Marched out at 4.30 p.m. to Xr where trenches were finally taken over from 6th CAMERON Hrs at 11-30 p.m.	f/13 f/13

Army Form C. 2118.

WAR DIARY
or
INTELLIGENCE SUMMARY.
(Erase heading not required.)

Page 26

Place	Date	Hour	Summary of Events and Information	Remarks and references to Appendices
IN TRENCHES	19/8/15		4th Cameron. Information received this morning that the Battn would remain in Trenches for 8 days instead of four as originally ordered. Lieut A.R. CHAPMAN A Coy wounded in trenches this morning while inspecting rifles. Bullet struck trench upright & travelled along its length.	MB
			One man wounded.	MB
	20/8/15		Capt E.K. CAMERON discharged from hospital returned to duty. One man of "B" Coy while placing sandbags on parapet was shot by an enemy sniper rising. The bullet on another man, who was immediately shook himself free from front & dropped to ground no harm being done. It took him ½ an hour to get through quickly & reappeared in the section of the enemy trenches. German working party fired on by A Coy.	MB. MB. pr. MB.

1577 Wt.W10791/1773 500,000 1/15 D. D. & L.   A.D.S.S./Forms/C. 2118.

WAR DIARY or INTELLIGENCE SUMMARY

Army Form C. 2118.

Page 27

Place	Date	Hour	Summary of Events and Information	Remarks and references to Appendices
In TRENCHES	20/8/15		On this day + previous one batteries of 71st Bde R.F.A. allotted to X2 have been registering on enemy line of trenches. Practice good.	M.T. Concerns
			Line is much extended by enemy sniping, & fixed rifles, & machine guns firing single shots. Bullets came 'from all directions' & there communicated at A work. There fell in QUALITY STREET small shells of a new variety of explosive & sound which are apparently the same as the 18 lb enemy shell reported to be fired from enemy parapet.	M3
	21/8/15		During previous night — about 2-4:30 am. A coy opened rapid fire — 3 rounds — on enemy working party. Rounds not known — one man of A Coy seriously wounded in head by bullet as he was preparing to loose the firing platform. Reported by O/C A Coy that trench mortar battery opposite him night centre was active. — D Bty, 71st Bde R.F.A, asked to retaliate.	

Army Form C. 2118.

WAR DIARY
or
INTELLIGENCE SUMMARY.
(Erase heading not required.)

Place	Date	Hour	Summary of Events and Information	Remarks and references to Appendices
IN TRENCHES (contd)			Pg 28	7th Camerons
	22/4/15		in less than 3 minutes of receiving request but shrapnel burst over the enemys trench about 50 yards to right. Aviv. Meyers connected. D Bty 73 Bde R.F.A. (Howitzer) also informed of exact location of enemy minenwerfer King & Pty dropped three bullets shells exactly on the spot where the trench mortar was seen to fire from. C Bty 71st Bde R.F.A. also sent three rounds of shrapnel with bellows on our left front where snipers were very active. The trench mortar was silenced & the sniping practically ceased for the remainder of the night. Draft of 38 men N.C.O.s & men arrived from 3rd Reserve Batt (8th (S) Bn CAMERON Hrs) about 2 p.m. 30 out of the 38 had previously been with the 7th Battalion.	MB MB MB
"	23/4/15	8 am	A Quiet day - our Artillery active & enemy wire much damaged. Batt Hqrs & Reserve Coy Billets in QUALITY ST. Shells - shells	MB

Army Form C. 2118.

WAR DIARY
or
INTELLIGENCE SUMMARY.
(Erase heading not required.)

Place	Date	Hour	Summary of Events and Information	Remarks and references to Appendices
IN TRENCHES (contd)	23/8/15		Page 29	7th Cameron
	24/8/14	about 18th	no casualties - Heavy shells burst near centre of support line in afternoon - Enemy working parties active at night repairing wire but no action other than emptying them as in Section to our left. Strong parties were out digging firing line to join up Sap-Pt.60 & seemed more or less in enemy line opposite X & has been inactive. Some howitzer shells were dropped on or near our Enemy's S.P. opposite P5 C.T. 9C has been advanced 10 yards. It is reported that new advanced trench has been begun by enemy opposite work in input that emply opposite left of X.	YB. YB. YB.
"		9.30pm	Enemy working parties shelled by R.F.A. About a dozen shells burst of Chapel burst opposite our left & interrupted their work.	YB.

1577 Wt. W10791/1773 500,000 1/15 D. D. & L. A.D.S.S./Forms/C. 2118.

Army Form C. 2118.

WAR DIARY
or
INTELLIGENCE SUMMARY.
(Erase heading not required.)

Instructions regarding War Diaries and Intelligence Summaries are contained in F. S. Regs., Part II. and the Staff Manual respectively. Title pages will be prepared in manuscript.

Page 30

Place	Date	Hour	Summary of Events and Information	Remarks and references to Appendices
IN TRENCHES	28/9/15		In trenches. Nothing special to report	7th Cameronians M3
"	29/9/15		10th GORDON HIGHRS relieved the Battn in trenches, beginning at 2 p.m. Battalion then marched from the trenches via lewes detachments to PHILOSOPHE where men had tea & cooked tea dinner when Battn proceeded to MAZINGARBE & went into billets in area C being up from 9th BLACK WATCH. In Billets at MAZINGARBE	M3 M3
MAZINGA-RBE	29/9/15 30/9/15	5pm	Battalion moved back to NOEUX LES MINES & took over billets of 11th ARGYLL & SUTHERLAND HIGHRS	M3
NOEUX LES MINES	30/9/15			
"	3/10/15		In Billets at NOEUX LES MINES - working parties of 300 all ranks each night	M3

44th Inf.Bde.
15th Div.

WAR DIARY

7th BATTN. THE CAMERON HIGHLANDERS.

S E P T E M B E R

1 9 1 5

Attached:
Report on Ops. 25.9.15.
Battalion O.Os.
Notes on Attack.

WAR DIARY.

WAR DIARY
or
INTELLIGENCE SUMMARY.

Army Form C. 2118.

Place	Date	Hour	Summary of Events and Information	Remarks and references to Appendices
NOEUX LES MINES	1/9/15		F 31	
			In Billets	
			Lieut Robertson, R.A.M.C., attached this Battalion left to join 46th Field Ambulance on 29th 2.9.8-15 Lieut ROWELL R.A.M.t. reported for duty same day in place	9/3
"	2/9/15		do	
"	3/9/15		do	9/3
"	4-9/15 to 5/9/15		do } Furnished working parties each night	
"	6/9/15			
"	7/9/15 - 5 p.m.	marched to MAZINGARBE + took over trenches x1 from Sep 18 to EC exclusive from 7th Royal Scot fusiliers	9/3
IN TRENCHES	8/9/15		in trenches.	
	9/9/15	7 p.m.	Trench mortar in German redoubt fired one shell about 7 p.m. Lt W.G. STUART info wounded in arm	9/3

Army Form C. 2118.

WAR DIARY
or
INTELLIGENCE SUMMARY.
(Erase heading not required.)

Place	Date	Hour	Summary of Events and Information	Remarks and references to Appendices
			Page 3 — Lieut. K.C.B. MACDONELL & Lieut. K. MACRAE in forearm & week, 1 offr & 1 man also wounded. Shell burst on parados at Support trench as officers were looking below while A Coy were in Support. 18 through hundreds of rifle grenades fired by enemy - Investigations showed that our men were killed, there also 2 wounded. Total 5 killed 2 wounded. Investigation showed that the party at the head of Sap 18, about 70 yards in front of the fire trench and the same distance from the enemy's front line — were together when a trench mortar or minenwerfer shell fell amongst them. The injuries to the dead & wounded that they must have been caused by something more powerful than a trench mortar but less powerful than a H.E.	7 Canadians W/3 W/3
In Trenches	19/9/15	2.15 p.m. 1.5 a.m.		

Place	Date	Hour	Summary of Events and Information	Remarks and references to Appendices
In Trenches (cont)	10/9/15		Page 33	7th Canadians

Shell - The S. Beven of A Coy & 2/Lt S Musgrave & Sgt Thevenleer proceeded to the head of the Sap & over & while attacking the wounded other, Shells burst near the Sap & one in it wounding one of the Stretcher bearers - 2/Lt Musgrave & everyone further back but himself with Sgt Thevenleer - Pte Paul went back & stay by the wounded. Pte Paul remained there & he often went up & down when one of the bombers of A Coy who was on duty at the first of the Sap when the first fright shell burst remained at his first all the time while relieving later in the day. Others specially mentioned on leaving Trenches were Pte R.S. Brown A Coy & L/Cpl Hotchkins S. Berry Su Battalion orders by 12-9-15 (app A) & Statement by of A Coy etc

appendix A
app B.

(app B)   (app B)

Army Form C. 2118.

WAR DIARY
or
INTELLIGENCE SUMMARY.
(Erase heading not required.)

Place	Date	Hour	Summary of Events and Information	Remarks and references to Appendices
In TRUCHES	10/9/15		Page 34 7th Cameron News of the Russian victories & captures in Galicia was given to men in trenches. At evening "Stand to" they cheered heartily for the Czar. As the cheering went up & down the line for a long distance the enemy opened fire with rifles & machine guns in anticipation of an attack in trenches - no incident.	AB
"	10/9/15		Relieved in XI by 13th Royal Scots & marched back to Verquin. Relief was delayed by members of relieving parties going into trenches at the same time as the Battn was coming out, causing blocking & confusion in communication trenches between support trench & Beuvrin Agnes main exit trench - no. 12.	AB
VERQUIN		11pm	2nd Relief Lieut W. G. STUART returned from Hospital to duty	MB
VERQUIN	13/9/15			

Army Form C. 2118.

WAR DIARY
or
INTELLIGENCE SUMMARY.

(Erase heading not required.)

7th Camerons

Place	Date	Hour	Summary of Events and Information	Remarks and references to Appendices
VERQUIN	14/9/15 – 18/9/15	Page 35 –	In Billets. The Pipes & Drums played each evening in the grounds of the Convalescent at the Brewery. Small working parties detailed each day.	
"	19/9/15	5 pm	The Pipes & Drums played in the afternoon at 5 pm. The band having a spare hour had done so. The 4th (T.F.) Battn. Camerons marched through VERQUIN on their way to the trenches about 10.30 am. They were played through the town by the pipes & drummers of the Battn. & were cheered by the men.	
add	19/9/15		The Pipes played outside BETHUNE & other convenient lively chance. They played in to Square which was kept clear of traffic for the occasion.	
VERQUIN	20/9/15			

Army Form 2118.

WAR DIARY
or
INTELLIGENCE SUMMARY.
(Erase heading not required.)

7th Cameroons

Place	Date	Hour	Summary of Events and Information	Remarks and references to Appendices
VERQUIN	Sept 21st	8 p.m.	O. 76. Moved to Vermelles - Spency Branch line of Trenches. Bombardment of enemy's trenches began that evening.	ya
GRENAY VERMELLES LINE	22/23/24		Occupied same line of trenches. Bombardment in full swing.	do
"	25th	4.45 a.m.	Moved up at 4.45 a.m. & the attack marching over. Found as far as mine in Quality Street, at which point trench Jonction of was entered. Head of Battalion found bar Trench 21 went in and they came in touch with Black Watch (9th) started to assault. Gas turned on at 6.30 a.m. for 40 minutes.	do
"	"	6.30 a.m.	Assault delivered at 6.30 am which was very successful to 16 fore & some confusion arose amongst front troops, some of them were gassed.	do
"	"		Assault delivered by Black Watch (9th) with right on	No

Army Form C. 2118.

WAR DIARY
or
INTELLIGENCE SUMMARY.
(Erase heading not required.)

Place: 7th Camerons

Date	Hour	Summary of Events and Information	Remarks and references to Appendices
		The Lens road. Seaforths (8th) left, 9 Black Watch, 7 Cameron followed in support, 10 Gordons a reserve.	W
		Assault went straight through German 1st line & Support trench without little opposition & kept on to Loos, when it was held up for a short time at German 3rd line by strong wire untouched by artillery. Some however to have firstly entered in LOOS, but both pressed on to HILL 70. This was the original objective of Division, which appeared an much as could be expected from the troops but an after order was issued giving as objective a point 2 or 3 miles further on. The impression I got from being a rider was that it sounded more alarming & in accordance with the offensive spirit so freely preached.	W

1577 Wt.W10791/1773 500,000 7/15 D.D. & L. A.D.S.S./Forms/C. 2118.

Place	Date	Hour	Summary of Events and Information	Remarks and references to Appendices
		038	The result of the changed order was that instead of moving from HILL 70 to the troops pierced an area the slope down towards ST LAURENT where we came met with the heavy machine gun fire. It is difficult to know how many men got in to the forward slope probably about 500. Few I have ever got back. Lieut Neill Sandilands DSO led 7th Camerons in taking up his own Battalion & reinforced two companies of the 7th Seth Fusiliers which lost who retreated keeping to the West of LOOS had which advanced this view & come straight on. Recognising to fact that the forward line was quite untenable but the troops to his disposal, Lt Col Fitz Sandilands gave orders to all troops to dig in & took up a position 200 or 300 yards down the reverse slope.	7th Camerons

Place	Date	Hour	Summary of Events and Information	Remarks and references to Appendices
7 Cameroons		9.39	As soon as the hit was fired, well established, when have kept out so that we left of the forward line to come in. This started a panic + an ugly rush + the rear of the left of the hill to take places. The men were however rallied & however that is to rally was played by the H.Q of the Flags to the Cameroons & to ? landing of one of the activity, yellow flags issued to & serving with a Rattan batten & lanced Tartan seen at 10 a.m. each side. This was planted on HILL 70 at 10 am of our ??? until 11 p.m. but night. These were two more scouts to the east from a so several large bodies of men shown top of retreat. The flags however was seen took to the men fled back.	1/10

Army Form C. 2118.

WAR DIARY
or
INTELLIGENCE SUMMARY.
(Erase heading not required.)

Instructions regarding War Diaries and Intelligence Summaries are contained in F. S. Regs, Part II. and the Staff Manual respectively. Title pages will be prepared in manuscript.

Place	Date	Hour	Summary of Events and Information	Remarks and references to Appendices
P 40			7th Camerons	
		3pm	About 3pm the hit settled down & he came into tent. The teams for rifle fire & some slight trouble for in certain amount of shelter but tried little damage. Rain fell heavily during the afternoon. The Regiment reported to HILL 70 during the afternoon & was 9th Black Watch 7th Cameron Hrs 6th Seaforths, 9th & 10th Gordons, 7th & 8th Pembrokes, 11th Argyll & Sutherlands. Received orders N.W. Landslops. D.S.O. commanded to HILL 70 from 10. a.m to 11 p.m then be lectured men & introd "ibd machine" 13th Royal Scots. At 6pm G.O.C. went to Brigade arived at LOOS. It was decided that 45th Brigade should take HILL 70 & what was left of the Camerons.	1/4

WAR DIARY or INTELLIGENCE SUMMARY

Army Form C. 2118.

Place	Date	Hour	Summary of Events and Information	Remarks and references to Appendices
P41 7th Camerons			night withdrew. The 62nd Brigade was ordered to take over Hill 70 & West of it, but unable to do it without relief. 7th Sunderland and Lieut ROLLO, W.G. STUART, W. GRAHAM, J.S. Robertson, D.F. JUTT & R.R. ANDERSON & 75 men missing. Otr Ranks trops LOOS to PHILOSOPHE. LOSSES to day 4 Officers killed, 6 Officers wounded, 4 Officers missing men killed 64, wounded 253, missing 217. Total other Ranks 534 = 14 Officers	NP
Sept 26	9am		Ordered up to help hold line of old British Trench. large numbers of men belonging to 21st Division were met retiring in confusion from la direction	NP

1577 Wt. W10791/1773 500,000 1/15 D.D.&L. A.D.S.S./Forms/C. 2118.

Army Form C. 2118.

WAR DIARY
or
INTELLIGENCE SUMMARY.
(Erase heading not required.)

Place	Date	Hour	Summary of Events and Information	Remarks and references to Appendices
			7th barracks	
Loos		9	Attack & hold support line the Germans Trench. (the boys return!) men returning. I should think about how them the by it was the brigade major was looking for the brigades. Panic attitude to rear troops, was a little bit scared last to pieces totally unused to shell fire & gas. Remember to lay a scene which is not a [unclear] at futur traditions to [unclear] by the who in a reserve keeps a German trench, on trench to keep our intervals ready to gas.	Jos
27/5 1.30 am			retired to withdraw & was injured, evacuated in a field, heavy rain.	NO

Army Form C. 2118.

WAR DIARY
or
INTELLIGENCE SUMMARY.
(Erase heading not required.)

Instructions regarding War Diaries and Intelligence Summaries are contained in F. S. Regs., Part II. and the Staff Manual respectively. Title pages will be prepared in manuscript.

Place	Date	Hour	Summary of Events and Information	Remarks and references to Appendices
	28th	9.30 am	Marched to Houchin, joining & arms. HdQrs at Houchin	7th Camerons
	29th			

REPORT ON OPERATIONS 25TH/26TH September.

Headquarters,

44th Infantry Brigade.

Reference S, 688, 27.9.1915.

My Battalion was formed up ready for the assault on the 25th about 6.15 a.m. At 6.30 the two Battalions in front of me went forward to the assault as ordered.

I remained at the junction of trench 21 and 6 and saw the whole of my regiment go forward over the parapet in four lines before I went on myself. I went straight forward to our original front trench, but there, however, I could not make out very clearly what was the situation so proceeded to G.28.c.9.1.of the German second line. On arrival there I halted to make detail reconnaissance. It could not then have been much more than about 8 a.m.

To my astonishment there were scarcely any signs of my own regiment in the immediate vicinity: they were all streaming through the German 3rd line, into the houses of LOOS. On my left I very soon distinguished a line of 15th Division troops ascending the slope towards Puit No. 14 bis. and in 25. c.

At that time I could see no signs of either the 47th or 1st Division. I went forward as arranged with my Company Commanders to LOOS Church, meeting with no opposition. The loss in the Brigade did not strike me as having been excessive at this point.

In LOOS itself there were still parties going about bombing and bayonetting Germans running out of houses, and also taking prisoners. I sheltered behind a strongly built house close to LOOS Church, but was very heavily shelled and went in search of cellars. I found one which was occupied by Germans who were killed, and this was used as my Headquarters for a quarter of an hour.

When one of my men with a Vermoral sprayer came along I sent him into the lower cellar of the house, where a German officer was found still telephoning to the enemy. He was killed.

About 9 o'clock I pushed on through LOOS by FOSSE Street towards hill 70, and finding about 2 Companies of the Scots Fusiliers without any particular orders I took them with me and went up to hill 70. On arrival about half-way up the slope of hill 70 I heard that a body of two or three hundred of the Brigade, including many of my own men, had pushed on too quickly, down the further slope of hill 70, where they were encountering the most serious resistance from the Germans round SAINT LAURENT, and could not get further. I proceeded further up the slope and getting reports that the position already referred to was becoming untenable decided to dig in at once with what troops I had on the reverse slope. I gave orders to this effect to all Officers I could find and a line was taken up roughly from G.36.d.2.5. to H.31.c.6.9., running on to H.31.b.27.

There was very heaving firing in front: the few Officers and men returning all stated that the line in front had been practically wiped out This influenced me further to hold on to the back line at all costs. By now the mixture of units made Command most difficult.

I would like to metion here that Colonel Wallace of the 10th Gordons rendered me great assistance in keeping the mixed units together and that the Scots Fusiliers stuck to me most staunchly and were in a great measure responsible for the hill being held. Finally the line settled down and became quite confident.

(continued)

2.

I remained myself on Hill 70 until about 8'clock p.m. when, hearing that the G.O.C., 44th Brigade was in LOOS, I went back to make a personal report on the situation.

At my interview with the General it was decided that I could withdraw 50 or 60 men of the CAMERON HIGHLANDERS who were all that remained of my Battalion on hill 70. I went back to get them out and in my opinion at 11 p.m. the line we had constructed was sufficiently strong to hold out against a large number of Germans should they attack it.

The left of my line was in touch with the 8th K.O.S.B's of the 46th Brigade near Puit 14 bis: my right was in touch with the London Regiment (19th ?) who were astride the DOUBLE CRASSIER. When I retired my men at 11 p.m. there were still no signs of the 62nd Brigade, who had been given orders to relieve us. I marched back with my party and, mistaking the road in the dark, came through MAROC. On my way I encountered quantities of men of the 62nd Brigade wedged up in trenches. They did not seem to know where they were going or what they were to do. I spoke to what Officers I could find and told them that they were badly wanted at Hill 70 but it appeared quite impossible to find anybody who would take the responsibility upon himself to take his men forward.

I returned to PHILOSOPHE about midnight, left my men there, and went to report at Divisional Headquarters at MAZINGARBE.

About 9 o'clock next morning I was ordered up into the old British line trenches. At 5 p.m. I was ordered to hold the old second line German trench north of the LENS ROAD. Owing to the presence of gas I found it necessary to dig myself in behind the rear parapet as the trench itself was untenable. The night was very quiet and there was scarcely any shelling in LOOS.

About 3 a.m. on the 27th I received the order to retire to MAZINGARBE. I regret to say that my Battalion has lost 15 Officers and 560 men, killed, wounded and missing including a very high percentage of senior N.C.O's. I am proud to say that I consider that all ranks fought with the greatest gallantry and determination, and that the spirit of the men has in no way been damaged by the heavy casualties.

Lieut-Colonel.
Commanding 7th Battalion Cameron Highlanders.

28th. September, 1915.

BATTALION OPERATION ORDERS.

BATTALION ORDERS BY LT-COLONEL J.W. SANDILANDS, D.S.O.,
COMMANDING 7TH (SERVICE) BATTALION CAMERON HIGHLANDERS.

SUNDAY, 12TH SEPTEMBER, 1915.

PART I.

DETAIL. Company for Duty Monday, "C" Company.
Company for Duty Tuesday, "D" Company.

(184)
SPECIAL   The Commanding Officer wishes to record the courage
ORDER.   displayed by the following Officer, N.C.O's and men
          during the unfortunate affair in Sap 18 on September
          10th, -

        2nd-Lieutenant S.   McDonald.
        No.13691 Sgt. I.H.   McCulloch.
           15434 L/Cpl.A.   Donald.
           13274 Pte. R.S.   Brown.
           13709 Pte. W.   Graham, S.B.
           15851 Pte. D.   Paul,   S.B.
           13203 Pte. D.   McNeil, S.B.
           16107 L/Cpl.J.A. Hutchison,S.B.

This order is to be read out on Parade.

                (Signed) JAMES BARRON, Major,
                        for Adjutant,
         7th Battalion Cameron Highlanders.

SECRET.   Copy No. 49. War diary

OPERATION ORDERS No 1.
BY
LT-COLONEL J.W. SANDILANDS, D.S.O.,
COMMANDING 7TH (SERVICE) BATTALION CAMERON HIGHLANDERS.

19TH SEPTEMBER, 1915.

1. The Battalion is to form part of an assaulting Column.

On the morning of the assault the Black Watch will be formed up, with their right on 6 A., i.e., just across main LENS Road, and left between 7 A. and 7 B. on a front of 2 Platoons.

The Seaforths will be on the left of Black Watch, also on a front of 2 Platoons, with their right touching the Black Watch and their left on 8 C.

The Black Watch and Seaforths will advance in 8 successive lines, followed by the Camerons, who will be followed by the GORDONS.

On the day of the assault the CAMERONS will march up Southern Up and turn to the left down C.T. No. 21, in the following order of Platoons:

No. 6
5
2
1

8
7
4
3

14
13
10
9

16
15
12
11

H.Q.

As the leading file of each group of four Platoons touches C.T. No. 23 it will halt; those in rear will close up until the rear file of the last Platoon is clear of the LENS Road.

As soon as this position has been taken up, the group of four Platoons will turn to their right and go straight over the Parapet across country and follow the assaulting column, their place in C.T. No. 21 being taken by another group of 4 Platoons, who will also follow on as above

2. The 46th Brigade is to assault the German line immediately on our left, and the 45th Brigade will move up in reserve.

Troops in the 15th Division will carry yellow flags Then flags

On the left of the 46th Brigade the 1st Division is to assault, and will carry Red flags with a whie stripe.

On our right the 47th Division is to assault, and will carry yellow flags with a black cross.

Page 2.

3. The line of advance of our Brigade is practically due EAST, straight through the village of LOOS and on to the hill about a mile behind the village.

If the LOOS Towers are still standing, they should be kept slightly on our right.

The main LENS Road, which is recognisable by a double border of trees, should not be crossed on any account, but should be kept about 400 or 500 yards outside our right flank.

4. The advance must be carried out in quick time and not at the double.

Men should not be allowed to lie down; the sooner everybody gets on the better.

The bayonet should be used as much as possible.

5. It should be remembered by all ranks that it will be impossible to get any order through to them during the assault, and probably for a considerable time afterwards. All ranks must do the best for themselves.

In a fight of this sort, Battalions, Brigades, and even Divisions will become mixed up.

All Commanders should endeavour to force their will on any men they come across, regardless of the regiments to which they belong.

6. In the event of Hill 70, about a mile EAST of LOOS, being carried, all ranks will at once proceed to dig themselves in, without further orders, on the reverse slope, i.e. on our side of the hill

7. N.C.O's and men should be warned not to touch their water-bottles or emergency rations until they are driven to do so. Is is impossible to say how long they may be left without food or drink.

8. No one is allowed to fall out to take wounded to the rear. A badly wounded man may be moved a few yards to a spot which would render it easier for him to be picked up by the stretcher-bearers.

The bodies of officers and men who have been killed should be at once lifted out of a trench and put over the parapet.

Ammunition should be taken off officers and men who have been killed or wounded, also water bottles and emergency rations,- waterproof sheets, etc., if required, from those killed.

9. No officer, N.C.O. or man should allow himself to be carried on a stretcher if he can possibly walk. It is considered a point of honour for a soldier to walk in if he can.

10. The Commanding Officer himself intends to march at the head of No 6 Platoon. He will take up his position in Trench No. 21 near the LENS Road, and will see each group of 4 Platoons start off. After that he will walk up Trench 7 and 7 a. with the Headquarters Staff, go straight over to the German line and establish his Headquarters at 28 C.91. He will then follow the regiment on to LOOS Church. Every endeavour should be made to send back information, especially as to progress.

(Signed) J.F. BUCHANAN, Captain and Adjutant,
7th (Service) Battalion Cameron Highlanders.

Copy No 23
War diary

OPERATION ORDER NO. 2.
BY LIEUT-COLONEL J.W. SANDILANDS, COMMANDING
7TH BATTALION CAMERON HIGHLANDERS.

REFERENCE 1/40,000 Map Sheet 36. b.   September, 20th 1915.

(1)
MOVE.   On the night of September, 22nd the 7TH CAMERONS will move
from VARQUIN to the GRENAY-VERMELLES branch line.
The Route to be followed will be the new road used by the
Divisional Transport when returning from the front line.
The Head of the Battalion will pass the cross roads S. of
VAUDRICOURT PARK (immediately N. of 4 in K.4) at 8 p.m. in
the following order of platoons at about 50 yards distances

HEADQUARTERS.
11
12
15
16
9
10
13
14
3
4
7
8
1
2
5
6

Lieut. Ogilvy will be responsible for guiding the column as far
as MAZINGARBE.   The 8th K.O.S.B's will follow the 7TH
CAMERONS.   On arrival at MAZINGARBE all ranks will take off
their packs, which will be stored under battalion arrangements.

(2)
ADVANCE   1 Officer per Company and 1 reliable N.C.O. per platoon will
PARTIES. report to Major Barron at 5 p.m. on the 22nd at BATTALION
HEADQUARTERS.

(3)
FORMING   The 7TH CAMERONS will remain in position in the GRENAY-VERMELLES
UP.   BRANCH LINE until the morning of the attack.
(4)
OFFICERS, N.C.O's AND MEN LEFT BEHIND.
(a) Captain T.L. Cunningham will be in charge of the Ammunition
Store at QUALITY STREET and will be assisted by the Regtl. Sgt-
Major, 7th Camerons.   They should proceed there about 4 p.m.
on the 24th instant.
Privates R.J. Marshall, T. Balls, J.Sweenie and J. Hynds of
the Reserve Machine Gun Section will report to Captain
Cunningham at QUALITY STREET at 8 p.m. on September, 24th.

This store will act as a feeder to the two forward S.A.
Ammunition Stores in Support Trench between 6 and 7 and junction
of trenches 8 and 26.

(continued)

OPERATION ORDERS NO. 2.   Copy No. 23

(b) Captain Bruce Johnstone, will report at 1st Line Transport at NOEUX-LES-MINES at 5 p.m. on the 24th September.

(c) Captain and Adjutant, J.V. Buchanan will remain behind with men who will be left in the trenches, when the advance takes place.

(d) The Drum-Major and the following N.C.O.'s and Men will be left in charge of the Packs stored at MAZINGARBE.
L/Cpl. Hutchieson, Piper A. Shand, Piper A. Smart, Dr. McIlwraith, Ptes. P. McFarlane, Pte. J. Fergusson, Pte. D.B. Brown, "D" Coy.

(e) The Provost Sergeant and the following police:-
Piper D. Scoular, Dr. A. McLetchie, Pipers Williamson and McKenzie, will report to CAPTAIN PEARSON, 10TH GORDONS at MAZINGARBE CHATEAU, at 6 p.m. on September, 24th and will remain there for the night.

(f) Privates R. Kirkwood and J. Ramsay will parade with the Battalion with bicycles. They will remain with Captain Buchanan when the Battalion moves forward.
Pte. W. Clark, J. McEwan, J. Donald, and J. McIntosh will go direct to the 1st. Line Transport, at NOEUX-LES-MINES, with their bicycles on September 24th.

(g) Lance/Cpl. Ross and Lance/Cpl. MacArthur, and the following Scouts (5) Cpl. H.N. Taylor, L/Cpl. Henderson, Pte. A. McDonald, Pte. A. McDermott, and Pte. J. Herd, will report at Brigade Report Centre by 4 p.m. on Friday 24th. instant.

(5) All the 1st. Line Transport is to remain parked at NOEUX-LES-MINES in its present position with the following exceptions.
One machine gun limber from each battalion will be brought up to the wall behind MAZINGARBE CHATEAU.
These four limbers will be under the charge of Lieut. Holmes 6th. Seaforth Highlanders. The Water Carts and Cookers will accompany the Battalion on September 25nd.
"A" and "B" Cookers and 1 Water Cart will proceed to the Railway Arch, which will be shown to them.
"C" and "D" Cookers and 1 Water Cart will proceed to G.19.d.9.4. The cooking utensils will be taken out and the limbers will return to NOEUX-LES-MINES. In addition to the above, 2 limbered wagons for Officer's Kits., etc., and 2 limbered wagons for machine guns will be required on September, 25nd. They should be at the Battalion Headquarters at 5 p.m.

(6) MEDICAL ARRANGEMENTS. On the night preceding the bombardment the following dressing stations will be established.
QUALITY STREET,   FOSSE,7.   BREWERY , PHILOSOPHE.
The Medical Officer of the 7th. Camerons will move with the Battalion and remain at QUALITY KEEP SOUTH.

(CONTINUED.)

OPERATION ORDER No. 2.   Copy No. ....23......

7.   TRAFFIC. Trenches will be reserved as follows:-
     For up traffic only - SOUTHERN UP, 1.a. and 6.
     For DOWN Traffic only - 2.
     The new evacuation trench which runs straight back from between
     8.b. and 8.c. and SOUTH OF QUALITY KEEP, EAST and the junction
     of 9. and 6; and trench No. 2 are for casualties only.

8.   SCALING LADDERS. 100 small scaling ladders have been provided.
     The O.C. 10th Gordon Highlanders will see that 80 of them are
     placed in the fire trench - one in each bay from 61 to 111 and the
     remaining 20 in reserve trench 21, from trench 6 to left of
     44th Brigade Area. These ladders are in addition to the steps
     in the trenches.
     VERMOREL SPRAYERS.   Vermorel Sprayers will be distributed along
     the front line trenches. It is the duty of the leading Battalion
     to take them on, but if they still remain in the trenches they will
     be taken forward by the men of the battalion.
     TOOLS. Nos. 11,12,15, and 16 Platoons will each carry 6 picks
     and 12 shovels, they should be carried slung across the back with
     rope slings.
     IRON RATIONS.   In the event of the Iron Rations having to be used
     only one tin in four should be opened at a time. Thus four meals
     can be provided without waste.
     EXPOSURE. During the bombardment men, especially in the rear lines
     are not to expose themselves. Haversacks, etc., are to be kept in
     the trenches and not on the parapet. All work must be done at night
     and men encouraged to sleep during the day.

9.   SIGNALLERS.   In addition to wire and telephones, signallers
     will carry lamps, glasses, telescopes, discs, shutters.

10. After the advance has begun reports will be sent as follows:
     The Commanding Officer and 2nd in Command will lead the Battalion
     up SOUTHERN UP AND ALONG TRENCH 21.
     They will take up their position at the junction of trench 7 and
     trench 21 and remain there until the whole of the battalion has
     gone forward.
     They will follow the line of trench 7 and 7 a. to the front
     line British Trench and move over to the German trenches following
     a line towards 28.c.9.1. after that they will follow on to LOOS
     CHURCH.
     MESSAGES SHOULD BE SENT BACK ALONG THIS LINE.

11. DESTRUCTION OF ORDERS. All copies of Orders in the possession of
     Officers, etc., must be destroyed before the attack begins.

                            (Signed) J.D. BUCHANAN, Captain and Adjutant,
                                     7th (Service) Battalion Cameron Highlanders.
     +++

COPIES TO: 1,2,3,4,5,6,7,8,9,10,11,12,13,14,15,16 Platoons, O.C. "A" Coy.
           O.C. "B" Coy. O.C. "C" Coy. O.C. "D" Coy. Commanding Officer,
           2nd in Command, War Diary (2 Copies) NILE.

NOTES ON ATTACK.

SECRET.　　　　7TH BATTALION CAMERON HIGHLANDERS.　　　War diary

NOTES ON ATTACK.

1. The following special stores will be issued if not already in possession:-
    (a) Large yellow flags, 2' x 2'.
    (b) Small   "   "   1' x 1'.
    (c) Wire cutters and lanyards.
    (d) Billhooks.
    (e) Hedging gloves.
    (f) Sandbags.
    They will eventually be issued as follows:-
    (a) One selected man per platoon.
    (b) One man of each bombing party.
    (c) 10 selected men per platoon.
    (d) 3 men per platoon in the two leading companies.(if available)
    (e) To all men carrying wire cutters or billhooks. (do.)
    (f) 2 per man throughout the Brigade.

2. A bombing squad of 1 N.C.O. and 7 men will be told off from every platoon.

3. The flags will be used as follows:-
    (a) Large ones by platoons to mark the progress of the platoon in the attack.
    (b) Small ones by one man per bombing squad to mark progress of his squad.
    These flags will be carried - never stuck in the ground.

4. Vermorel Sprayers will be taken forward. They must be examined and a report sent in that they are properly equipped with vermoral.

5. "C" and "D" Companies of the Battalion will carry a proportion of picks and shovels.

6. Every infantryman will carry:-
    Rifle and equipment, less pack.
    2 bandoliers of S.A.A. in addition to equipment ammunition. (220 rounds in all).
    2 sandbags in belt.
    Smoke helmet.
    N.B. Haversacks will be carried on the back.
    Bombing squads will only carry equipment ammunition.

7. Battalions will take forward with them two light wires for telephone communication back to Brigade Headquarters.
    4 men per company and 6 men per battalion Headquarters will be selected as runners to supplement means of communication.

8. Steps in parapet, or sandbag steps will be made, and stakes driven into top of parapet for men to pull themselves up out of trenches.

9. Trench Mortar Batteries will have the call on the nearest Infantry to help move their guns.

　　　　　　　(Continued)

7TH BATTALION CAMERON HIGHLANDERS.   NOTES ON ATTACK.

PAGE II.

10.   Packs and greatcoats will not be taken to forming up positions on the night preceding an assault, but will be labelled and left under guard in selected houses or dugouts.

11.   Grenades will be served out to all bombing parties on a day and hour to be fixed.   For 44th Infantry Brigade from H.Qrs., 73rd Field Coy. R.E. at SAULCHOY FM.

12.   Special Stores of grenades and S.A.A. will be formed in the trenches and marked, but will not be touched without orders.

13.   All papers and orders are to be destroyed before an advance. No papers will be carried by Officers or men except the 1/10000 trench map recently issued showing German trenches only, and the 1/40000 map, Sheet 36.c.N.W.
        All messages and reports will refer to one or other of these maps.

                                  (Signed) J.F. BUCHANAN,
                                              Captain and Adjutant,
                          7TH BATTALION CAMERON HIGHLANDERS.

7th Camerons

7444/10/

October 1915.

Army Form C. 2118.

WAR DIARY
or
INTELLIGENCE SUMMARY.
(Erase heading not required.)

Instructions regarding War Diaries and Intelligence Summaries are contained in F. S. Regs., Part II. and the Staff Manual respectively. Title pages will be prepared in manuscript.

Page 44.

Place	Date	Hour	Summary of Events and Information	Remarks and references to Appendices
Houchin	Oct. 2		Billets.	
"	" 3		do	
Lillers	" 4		Marched to Lillers and went into Billets.	
"	" 5		Billets.	
"	"		Lieut-Col Sandilands went on leave, Capt. P. L. Cumming having assumed command of the Batt. during Col Sandilands' absence.	
"			The following Officers joined the Batt?	
"			2nd Lieut J. McSwein	
"			" " A. Fairlie	
"			" " M. Murchison	
"			" " H. McLean	
"			" " D. McDonald	
"			" " J. McFarlane	
"			" " D. Forbes	
"	" 6		A Draft of 200 N.C.O's & men was received. Billets.	

1577 Wt.W10791/1773 500,000 1/15 D. D. & L. A.D.S.S./Forms/C. 2118.

WAR DIARY or INTELLIGENCE SUMMARY

Army Form C. 2118.

Place	Date	Hour	Summary of Events and Information	Remarks and references to Appendices
Lillers	Oct 7		Page 45.	
			Maj General S.W. McCracken C.B. DSO. commanding 15th Div. inspected Officers & men of the New Draft.	
			The following officers joined the Batt?	
			2nd Lieut A.N. Baim	
	"		" S.A. Queen	
"	" 8	Billets		
"	" 9	Billets	M.O. Lieut H.A. Powell went on leave. Lieut J. Fraser 35th RAMC FA took his place.	
"	" 10	Billets		
"	" 11	Billets		
"	" 12		Lieut Col Sandilands returned from leave.	
			The Batt? proceeded to Noeux les Mines by Rail at 5.30 PM.	
Noeux les Mines	" 13	Billets		
"	" 14	Billets	2nd Lieut A.N. Baim 10th Gordons ceased to be attached to this Batt?	
"	" 15		2nd Lieut G.B Hilton joined the Batt?	
	"		A Draft of 17 NCO's recon joined the Batt?	

WAR DIARY
or
INTELLIGENCE SUMMARY.

Place	Date	Hour	Summary of Events and Information	Remarks and references to Appendices
hoeur le haine	Oct 16- h		Billets.	
	19th		Lt M. Swatland & D.S.O. assumed command of 4th Bn the vice Major G. Wilkinson to command of XV Division — until Oct 25 th.	
	23rd		Lt Rush made C.T. Cowan acting assumed duties of Adjutant vice Capt. Rackman, who is temporary of an function, and in that leave, has not been able to return. Draft of 40 men arrived.	
	24th 25th		2nd Lieut. S. Wallace joined the Battalion. T. C.	

WAR DIARY
or
INTELLIGENCE SUMMARY.
(Erase heading not required.)

Place	Date	Hour	Summary of Events and Information	Remarks and references to Appendices
Noeux les mines	26th Oct		Page #7	
			Left Noeux les mines 12.40 pm for tour in trenches 75% of officers & men had never been under shell or rifle fire & had not seen a trench. Company Commanders "A" Rollo. B. O'Libry C. Johnstone D. Stuart. 2nd in command Captain Cunningham Lieut. & 2nd Lieut. Isnam proceeded to trenches in abstract. Took over line from 6th Camerons, pouring rain + bad trenches especially on the right too dring HULLOCH Road. Quiet it is dead lying interred, — even in trenches 6th Cameron like ourselves new troops. Right section I am line, and German gun emplacements in a battery very much knocked about. Infantry told this returned by us about — ammunition — clothing — all this From a medical point of view very unsatisfactory, but len oftener than in billets.	

Army Form C. 2118.

WAR DIARY
or
INTELLIGENCE SUMMARY.
(Erase heading not required.)

Instructions regarding War Diaries and Intelligence Summaries are contained in F. S. Regs., Part II. and the Staff Manual respectively. Title pages will be prepared in manuscript.

Page 48

Place	Date	Hour	Summary of Events and Information	Remarks and references to Appendices
	27		Weather horrible - in & out rain.	
	28		Little unusual happened, hindering the battalion quite new at it etc, - did very well.	Mr
	29		by the younger members, he too will bring in scares. Returned 4 O/R infants sent back - old German trenches held by from before Sept 25th.	
	30		A good deal of shelling but little damage done.	
	31		Our artillery now opens sudden bursts of intense fire at uncertain intervals - every sort of gun appears to open fire. German general a we look, he it is beginning to have the "distinct appearance" look us have repeatedly all round.	MO.

7th Camerons

November 1915.

Army Form C. 2118.

WAR DIARY
or
INTELLIGENCE SUMMARY.
(Erase heading not required.)

Instructions regarding War Diaries and Intelligence Summaries are contained in F.S. Regs., Part II. and the Staff Manual respectively. Title pages will be prepared in manuscript.

Page 49

Place	Date	Hour	Summary of Events and Information	Remarks and references to Appendices
Trenches	Nov 1.		Relieved 8th Seaforths in front line trenches. The right sector formerly occupied by A Co was taken over by 10th Gordons, our front line was held, on the left, by 3 Platoons of B Co with one in support, and, on the right, 3 Platoons of C Company with one in support, the remainder of the support trench was held by D Co to cover gap between 10th Gordons and our right. A Co was in local reserve line previously held by B Co. – In the machine gun section in C Co's line 3 men were buried by an enemy shell one of whom was killed. Weather wet + cold, trenches also bad.	
	" 2.			
	" 3.		In the afternoon a heavy gun situated to the right of our line in the direction of Hulluch opened an enfilading fire on the right of B Co's line, killing 11 men and wounding 19 + doing considerable damage to trench. Frost during night, morning very thick + misty. One man of C Co was killed and 3 men of various Co's wounded	
	" 4.		Relieved by 8th Seaforths in front trenches + occupied Old German trenches as on 29th ult. working parties improving communications Draft of 64 men joined the Battn. remaining at Philosophe until our relief.	

1577 Wt. W107911773 500,000 1/15 D.D. & L. A.D.S.S./Forms/C. 2118.

Army Form C. 2118.

WAR DIARY
or
INTELLIGENCE SUMMARY.
(Erase heading not required.)

Page 50.

Place	Date	Hour	Summary of Events and Information	Remarks and references to Appendices
Noeux-les-Mines	Nov.5		Buried many of the bodies lying about between the trenches	
	6		Working parties.	
	7		Relieved by 8th K.O.S.B's and marched to Noeux-les-Mines taking over their billets as occupied by us before this tour	
	8		Billets	
	9		" Draft of 65 men joined the Battalion.	
	10		"	
	11		"	
	12		"	
Trenches D.1	13		Marched from Noeux les Mines to Trenches Sector D1. relieving 13th Royal Scots in support. B Co in old British Support-line A & C Companies in billets in Grenvilles, D.Co in La Philosophe.	
	14		Trenches	
	15		" one man in D.Co wounded	
	16		Relieved 8th Seaforths in front line, 9th Black Watch on our right. Scottish Rifles (46th Brig) on our right, D.Co on the left, A Co on the right, C.Co in support in old German front line	

1577 Wt.W10791/1773 500,000 1/15 D. D. & L. A.D.S.S./Forms/C. 2118.

Army Form C. 2118.

WAR DIARY
or
INTELLIGENCE SUMMARY.
(Erase heading not required.)

Place	Date	Hour	Summary of Events and Information	Remarks and references to Appendices
Trenches	Page 51.			
Trenches	Nov 16		B Co in reserve. 1 man A Co. 1 man B Co wounded	A6
	" 17		Trenches. Captain R.B.C. Raban joined the Battalion as Second in Command. 2nd Lieut-Suttie invalided to England.	
	" 18		"	
	" 19.		Relieved in firing line by 8th Seaforths, went into reserve in Billets at Noyelles 2nd Lieut D Fowlis wounded	
	" 20			
	" 21			
	" 22		Relieved 8th Seaforths in trenches, 10th Gordons on our left, 6th Camerons on our right. C. Co on the left. B Co on the right; A Co in Old German front line, D Co in reserve.	
	" 23			
	" 24		Relieved by 13th Royal Scots, - Lieut Maxwell Pearson killed. - Marched to Noreuil -	
Noreuil	25		les Mines - Draft of 49 men joined the Battalion.	
	26		Billets	
Sailly la Bourse	27		Marched to Sailly la Bourse.	
	28		Billets	
	29		do Colonel Sam Wilands reconnoitred the German lines from an aeroplane. Lieut-Humphrey Davies " 2nd Lieut-Hobbs. 2nd Life Guards were attached for 5 days instruction in trench warfare	A6
	30		Trenches to-morrow	

7th Cameron High'rs
No: 6

121/7931

7th Camerons

December 1915.

15th/K31
44th Bde.

Q5

Army Form C. 2118.

WAR DIARY
or
INTELLIGENCE SUMMARY.
(Erase heading not required.)

Instructions regarding War Diaries and Intelligence Summaries are contained in F. S. Regs., Part II. and the Staff Manual respectively. Title pages will be prepared in manuscript.

Place	Date	Hour	Summary of Events and Information	Remarks and references to Appendices
Trenches C.1.	Dec.1.		Marched from Sailly Labourse into Trenches Sector C.1. relieving 11th Argyll Sutherland Highlanders, on our left 4th Black Watch, on our right-London Scottish (I.Div) - 'A' Coy on the right of firing line. 'B' Coy on the left, firing line extending from Devonshire (excl.) on the right to Gordon Alley (excl.) on the left. 'C' Coy in support in Old German Front line. 'D' Coy in Reserve in O.B.5.	
	" 2.		Raining - Trenches very wet - Heavy Shelling. A. Co had 3 men wounded - B.Co. 1 man wounded - 'C' Coy 1 man killed and 3 wounded Trenches. 'B' Coy 1 man killed.	
	" 3.		Capt H. Bruce Johnstone struck off the strength of the Batt'n "unfit to return to duty"	
	" 4.		Relieved by 8th Seaforths. Batt'n proceeded to Nogelles in Brigade Reserve.	
	" 5.		Nogelles. Church Parade at Chateau. 2nd Lieut J.C. Cattanach joined. 2nd Lieut D Anderson, 2nd Lieut J.K. MacDonald joined. 2nd Lieut J.F. Briggs North Somerset Yeomanry & 2nd Lieut W.A. Jacob Essex Yeomanry were attached to the Batt'n for instruction in Trench warfare. - Lieut Humphrey Davies and 2nd Lieut Hobbs 2nd Life Guards ceased to be attached.	
	" 6.			
	" 7.		Moved into Trenches relieving 8th Seaforths. 'C' Coy on left of firing line, 'D' Coy on the right 'B' Coy in support in Old German Frontline and 'A' Coy in reserve in O.B.5.	
	" 8.		Trenches	

WAR DIARY
or
INTELLIGENCE SUMMARY.

(Erase heading not required.)

Army Form C. 2118.

Page 58.

Place	Date	Hour	Summary of Events and Information	Remarks and references to Appendices
Trenches	Dec 9		Trenches	
	" 10		do	
	" 11		Relieved by 8th Seaforths. 'B' 'C' 'D' Coys went into Billets in Philosophe. 'A' Coy remained in O.B.5. Battn Headquarters Wilkie's Folly. Heavily shelled.	
	" 12		do 2nd Lieut G. Findlay & 2nd Lieut J.H. McKenzie joined.	
	" 13		do	
	" 14		44th Brigade relieved by 141st Brigade. 7th Camerons relieved by 19th County of London. Battn marched to Noeux les Mines and there entrained for Lillers and marched thence to Allouagne.	
Allouagne	" 15		Billets cleaning up	
	" 16		Captain R.B.C. Polson 1st Camerons promoted to the temp rank of Major whilst holding the appointment of 2nd in command of the Battn. Major Gen Wilkinson proceeded to England on leave and Lieut-Col J.W. Sandilands D.S.O. assumed command of the 44th Brigade. Major Polson assumed command of the Battn.	
	" 17		Billets	
	" 18		Billets. 2nd Lieut J.B. Middleton joined the Battalion	

Army Form C. 2118.

WAR DIARY
or
INTELLIGENCE SUMMARY.

(Erase heading not required.)

Instructions regarding War Diaries and Intelligence Summaries are contained in F. S. Regs., Part II. and the Staff Manual respectively. Title pages will be prepared in manuscript.

Page 54.

Place	Date	Hour	Summary of Events and Information	Remarks and references to Appendices
Allouagne	Dec 19	Billets		
	" 20	do	A Draft of 47 men arrived this day.	
	" 21	do		
	" 22	do		
	" 23	do		
	" 24	do		
	" 25	do	⎫	
	" 26	do	⎪	
	" 27	do	⎬ Platoon Company Battalion & Brigade training.	
	" 28	do	⎪	
	" 29	do	⎪	
	" 30	do	⎭	
	" 31	do		

The Lawrence Hoyden
Vol. 7

Army Form C. 2118.

WAR DIARY
or
INTELLIGENCE SUMMARY.

7th (SERVICE) Bn. CAMERON HIGHLANDERS.

(Erase heading not required.)

Instructions regarding War Diaries and Intelligence Summaries are contained in F. S. Regs., Part II. and the Staff Manual respectively. Title pages will be prepared in manuscript.

Page 55

Place	Date	Hour	Summary of Events and Information	Remarks and references to Appendices
Allouagne	1916 Jan 1.		Billets. Football Match v 9th Gordons.	
	" 2		do	
	" 3		do. A Draft of 12 men joined the Battalion	
	" 4		do	
	" 5		do. A three day Divisional Exercise commenced, the idea being that the 15th Division were moving WEST with the First and 47th Divisions on parallel roads on the right and left respectively. The Battn. marched from ALLOUAGNE at 8 A.M via BURBURE – ECQUEDECQUES – LIERES and AUCHY au BOIS arriving at RELY at 3.45 P.M. where billets had been arranged by a Brigade billeting party detached from the Regiments of the Brigade	
RELY	" 6.		The Battalion marched from RELY at 7.30 A.M. and joined the 44th Brigade at CUHEM, the starting point, marching thence through BOMY until the head of the column reached COYECQUE, when the order was received about turn and proceed to the billets of the preceding night reached RELY at 6 P.M.	
	" 7		The return march to ALLOUAGNE commenced at 8 A.M, Brigade starting point AUCHY au BOIS, thence by BILLERY – HURIONVILLE – BURBURE, arriving at ALLOUAGNE at 12.15 noon. The weather was good on the 5th and 7th but on the 6th there was high wind & driving rain most of the day.	

1577 Wt. W10791/1773 500,000 1/15 D. D. & L. A.D.S.S./Forms/C. 2118.

WAR DIARY
or
INTELLIGENCE SUMMARY.

(Erase heading not required.)

Army Form C. 2118.

7th (SERVICE) Bn. CAMERON HIGHLANDERS

Page 56

Place	Date	Hour	Summary of Events and Information	Remarks and references to Appendices
ALLOUAGNE	1916 Jan 8		Billets. A two day Boxing Tournament commenced, the events being for Lightweights, Welters, Middles and Heavies. Competitors from the 4 Battns of the Brigade and the 45th Field Ambulance taking part.	
	" 9		do. Divine Services in Recreation Room	
	" 10		do. The Second day of the Boxing Competition when the finals were contested and a special 10 round bout was fought between Pte O'Rorke 7th Camerons and Sergt McLeod 8th Seaforths resulting in a decision on points in favour of Sergt McLeod. A Stage rung for the Competition was erected for us by the 93rd Field Co R.E. in the school square.	
	" 11		do Baths at Marles-les-Mines cleaning up Billets, etc	
	" 12		do	
	" 13		do 1 man Transport (A Co) wounded.	
TRENCHES LOOS.	" 14		The Battalion marched from ALLOUAGNE at 8.15 AM to LILLERS and entrained at 10AM for NOEUX les MINES arriving there at 11AM. Close billets in NOEUX until 4.30 PM then marched to PHILOSOPHE thence by LENS Rd + BENIFONTAINE Rd to LOOS where we relieved the 2nd K.R.R and occupied positions for the night as follows. Headquarters in the TRAIT de L'UNION, A Co GUN ALLEY and RESERVE TRENCH, B & D Cos GUN ALLEY and C Co in LENS Rd Redoubt, 65 METRE POINT and NORTHERN SAP Redoubt.	

Army Form C. 2118.

WAR DIARY
7th (SERVICE) Bn. CAMERON HIGHLANDERS
or
INTELLIGENCE SUMMARY.
(Erase heading not required.)

Place	Date	Hour	Summary of Events and Information	Remarks and references to Appendices
TRENCHES LOOS. Hill 70. Section 14 Bis	1916 Jan 15		Page 57.	
		At 6 P.M. A Co, B Co and D Co less two Platoons, took over the firing line between BOYAU des ANGLAIS and the LOOS - LAURENT road on the left and right respectively. B Co relieving the 8th Seaforths on our left. D Co (2 Platoons) in centre, A Co on the right. The two latter relieving the 15th London Regiment. On the left of our line 8th Sea-forths on the right - 6th London Regt (140th Brigade). Headquarters in cellars on Loos with two Platoons of D Co. C Coy moved from Redoubt in 10A AVENUE to GUN ALLEY.	
	" 16		Two platoons of C Coy relieved two Platoons of 8th Seaforths in cellars about Headquarters. One Company (C) of 6th Royal Irish Regiment was attached to the Battn. (1 Platoon per Company) for instruction in Trench warfare.	
			2 men killed and 4 men wounded in B Coy. 1 man wounded in A Coy.	
	" 17		B Co came back to GUN ALLEY, the front line being held by 2 Companies only, the 2 Platoons of D Co in the cellars proceeding to the firing line.	
			1 man B Co wounded	
	" 18		C Coy relieved A Coy. A Co moving back to cellars about Headquarters	
			1 man A Co wounded	
	" 19		2 men killed and 1 man wounded in B Coy	
			1 man killed and 1 man wounded in D Coy. 1 man wounded in C Coy	

Army Form C. 2118.

WAR DIARY
7th (SERVICE) Bn. CAMERON HIGHLANDERS.
or
INTELLIGENCE SUMMARY.
(Erase heading not required.)

Instructions regarding War Diaries and Intelligence Summaries are contained in F.S. Regs., Part II. and the Staff Manual respectively. Title pages will be prepared in manuscript.

Place	Date	Hour	Summary of Events and Information	Remarks and references to Appendices
			Page 58.	
TRENCHES. LOOS. HILL 70. Sec.14 Bis.	1916 Jan 20		B.Co relieved D.Co on the left of the firing line, D Coy moving back to GUN ALLEY.	
	" 21		1 man killed and 4 men wounded in C. Coy.	
	" 22		1 man wounded in B. Coy.	
	" 23		The Battalion was relieved by 8th Seaforths and went into Reserve in 10th AVENUE. Headquarters in PONT STREET, Battn Area from VENDIN ALLEY on the left to CHALK PIT ALLEY on the right. B.Co on the left. C next then D and one Platoon of A.Co. 1 Platoon of D Co in NORTHERN SAP Redoubt. 1 Platoon of A.Co in 65 METRE POINT Redoubt and one in LENS ROAD Redoubt.	
	" 24		Large working parties. 2nd Londons & C Welch joined the Bn?	
	" 25			
PHILOSOPHE.	" 26		Battalion was relieved by the 4th Suffolks and proceeded to PHILOSOPHE where, on orders from 15th Div it was claimed in Billets for the night owing to enemy activity.	
NOEUX les MINES	" 27.		Battalion marched at 9.15 A.M from PHILOSOPHE to NOEUX les MINES and went into Billets, taking over from 8th KOSB's - orders were received at 5.30 P.M for the Battalion to stand to in readiness to march at once. The reserve machine gun section was ordered to MAZINGARBE. Stand down ordered at 9 P.M.	

Army Form C. 2118.

WAR DIARY
or
INTELLIGENCE SUMMARY.

7th (SERVICE) Bn. CAMERON HIGHLANDERS.

(Erase heading not required.)

Place	Date	Hour	Summary of Events and Information	Remarks and references to Appendices
	1916		Page 59.	
NOEUX LES MINES	Jan 28		Billets – Stand to again ordered and afterwards cancelled.	
"	29		do normal. working party of 650 am on, half by day half by night.	
"	30		A Draft of 39 men joined the Battn. Captain A.C. Bateman RAMC SP relieved Lieut Powell RAMC as MO to the Battn.	
"	31		do Divine Services in Cinema House	

7th Bn
Cameron Highlanders

February 1916

Army Form C. 2118.

WAR DIARY
or
INTELLIGENCE SUMMARY.
(Erase heading not required.)

7TH (SERVICE) Bn. CAMERON HIGHLANDERS.

1916

Page 60

Place	Date	Hour	Summary of Events and Information	Remarks and references to Appendices
	Feb.			
HULLUCH SECTION	1.		Batt. relieved 11th Argyll & Sutherland Highrs of 45th Infty Bde. in left sub. section of HULLUCH section. 'A' & 'D' companies in firing line – 'B Co' in support line – C Co in reserve line. The reserve line was taken over from 6th Cameron Highrs. Battalion march from NOEUX-LES-MINES at 2–30 p.m. The line on our right was taken over by 8th Seaforth Highrs – that on our left was held by Cavalry Division.	
"	2.		1 man of A Co. wounded.	
"	3.			
PHILOSOPHE	4.		Batt. was relieved in the evening by 10th Gordon Highrs & moved into brigade reserve at PHILOSOPHE. A draft of 30 other ranks joined battalion.	
"	5.		Billets at PHILOSOPHE. 1 man of B Company wounded. Lt.Col. Sandilands rejoined from leave in the evening but both our commanding of brigade following day. 2/Lt W.BLACK joined battalion + posted to B company. 2/Lt D. ANDERSON struck off strength + transferred to B/44 Light Mortar Battery.	
"	6.		Divine service.	
HULLUCH SECTION	7.		Batt. relieved 10th Gordon Highrs in left sub-section. B & C companies in firing line – A company in support line + D company in reserve line. 8th Seaforth Highrs on right + Cavalry Divn on left.	

1577 Wt. W10791/1773 500,000 1/15 D. D. & L. A.D.S.S./Forms/C. 2118.

Army Form C. 2118.

WAR DIARY
or
INTELLIGENCE SUMMARY.

(Erase heading not required.)

7th (SERVICE) Bn. CAMERON HIGHLANDERS.

Instructions regarding War Diaries and Intelligence Summaries are contained in F.S. Regs., Part II. and the Staff Manual respectively. Title pages will be prepared in manuscript.

Place	Date	Hour	Summary of Events and Information	Remarks and references to Appendices
			Page 61.	
HULLUCH SECTION.	Feb. 7 (cont).		1 man of O.R. accidentally wounded	
" "	8.		1 man of B.W. + 1 man of D.W. wounded. 2/Lt. D. McDONALD struck off strength.	
" "	9.		1 man of B.W. wounded.	
" "	10.		2/Lt. F.C.M. TINLINE invalided to England & struck off strength. Battalion relieved by 10th Gordon Highrs in the evening & relieved 9th Black Watch in TENTH AVENUE as Brigade Support.	
" "	11.		1 killed - 2 wounded - 1 accidentally wounded (all of B.W.)	
" "	12.		2/Lt. J.C. CATTANACH & 2 A.W. accidentally wounded at Grenade School at NOEUX-LES-MINES. 1 man of B.W. wounded.	
NOEUX-LES-MINES.	13.		Battalion relieved by 8th K.O.S.B.s of 46th Brigade in the evening & marched to NOEUX-LES-MINES. 1 man of B.W. wounded	
" "	14.		Billets - Baths.	
" "	15.		Billets.	
" "	16.		Billets. Large working parties found - 10 officers + 500 other ranks.	
" "	17.		Billets. A Draft of 38 other ranks joined battalion. Lt. Col. Sandilands resumed command of battalion in the evening.	

WAR DIARY or INTELLIGENCE SUMMARY

Army Form C. 2118.

7th (SERVICE) Bn. CAMERON HIGHLANDERS.

Page 62.

Place	Date	Hour	Summary of Events and Information	Remarks and references to Appendices
	Feb.			
NOEUX-LES-MINES	18.		Gas Demonstration attended by all available officers + other ranks.	
14 BIS SECTION.	19.		Batt. relieved 6th Cameron Highrs of 45th Brigade in left sub-section of 14 BIS section. Front entered from VENDIN ALLEY to POSEN ALLEY. A + D lies in firing line - C Coy in support line + B Coy in reserve line 9th Black Watch on NFN + 4 B/H Brigade on left. Batt. moved from NOEUX-LES-MINES at 4pm	
Do.	20.			
Do.	21.			
Do.	22.		10th Gordon Highrs relieved 9th Black Watch on our right. C. Coy relieved A Coy in front line. 1 Sergt. A Coy wounded (viz Johnny Gay) + 2 of A Co. 1 of B Co. + 3 of C Co. wounded.	
Do.	23.		Capt. G.A.C. DAVY + Lt. K. McRAE joined battalion + posted to C + A Cos respectively.	
Do.	24.			
Do.	25.		Batt. relieved by 9th Black Watch + moved into Brigade support in TENTH AVENUE with one company (A) in GUN TRENCH. The left of 44th Brigade changed to POSEN ALLEY — the portion between POSEN ALLEY + VENDIN ALLEY being taken over by 45th Brigade. 2 men of C Co. wounded.	

Army Form C. 2118.

WAR DIARY
or
INTELLIGENCE SUMMARY.
(Erase heading not required.)

7th (SERVICE) Bn. CAMERON HIGHLANDERS.

Page 63.

Place	Date	Hour	Summary of Events and Information	Remarks and references to Appendices
	Feb.			
14 BIS SECTION A	26		1 officer + 50 other ranks proceeded to M/W sub-section to form part of a permanent working party.	
"	27.		2/Lt. M.N. McLEAN wounded + 2 N.C.O.s killed all of C. Coy. hit with machine gun fire from Guitard.	
"	28.		Batt. relieved B E Seaforth Highrs in M/W sub-section in the evening. A + B Companies in firing line – C Coy in support line + D Coy in reserve in cellars in LOOS. 1st Division on our right – 10th Gordon Highrs on our left. 1 man of A Co. killed.	
"	29.		Quiet day : no casualties.	

7th Bn
Cameron Highlanders

March 1916

XV. 44.

7. Camerons
Vol 9

Army Form C. 2118.

WAR DIARY
or
INTELLIGENCE SUMMARY.
(Erase heading not required.)

Page 64.

Place	Date	Hour	Summary of Events and Information	Remarks and references to Appendices
	March			
14 BIS SECTION	1.		3 men wounded, one each in A, B, C & D Coys.	
MAZINGARBE.	2.		Batt. relieved by 12th H.L.I. of 46th Brigade in the evening & marched to MAZINGARBE.	
Do.	3.		1 man of B Co. wounded.	
Do.	4.		Athletic Matches.	
Do.	5.		Working party of 150 men supplied.	
Do.	6.		Divine service cancelled owing to shelling. Working party 150 men supplied.	
Do.	7.		Baths. Working party 150 men supplied. Working party 150 men supplied. 2/Lt. F. MACFARLANE struck off strength (invalided to England). 2/Lt. J. H. MAUCHLEN joined battalion & appointed transport officer. 2/Lt. A. FAIRLIE struck off strength from 29th Feb.	
HULLUCH SECTION	8.		Battalion relieved 7th Royal Scots 7 midland in left sub-section of the HULLUCH sector. Marched out of MAZINGARBE at 8.30 a.m. C & D Coys in firing line, B Co. in support & A Co. in reserve line. 12th Division on our left – 10th Gordons on our right. 1 man (B Co.) killed.	
"	9.			
"	10.		Draft of #(R) 12 men joined from base.	

WAR DIARY or INTELLIGENCE SUMMARY

Army Form C. 2118.

Page 65.

Place	Date	Hour	Summary of Events and Information	Remarks and references to Appendices
HULLUCH SECTION	March 11.		A.G. changed position with D Co. in the morning — other companies shoot late. Gate Sent section now occupied by 2 Cos. of 10th Gordons + 2 Cos. of 8th Inniskilling Fusiliers. 1 man of C Co. wounded.	
"	12.		Change in weather; a nice sunny day. C Company's line blown in in 11 places in the afternoon + trench considerably damaged. Lt K.C.B. MACDONELL + 2/Lt G.J.S. LUMSDEN (10th GORDONS) reported themselves from hosp. — joined posted to D Co. late took over duties of signalling officer. In A Coy. 1 man killed + 1 wounded. In C Coy 2 men wounded. 1 man killed. In D Coy 1 man wounded.	
"	13.		Bright sunny day. Support line blown in in 4 places in the afternoon + communication trenches. Damage done. A draft of 71 men arrived from base.	
PHILOSOPHE	14.		Proceeded into Brigade Reserve at PHILOSOPHE in morning — relieved by 3 Cos. 10th Gordons + 1 Coy. 8th Inniskilling Fusiliers.	
"	15.		2 billets. Day working parties of 205 men supplied. Lecture on discipline by C.R.A.	
"	16.		Large number of men in baths at MAZINGARBE. Day working parties of 85 men. Remainder of men batting. Three men of C Coy wounded by shell fire in PHILOSOPHE.	

Army Form C. 2118.

WAR DIARY
or
INTELLIGENCE SUMMARY.
(Erase heading not required.)

Page 66.

Instructions regarding War Diaries and Intelligence Summaries are contained in F. S. Regs., Part II. and the Staff Manual respectively. Title pages will be prepared in manuscript.

Place	Date	Hour	Summary of Events and Information	Remarks and references to Appendices
	March			
HULLUCH SECTION.	17.		Batt (less D Coy) went into Brigade support in TENTH AVENUE, relieving 8th Inniskilly Fusiliers. D Coy in reserve line of centre sub-section & under orders of OC 8th Seaforths.	
"	18.		1 Coy of D Coy wounded. Large quantities of trolley deep & other Govt property salved.	
"	19.		All available men on working parties. Salving operations continued.	
NOEUX-LES-MINES.	20.		Relieved by 12th H.L.I. & 4th Brigade in the morning & marched to NOEUX-LES-MINES. D Coy out relieving till afternoon. A draft of 12 men joining battalion.	
"	21.		Batts. allotted to battalion. Capt. C. J. COWAN attached to 1st Division.	
"	22.		Batts continued in training. Light working parties of 6 officers + 200 men supplied.	
"	23.		B Coy proceeded to LABUISSIERE to go on duty at 1st Corps Headqrs. During the next period ordered for Corps Commander cancelled.	
"	24.		Snowed all the morning. An inspection ordered for Corps Commander cancelled.	
ALLOUAGNE	25.		Batt. moved to ALLOUAGNE & occupied billets previous rest. Batt. routed to LILLERS & marched from there. Transport proceeded by road.	
"	26.		Divine service at 10.45 a.m. in recreation room. A parade had been ordered for OC Troops, but it was cancelled owing to inclement weather.	
"	27.		Platoon training.	

WAR DIARY
or
INTELLIGENCE SUMMARY.

Page 67.

Place	Date	Hour	Summary of Events and Information	Remarks and references to Appendices
ALLOUAGNE	March 28.		Ceremonial parade at LILLERS at 3 p.m. The brigade (strength 160 per coy) formed up on 3 sides of the square - G.O.C. 1st Army distributed some medals + afterwards the brigade marched past in column of fours.	
	29.		Platoon training.	
	30.		Drafts of 63 joined battalion. Re-inoculation for enteric fever.	
	31.		Baths allotted to Batt. at AUCHEL. Re-inoculation for enteric fever. Platoon training - musketry - Re-inoculation for enteric fever.	

7th Bn Cameron Highlanders

April 1916

1916
January Vol 10

Army Form C. 2118.

WAR DIARY
or
INTELLIGENCE SUMMARY.
(Erase heading not required.)

XV

Page 68.

Place	Date	Hour	Summary of Events and Information	Remarks and references to Appendices
ALLOUAGNE	April 1		Officers & men who had not been inoculated within a year, re-inoculated	
	2		Divine Service in Recreation Room at 10:15 AM	
	3		Wiring Course commenced. Musketry at range at BURBURE. Major R.B.C. RABAN (2nd in command) posted to command 13th (S) Bn Royal Scots and accordingly struck of the strength. 2nd Lt O.F. SUTTIE joined from the Base taken on strength. Captain Q.R. CHAPMAN appointed Adjutant from 24/3/16	
	4			
	5			
	6		Baths at AUCHEL	
	7		Divisional exercise commenced. Battn passed the Orderly Room at 4.10 am following 10th Gordon Highrs and marched via LOZINGHEM, AUCHEL, CAUCHY à la TOUR, FERFAY, BELLORY, AUCHY au BOIS to FEBVIN PALFART arriving at 1.30 pm & billeted	
	8		Marches from FEBVIN PALFART via FLECHIN, CUHEM to ENQUIN-les-MINES where a Battn attack was practised in the forenoon, witnessed by Gen Cavanagh, the Commander of the 1st Corps. After lunch the Battn took part in a Brigade attack afterwards returning to billets in FEBVIN PALFART.	

Army Form C. 2118.

WAR DIARY
or
INTELLIGENCE SUMMARY.
(Erase heading not required.)

Instructions regarding War Diaries and Intelligence Summaries are contained in F. S. Regs., Part II. and the Staff Manual respectively. Title pages will be prepared in manuscript.

Page 69

Place	Date	Hour	Summary of Events and Information	Remarks and references to Appendices
	April 6		A draft of twenty men arrived at ALLOUAGNE	
	9	9.10 AM	Marched from FEBVIN PALFART to Brigade Starting Point and proceeded thence to ALLOUAGNE by the route taken in the way out, arriving at ALLOUAGNE at 2 p.m. Weather clear and sunny throughout. Divisional Reserve.	
ALLOUAGNE	10	11 AM	A smoke demonstration at which the Battn. was present took place at the trenches on the high ground one mile South of BURBURE.	
	11.		Battn. practised Physical Drill and Wiring Musketry at Range at BURBURE	
	12		Baths at AUCHEL. Lt Col J.W. SANDILANDS, C.M.G., D.S.O. this day relinquished command of the Battn. on being promoted Brig-Gen. commanding 104th Infantry Brigade. Major J.L. Cunningham assumes command.	
	13.		Musketry at BURBURE. Practice in Wiring and Assault	
	14.		Wiring and Assault practices.	
	15		Divine Service in Recreation Room	
	16		Wiring practices. Battn. at Range at Burbure	
	17			

Army Form C. 2118.

WAR DIARY
or
INTELLIGENCE SUMMARY.
(Erase heading not required.)

Place	Date	Hour	Summary of Events and Information	Remarks and references to Appendices
			Page 70	
ALLOUAGNE	April 18		Wiring and Physical Training Practice. Capt J.H.B. JOHNSTONE rejoins Batt.	
	19		Wiring and Physical Training Practice.	
	20		Capt J.H.B. Johnstone took over command of 'C' Coy.	
	21		Coy drill. Wiring and Assault practice.	
	22		Inspection of Companies by G.O.C. 15th Division.	
	23		Divine Service in Recreation Room.	
	24		2nd Lt M.S. MACKAY joined the Battn and was posted to "A" Coy. Musketry at BURBURE. Assault practice. The following officers joined the Battn and were posted as follows:- 2nd/Lt T. ORR to 'A' Coy. 2nd/Lt J.D.W. McCRACKEN to 'B' Coy. 2nd/Lt J.W. MACKAY to 'C' Coy. 2nd/Lt R.A.M. McCROSTIE to 'C' Coy. 2nd/Lt H.B. GOUDIE to 'D' Coy. 2nd/Lt A. FRASER to 'D' Coy.	
	25.	12 noon	A. C & D Coys moved out of rest billets at Allouagne and marched to LILLERS. Entrained there for NOEUX-les-MINES. Marched from Noeux-les-Mines to reserve billets at ANNEQUIN. B Coy marches from LABUISSIERE to Annequin	

WAR DIARY
or
INTELLIGENCE SUMMARY.

(Erase heading not required.)

Army Form C. 2118.

Place	Date	Hour	Summary of Events and Information	Remarks and references to Appendices
Vermelles Left Sub-section Quarry Sector			Page 41.	
	26		Relieves 4th Royal Sussex Regt. in Left Sub-section QUARRY Sector. Disposition 'A' Coy on the left, 'D' Coy in the Centre, 'B' Coy on the Right finding their own supports with 'C' Coy in Reserve in O.G.1. Right of front from Southern Junction of Sussex Loop and Boyau 6 trench (inclusive) to Rifleman's Alley (inclusive) Headquarters in O.G.1. at Pt.G.11.d.3.9. 9th Black Watch on our Right. 8th K.O.S.B. on the Left. 8th Seaforths in Support and 10th Gordon H'rs in Reserve. Quiet all day with exception of a few trench mortar fires at our front trenches in the evening.	
	27	5am	Enemy commenced shelling our Right Coy and H.Q. Black Watch on our Right with shrapnel followed by Chlorine Gas Shells which necessitated the use of Gas Helmets. Enemy also shells Communication trenches and Vermelles.	
		6am	Engineers explodes a mine in our Sub section at G.11.d.9.4. about the Right Leg of the HAIRPIN. Our Bombers and Artillery co-operated.	
		7am	After this hour the Artillery bombardment gradually decreased. After 9am all quiet with exception of intermittent trench mortar fire. Casualties: Officers hit Other Ranks. Killed. A Coy 1. C Coy 1. D Coy 3 Wounded B Coy 3. D Coy 1. D Coy 10. Shellshock C Coy 1. D Coy 4.	
	28		A draft of 30 Other Ranks arrives from the Base.	

WAR DIARY
INTELLIGENCE SUMMARY.
(Erase heading not required.)

Army Form C. 2118.

Place	Date	Hour	Summary of Events and Information	Remarks and references to Appendices
	April 28		Intermittent shelling of our front and support trenches with Trench Mortars, Rifle Grenades and Aerial Torpedoes.	
		6.30 pm	Our front trenches were shelled by Trench Mortars opposite the HAIRPIN. Our Artillery retaliated with Field Guns. The enemy replied with things Bangs and Howitzers on our dugout and Communication Trenches, leaving them in several places. Bombardment ceased about 9 pm. Casualties Officers nil. Other Ranks Killed A Coy 1 C Coy 1 Wounded A Coy 2 C Coy 4 C Coy 1 D Coy 2	
	29	4 am	Enemy commenced heavy bombardment of trenches held by 16th Division (on Right of 9th Black Watch). Gas was reported from our Brigade 145 Bde but none came over our lines. This was followed by considerable rifle & machine gun fire. By 5.30 am all was quiet. During the evening the enemy fired Trench Mortars & rifle grenades into our front lines. Casualties 2nd Lieut. J.C. WELCH Killed. Other Ranks Killed nil. Wounded A Coy 1 B Coy 1	
	30		Shellstruck A Coy 1 B Coy 1. After dawn enemy fired Trench Mortars & Rifle Grenades into our front lines. Relieved by 10th Gordon Hghrs. Battn in Brigade Reserve. Disposition A & C Coys in Billets in VERMELLES. HQ & B D Coys in Billets in NOYELLES. Casualties Officers nil. Other Ranks Killed D Coy 1 Wounded D Coy 2.	

W. Manning Major
Cmdg 9 Cameron Highlanders

7th Bn Cameron Highlanders

May 1916

WAR DIARY
or
INTELLIGENCE SUMMARY

Army Form C. 2118.

T. Commons
Vol II
Q9

Place	Date	Hour	Summary of Events and Information	Remarks and references to Appendices
NOYELLES VERMELLES	1916 May 1, 2, 3		Battalion in Brigade Reserve. Battⁿ H.Q^{rs} and B & D Coys in billets in NOYELLES. A + C Coys in billets in VERMELLES.	
Left Sub-Section Quarry Section	4	10.30 a.m.	Relieves 10th Gordon Highlanders in Left Sub Section, Quarry Section. Disposition: A Coy on the Left, C Coy in the Centre and B Coy on the Right finding their own Supports. D Coy in Reserve in O.G.I. Battⁿ H.Qrs in O.G.I. at Pt G.11.d.3.9. Extent of front – from Southern junction of SWINBOURNE LOOP and BROOKWOOD TRENCH (inclusive) to RIFLEMANS ALLEY (inclusive). 9th Black Watch on our Right. 13th Royal Scots (45th Bde) on the Left. 10th Gordon Highr in Brigade Support. Quiet until 5 p.m. when enemy shelled O.G.I with whiz bangs and 4.2 Howitzers.	
		7 p.m.	Our Engineers exploded three mines at the HAIRPIN. Our bombers advanced and occupied the near lip of the Crater. The enemy bombers attacked the Crater but were driven off by our bombers. Immediately after explosion enemy bombarded our front lines with trench mortars + rifle grenades and our communication and reserve trenches with whiz bangs and Howitzers. Our Artillery retaliated and enemy bombardment decreased. The enemy continues firing Trench Mortars + Rifle Grenades into our front lines until about 11.0 p.m. Thereafter they fired Rifle Grenades into the crater until about midnight. Casualties Officers Nil. Other Ranks. Killed A Coy 1, B Coy 1, C Coy 2, Wounded A Coy 11, B Coy 3, C Coy 12, D Coy 2	

WAR DIARY or INTELLIGENCE SUMMARY

Army Form C. 2118.

Place: Left Subsection, Quarry Section
Page 74

Date	Hour	Summary of Events and Information	Remarks and references to Appendices
1916 May 5.		All quiet in forenoon. In the afternoon the enemy fired several Trench mortars at our front line. They also bombarded OG.1 between FOSSE WAY and BRESLAU AVENUE at intervals with 4.2's, trench mortars and howitzers which did no damage. Our Artillery retaliated with 18 Pounders and Howitzers. During the evening the enemy fired a few Trench mortars & Rifle Grenades into our front trenches. Otherwise the rest of the day was quiet. Casualties. Officers. Nil. Other Ranks. Killed. S.C Coy 1 Wounded S.C Coy 2, B Coy 1	
6.		Draft of 40 other Ranks arrived from the Base. Between 7.30 and 5.8 am the enemy heavily bombarded the junction of OG.1 and BRESLAU AVENUE doing only very slight damage to the trenches. From 3 pm to 3.30 pm our Artillery (Right and Left Groups) bombarded the enemy's front trenches and works opposite the KINK. The enemy retaliated only slightly. During the evening the enemy fired fewer trench mortars and rifle Grenades than usual. Casualties nil.	
7.		The enemy again shelled OG.1 between 6.30 and 7.30 am with whiz bangs and howitzers. The rest of the day was quiet.	
	10.30 am.	Orders received from Brigade to try to blow away for life of Left Hawthorn Crater tomorrow morning. Orders issued to Heavy and Light Trench Mortar Battery Officers to carry this out at 5 am.	

Army Form C. 2118.

WAR DIARY
or
INTELLIGENCE SUMMARY.
(Erase heading not required.)

Page Y5.

Place	Date	Hour	Summary of Events and Information	Remarks and references to Appendices
Left Out Section Quarry Section May	1916 May 8.		From 5 to 5.45 am our Heavy & Light French Mortar Batteries bombards for life of Leff Hairpin Crater but were unsuccessful in destroying it. No direct hits being obtained.	
		10.30 am	Relieved by 10th Gordon Highrs and moves into Brigade Support Disposition. C Coy in O.B.1. left of Loose Way. B Coy in O.B.1. right of Loose Way. D Coy in O.B.4 & O.B.5. A Coy in CURLEY Crescent. Battn. H.Qrs. at junction of Loose Way and Curley Crescent	
			Working parties found for the following:- 180th Tunnelling Coy RE: 253rd Tunnelling Coy RE and 93rd Field Coy RE.	
	9.		Above working parties found. Cleaning & repairing Communication Trenches up to O.G.1. 2nd Lieut D. TAYLOR reports from Cadet School and posted to D Coy.	
	10.		Above working parties again found. Work on Communication Trenches continues.	
	11.		Relieved by Yk. Bn. K.O.S.B. and proceeds to LABOURSE (Divisional Reserve). Arrives in Billets at 1.45 pm.	
		4.30 pm	Order to Stand To received from Brigade. Enemy having attacked Junction of 45th & 46th Brigade and succeeded in entering front and support.	
LABOURSE	12.		Battn. Standing to until 2.45 pm when order to "Stand Down" received.	
	13.		Parades put off on account of rain. In afternoon Battn. had Bath Parade at Baths at Labourse. Working party of 40 officers and 200 other ranks proceeds to Trenches. Major C.H. MARSH D.S.O. late of 16th Lancers & Y. K.O.S.B. assumes command of the Battn.	

Army Form C. 2118.

WAR DIARY
or
INTELLIGENCE SUMMARY.
(Erase heading not required.)

Instructions regarding War Diaries and Intelligence Summaries are contained in F. S. Regs., Part II. and the Staff Manual respectively. Title pages will be prepared in manuscript.

Page 46

Place	Date	Hour	Summary of Events and Information	Remarks and references to Appendices
LABOURSE	1916 May 14		Divine Service at 10 am	
		1.15 pm	Orders received for 2 officers and 100 men to proceed at once to trenches to report to 46th Bde.	
		2.50 pm	Orders received for two Coys to proceed to the trenches under orders of 46th Bde. The other two Coys and HdQrs to proceed to NOYELLES & be under orders of 46th Bde. C & D Coys proceeds to trenches and receives orders to occupy LANCASHIRE Trench. Bn. HdQrs & A & B Coy proceeds to billets at NOYELLES.	
NOYELLES		6 pm	Orders received from 46th Bde that A Coy occupy part of VILLAGE LINE. B Coy occupy billets in VERMELLES. Bn HdQrs to be in LANCASHIRE TRENCH. Orders carried out by 7.30pm	
	15	9 am	Orders received from 46th Bde for A & B Coys and HdQrs return to billets in NOYELLES. Arrives in billets at 10.45 am	
	16			
	17		A & B Coys relieves C & D Coys in Lancashire trench. C & D Coys took over billets of A & B Coys in NOYELLES. Enemy put seven large Howitzer Shells in the vicinity of the Chateau in the afternoon.	
	18			
	19		In the afternoon the enemy again put a few shells near the Chateau.	

WAR DIARY or INTELLIGENCE SUMMARY

Army Form C. 2118.

Place	Date	Hour	Summary of Events and Information	Remarks and references to Appendices
Left Sub-section Hohenzollern Section	1916 May 19		Page 77. Battn relieved 11th Argyll Sutherland Highrs in Left Sub-section, Hohenzollern Section. Disposition: "C" Coy on the Right: "D" Coy by the Centre: "A" Coy on the Left finding their own Supports, with "B" Coy in Reserve. 8/10th Gordon Highrs on our Right. 2nd Royal Welsh Fusiliers on our Left. Echelon of Front from Boyan 109 (exclusive) to MUD ALLEY (G4 & B.B)(inclusive)	
	20.		Enemy Shaky French intermittently throughout the day with Aerial darts. In the evening they put over a few French Trench Bombs & Rifle grenades into our front and support trenches. Casualties: Officers nil. Other Ranks: wounded 2 "A" Coy "B" Coy 1. Our Stafhead at G4. a. 8½. 8½. blown in by enemy T.M. Bombs. Things were quiet throughout the whole day. In the evening the enemy as usual fired a few French Trench Bombs, Rifle Grenades and Aerial Darts. We retaliated with Rifle Grenades etc which considerable losses enemy fire. Casualties: Officers nil. Other Ranks: wounded "A" Coy 1 B Coy 3 D Coy 3	
	21.	12:45 p.m.	The enemy sprang a mine between Craters 3 and 4. Most of the earth fell in a Southerly direction filling up our sapo and the French connecting Crater 3 to Crater 4. A lively bombing fight ensures in which our bombers held their ground and silenced the enemys bombers. By 4 p.m. all damage to our trenches had been repaired. The explosion of this mine has made no tactical difference to our position. Hostile artillery, Trench Mortars and rifle grenades were quiet throughout the day. (Casualties)	

Army Form C. 2118.

WAR DIARY
or
INTELLIGENCE SUMMARY.
(Erase heading not required.)

Instructions regarding War Diaries and Intelligence Summaries are contained in F. S. Regs., Part II. and the Staff Manual respectively. Title pages will be prepared in manuscript.

Place	Date	Hour	Summary of Events and Information	Remarks and references to Appendices
Left Sub-Section Hohenzollern Section			Page 78.	
	21		Casualties Officers: 2/Lt. J.S. ROBERTSON, killed. Other Ranks: killed C Coy 3, wounded B Coy 4 / D Coy 2 / C Coy 8 / D Coy 7	
	22	11:15 am	Our Engineers exploded a mine in the Centre Sub-section in front of the junction of FOSSE & POKER Streets and the fire trench. The explosion did no damage to our trenches. Hostile artillery is were quiet throughout the day. Casualties: nil.	
	23	7:30 am	The enemy exploded a mine at point G.4.d.6.5½. The explosion causes gaps 9' deep 9'. Argyle Sap, Hogs Back and part of Northampton trench to fillis in with debris. It was a complete surprise and many of the men were buried & injured by the falling debris. The 8/10th Gordon Hydr. afforde whose section the mine went up, occupies the new L.H. of Crater. This explosion causes our relief by the 8th Seaforth Highrs which has been arranged to commence at 9 am. as his Coys held the fields in parts of the trenches before handing over.	
		1 pm	Battn. relieved by 8th Seaforth Highrs. Battn. moved into Brigade Support. Disposition: A Coy. 1 platoon in JUNCTION KEEP, 3 platoons in LANCASHIRE TRENCH / B Coy. 1 platoon in CENTRAL KEEP, 3 platoons in RAILWAY RESERVE TRENCH / C Coy. in LANCASHIRE TRENCH / D Coy. in LANCASHIRE TRENCH / Battn. Headquarters at pt G.3.c.8.2. Casualties/	

WAR DIARY
or
INTELLIGENCE SUMMARY.
(Erase heading not required.)

Army Form C. 2118.

Place	Date	Hour	Summary of Events and Information	Remarks and references to Appendices
BRIGADE SUPPORT HOHENZOLLERN SECTION	1916 May 23		Page 79. Casualties: Officers nil. Other Ranks killed "C" Coy 3 - Wounded "B" Coy 4, C Coy 35, D Coy 4	
	24		Every available man employed in working parties. Casualties nil.	
	25		Every available man again employed in working parties. Casualties nil.	
	26		Working parties again found. Casualties nil.	
Right Subsection Hohenzollern Section	27		Battn relieved 9th Black Watch in Right Subsection, Hohenzollern Section. Disposition: B Coy on the Right. A Coy in the Centre. D Coy on the left finding their own supports with C Coy in reserve. Extent of front. From the junction of Sackville Street and Hulluch Alley on the left to the junction of Quarry Bay and Alexander Trench on the Right. Message received from Brigade the Aerial Reconnaissance reports abnormal railway traffic opposite our front. Eleven trains seen in the morning arriving at stations opposite Loos Salient. Enemy attack suspected.	
		9pm	Observed large enemy working party opposite RABBIT'S Hole. Shrieks + groans heard throughout the enemy artillery were significantly quiet. Two intelligence reports with statements of two prisoners received which shows that enemy intends to attack + were intending to use gas. Casualties: Officers nil. Other Ranks: B Coy missing believed killed 1. B Coy wounded 4.	
	28			

WAR DIARY or INTELLIGENCE SUMMARY

Army Form C. 2118.

Place	Date	Hour	Summary of Events and Information	Remarks and references to Appendices
Regtl Subsection Nothinghen Section	1916 May 28		Page 80.	
		8 p.m.	Everything very quiet throughout the day. Air reconnaissance reported abnormal transport moving in the direction of HAISNES also about 5000 men seen moving in a southerly direction towards South of that 5000 men were seen moving across the open. In the evening our centre Coy were much troubled by enemy trench mortars, our artillery retaliated on enemy's front line. After a few rounds enemy trench mortars ceased. Casualties Officers nil: Other Ranks: wounded B Coy 1 C.E.1 M.G. Detachment 1.	
	29	3.45 a.m.	Artillery frightfulness by our Right and Left Groups from 3.45 a.m. till 4.15 a.m. Enemy only retaliated slightly with Minnies on our Left Sub. Section.	
		9.45 a.m.	Enemy shells junction of Gose Way and O.B.1 with 4.2 Howitzers, our 18 Pounders retaliated on our front line. Casualties Nil –	
	30	1.30 p.m.	Enemy trench North of the HAIRPIN Crater. Enemy snarked around our Ancient fire. Enemy party repairing this snarking height were sniped by our snipers.	
		5 p.m.	Enemy shelled HULLUCH ALLEY and rifle grenaded RABBIT HOLE. Enemy shows two yellow flags with red St. Andrew's cross over his parapet at the Shrine.	

WAR DIARY
or
INTELLIGENCE SUMMARY
(Erase heading not required.)

Army Form C. 2118.

Place	Date	Hour	Summary of Events and Information	Remarks and references to Appendices
Right Sub Section HOHENZOLLERN Do Section	May 1916		Page 81	
	30		A heavy trench mortar bomb fell on top of one of our mine shafts heads in the front line. The shaft was collapsed, burying 20 of men who were as the time carrying sandbags from the mine. Casualties O.R. 1 killed "D" Coy 1 shock "D" Coy. 2 wounded "C" 1 crush "A" 1 wounded "B" 1 do "D" 2 shock "B"	
	31	9am to 10am	Rapid bg of HAIRPIN and front line behind Craters known there to enemy (T.M. Bombs)	
		11am	Enemy heavy shells FOSSE WAY, STANSFIELD ROAD & HULLUCH ALLEY	
		9pm	Enemy front line North of HAIRPIN craters fully traversed around by our heavy artillery. Our snipers dispersed enemy party, who were attempting to make good the damage. Casualties Nil. O.R. 1 wounded "C" Coy	

C.F.Walsh Lt Colonel
2nd CS Bordener Highlanders

7th Bn Cameron Highlanders

June 1916

1916

WAR DIARY
or
INTELLIGENCE SUMMARY

Army Form C. 2118.

Kens
7th Camerons
Vol 12

Place	Date	Hour	Summary of Events and Information	Remarks and references to Appendices
Right Sub Section HOHENZOLLERN Section	June 1		Extract from London Gazette of 31st May:- 2/Lt E J S LUMSDEN from Gordon Highrs to be Lieut. dated 2nd March 1916	
	2		2nd Lieut A Macniven rejoins the Battn.	
	3			
BETHUNE	4		Relieved by 1/6 K.O.S.B. "A" Coy proceeded to GOSNAY. The remainder of the Battn. proceeded to BETHUNE and went billeted in the Tobacco Factory (Rue de Lille) Here the following appeared in the Birthday Honours List:- "The King has been pleased to approve of the undermentioned rewards for Distinguished Service in the Field D.S.O. Major J.L. Cunningham D.C.M. S/1364Y Bath. Sgt Major A.K. Scott The G.O.C.-in-C. has under authority granted by His Majesty the King, awarded the following decorations:- D.C.M. S/3635 C.S.M. C.I.B. Davie Military Medal. S/11957 L/Cpl J McDougall S/13704 L/Cpl G.I. Sutherland S/16816 L/Cpl D Gardner	
	5			
	6		In Billets:- Day devoted to Batt Parade and cleaning-up	

Army Form C. 2118.

WAR DIARY
or
INTELLIGENCE SUMMARY.
(Erase heading not required.)

Place	Date	Hour	Summary of Events and Information	Remarks and references to Appendices
BETHUNE	June 6.		Page 63. In Billets: Companies paraded under Programme. Draft of 90 Other Ranks arrived from Base.	
	7.		In Billets: Companies carried out work under Programme. 2/Lt. J. Drew joined the Battn. from the Base.	
	8.		Do.	
	9.			
	10.		"A" Coy rejoined Battn. in Bethune	
	11.		Divine Service in Tobacco Factory	
Brigade Support HULLUCH SECTION	12.		Relieved 6/7 Royal Scots Fusiliers in Brigade Support: Disposition. "A" Coy in CURLEY CRESCENT. "B" Coy 2 platoons in O.B.1. 2 platoons in O.B.5. "C" Coy, Sixth Avenue between Hay Alley and Hulluch Road. "D" Coy 2 platoons in Sixth Avenue between Verdun Alley + Hay Alley. 2 platoons in Lone Tree Redoubt. Battn. Hd.Qrs at Junction of Curly Crescent + Gravel Way. Four platoons of 1/1 K.O. Royal Lancashire Regiment attached for four days for instruction.	
	13.		Battn. on Working Parties.	Casualties Wounded "D" Coy 1 other Rank. Do. "B" Coy 1 Do.
	14.		Do.	
	15.		Do.	
Right Sub-Section HULLUCH SECTION	16.		Relieved 8th Seaforth Hrs. in Right Sub-Section: Disposition "C" Coy on the Left. 2 platoons of "B" Coy in the Centre "D" Coy on the Right finding their own Supports. "A" Coy + 2 platoons of "B" Coy in Reserve Dispot. between Wings Way + Verdun Alley. 16th Division on the Right, 9th Black Watch on the Left.	Casualties Wounded "D" Coy 3 other ranks.
	17.			

Army Form C. 2118.

WAR DIARY
or
INTELLIGENCE SUMMARY.
(Erase heading not required.)

Instructions regarding War Diaries and Intelligence Summaries are contained in F.S. Regs., Part II. and the Staff Manual respectively. Title pages will be prepared in manuscript.

Place	Date	Hour	Summary of Events and Information	Remarks and references to Appendices
RIGHT SUBSECTION HULLUCH SECTION	June 17		Page 84	
			4 Platoons of 11th K.O.R. Lancashire Regt. rejoined their Battn. being relieved by one Coy of 13th 2nd London Regt. Draft of 20 other ranks arrived from Base. Casualties. Wounded D Coy 1 (Lce Cpl M.G.Coy)	
	18		Casualties. Killed D Coy 1 other rank. Draft of 15 other ranks arrived from Base.	
	19.		2/Lieut J.A. Macdonald invalided sick, struck off strength. Casualties Wounded D Coy 4 other ranks	
	20.		Casualties Wounded C Coy 3 other ranks	
	21.		Casualties Other Ranks Killed C Coy 1. Wounded C Coy 3 D Coy 3	
	22.		The Disposition of Companies changed to the following:- B Coy on the Left, 2 Platoons of 13th Surrey Regt. on the Centre, A Coy on the Right, finding their own Supports. 2 Coy 13th Surrey Bt. C and D Coys in Reserve Trench. Casualties other Ranks Killed A Coy 1. Wounded A Coy 1. B Coy 3	
	23.		2/Lieut R.B. Prudent & D mais joined from the Base. Draft of 40 other Ranks arrived from Base. Casualties other Ranks Wounded A Coy 1. B Coy 3. Shellshock B Coy 1	
	24.		2/Lieut G.C. McLeod joined from the Base. Casualties other Ranks Killed B Coy 1. Wounded A Coy 1. C Coy 2.	
	25./			

WAR DIARY or INTELLIGENCE SUMMARY

Page 85

Place	Date	Hour	Summary of Events and Information	Remarks and references to Appendices
RIGHT SUB-SECTION HOHENZOLLERN SECTION	June 25		Casualties Other Ranks. Wounded A Coy 1; Lewis Gun Detachment 1; Shell Shock, A Coy 2.	
	26		Casualties Other Ranks. Wounded B Coy 2, D Coy 1; Coy of 11th East Surrey Regt. left the trenches and rejoined their Battalion. 2/Lt Macauley, sick, struck off strength.	
	27		Casualties Other Ranks, wounded B Coy 1; C Coy 1; D Coy 1.	
	28	11.30 pm / 1 am	After discharge of gas from patrols of 30 men, 2/Lts Drew, Condie, Curry and McCrosti attempted to raid enemy lines. Owing to the enemy's wire not being cut only one patrol under 2/Lt Condie was able to reach German front line. This Coy bombed and returned to our own lines leaving 2/Lt McCrosti dead. 2/Lt Condie Sgt Small afterwards tried to bring back the body but after getting it back so far had to abandon attempt owing to enemy heavy machine gun fire. Casualties Other Ranks. Killed. B Coy 1; C Coy 6; D Coy 2; Wounded A Coy 1; B Coy 1; B Coy 2; C Coy 5; D Coy 9 Crushed, D Coy 1. Accidentally wounded C Coy 1.	
	29		Relieved by 10/11th Scottish Rifles. Battalion went into Billets. A & C Coys at the Orphanage, Bethune. B & D Coys in Vinquinoul. H.Q. & Coys in Bethune.	

Army Form C. 2118.

WAR DIARY
or
INTELLIGENCE SUMMARY.

(Erase heading not required.)

Instructions regarding War Diaries and Intelligence Summaries are contained in F. S. Regs., Part II and the Staff Manual respectively. Title pages will be prepared in manuscript.

Page 86.

Place	Date	Hour	Summary of Events and Information	Remarks and references to Appendices
BETHUNE & VERQUINEUL	June 29		In Billets. Day devoted to cleaning up. Chenekio accidentally wounded by bomb explosion. B Coy 2.	
	30.		In Billets. Companies carried out work laid down in programme.	

C.H. Marsh Lieut. Colonel
Cmdg 9th (S) Bn. Cameron Highrs.

7th Bn Cameron Highlanders

1916

15 July
7 Cameron

Vol 12

C 11

WAR DIARY
or
INTELLIGENCE SUMMARY.
(Erase heading not required.)

Army Form C 2118.

CONFIDENTIAL

War Diary
of
Seventh (S) Battalion Cameron Highlanders
From 1st July, 1916 to 31st July, 1916.

Army Form C. 2118.

WAR DIARY
or
INTELLIGENCE SUMMARY.
(Erase heading not required.)

Page 84

Place	Date	Hour	Summary of Events and Information	Remarks and references to Appendices
BETHUNE & VERQUINEUL	July 1, 2, 3, 4, 5		In Billets. Company training.	
LEFT SUB-SECTION HOHENZOLLERN SECTION	6.		Relieved 6/Y Royal Scots Sucking in Left Sub Section Hohenzollern Section. Disposition D Coy on the Left, C Coy in the Centre, A Coy on the Right finding their own supports. B Coy in Reserve. 8/10 Gordon Highrs on the Right. 3 4" Bde on the Left. 6th Seaforth Highrs on different. Staff of P.6. Other Ranks arrived from the Base. Quiet day.	
	7		Enemy shelled junction of MUD ALLEY, STICKY TRENCH & NORTHAMPTON TRENCH with heavy French Mortars doing considerable damage. Casualties. Other Ranks. Wounded A Coy 1. D Coy 1. Crushed A Coy 1.	
	8		In the forenoon MUD ALLEY and the QUARRY shelled with H.E.	
		10-11 pm	The Batt" stood to" owing to Brigade on Right being attacked. 4 of Enemy seen in the trenches wearing khaki caps similar to those worn by our infantry.	
		11.15 pm	A large mine was exploded in front of the Bde on our Left. Casualties. Other Ranks. Wounded B Coy 1. Crushed C Coy 1.	
	9	3.42 pm	All quiet until 3.42 pm when front line & heavy shelled with aerial darts and light mortars & the support lines with heavy mortars. This appears to be in retaliation for heavy mortars on enemy front line. Enemy's bombardment did considerable damage to the trenches but caused no casualties. Other Ranks. Wounded D Coy 2. Crushed A Coy 1. Shellshock A Coy 1.	
	10.			

A.D.S.S./Forms/C. 2118.

WAR DIARY or INTELLIGENCE SUMMARY

Army Form C. 2118.

Page 88

Place	Date	Hour	Summary of Events and Information	Remarks and references to Appendices
Left Sub-Section Hohenzollern Section	July 10	11.30 a.m.	Battn. due to be relieved by 6th Seaforth Highrs but owing to that Battn. carrying out a raid this night only the Right Left Centre Coys relieved. at at G.4.b.3.4.&5. 6th Seaforth Highrs raided enemys front line following explosion of mine. Enemys retaliation appears weak, most damage being done by his heavy mortars on our front line. During the raid enemy sent up numerous red rockets. Casualties: Other ranks wounded A Coy 1, C Coy 2. Crushed C Coy 1.	
Brigade Support Hohenzollern Section	11.		Right Coy, Reserve Coy & Headquarters relieved by 6th Seaforth Highrs. Battn. in Bde Support. Disposition A Coy, B Coy & 3 Platoons of D Coy in Lancashire Trench. C Coy in Railway Reserve trench and Central Keep. 1 Platoon D Coy in Junction Keep. Battn. found working parties. Casualties: Lieut J H MAUCHLIN wounded.	
	12.		Working parties. Casualties: Other ranks wounded A Coy 1.	
	13		Working parties. Casualties: Other ranks crushed C Coy 1.	
	14.		Working parties. Casualties: Other ranks wounded C Coy 1.	
Right Sub-Section Hohenzollern Section	14.		Relieved 9th Black Watch in Right Sub-Section. Disposition B Coy on the Right, D Coy in Centre, C Coy on the Right. Finding men over supports. A Coy in Reserve. With exception of occasional aerial darts the day was very quiet. Casualties: Other ranks wounded B Coy 1, C Coy 1.	
	15	4.40 a.m.	Enemy exploded a small mine near dug 96A opposite Centre Coy. No damage was done to our trenches. In the evening the enemy fired some heavy shrapnel over our support trenches. Casualties: Other ranks B Coy 1, C Coy 1.	
	16.	1.30 p.m. 4.30 p.m. 9-9.30 p.m.	Our Artillery carries out a programme laid down. Enemy retaliates on Crown Border trenches with 4.2 + 5.9 Howitzers doing considerable damage to Howitzers doing considerable damage	

WAR DIARY or INTELLIGENCE SUMMARY

Army Form C. 2118.

Place	Date	Hour	Summary of Events and Information	Remarks and references to Appendices
Right Sub Section Hohenzollern Section	July 16.		Page 89	
			Casualties: Other Ranks Killed C'Coy 1, D Coy 3. Wounded B Coy 5, C Coy 2, D Coy 2. Gas Shellshock C Coy 2.	
	17.	4 am	The enemy exploded a mine in the vicinity of Right Crater of the Hairpin.	
		12 noon	Our Engineers exploded two mines among the Hairpin Craters. Shellcraters were filled in part of our trenches around the left leg.	
			Artillery programme for this morning put off on account of mist. The day was quiet until	
		9 pm to 10.15 pm	9 pm when enemy commenced heavy bombardment of the front & support lines of the left and centre. This bombardment lasted until about 10.15 pm. During the bombardment a party of the enemy raided our trenches in the vicinity of ALEXANDER SAP and took one officer and 12 other ranks of this Bat.n. and three other ranks of the Queens prisoner. The officer and staff were patrolling the line at the time. The enemy left several bags of stick grenades in the sap. Our artillery was used for enemy bombardment.	
			Casualties: Killed Other Ranks B Coy 1, D Coy 2. Wounded B Coy 1, D Coy 1, D Coy 2. Shellshock D Coy 2. Missing believed prisoners of war: 2/Lt D TAYLOR, other ranks D Coy 12.	
	18.	6 pm	Our Engineers exploded two mines sites at the junction of RIFLEMANS ALLEY and ALEXANDER TRENCH. These explosions destroyed BORDER REDOUBT and the above junction and ALEXANDER SAP. Two craters were formed the left Crater being the larger. Immediately on the explosion our bombers rushed out and occupied the far lip of the Left Crater & tried to hold the Right Crater which was found unsuitable enough Rifle Grenades and Aerial darts. A Bombing fight was carried out on the top of the left Crater and the work of consolidating the Craters begun. The enemy did not attempt to occupy the new Craters but heavily bombarded them throughout the rest of the day with Rifle Grenades and Aerial darts.	
			Casualties: Killed 2/Lt M.D. MACDONALD. Other Ranks B Coy 1, D Coy 1. Wounded: Major T.L. CUNNINGHAM D.S.O. 2/Lt A. McNIVEN 2/Lt T. ORR 2/Lt G.C. MACLEAY. Other Ranks: A Coy 3, B Coy 6, C Coy 1, D Coy 2, D Coy 21. Crushed: Other Ranks C Coy 1. Shellshock: Other Ranks D Coy 1.	
	19			

Army Form C. 2118.

WAR DIARY
or
INTELLIGENCE SUMMARY.
(Erase heading not required.)

Instructions regarding War Diaries and Intelligence Summaries are contained in F. S. Regs., Part II. and the Staff Manual respectively. Title pages will be prepared in manuscript.

Page 90.

Place	Date	Hour	Summary of Events and Information	Remarks and references to Appendices
Right Sub Sector Hingette Section	July 19	12 noon to 3.45pm	Our Artillery carries out programme shelling enemy wire, front, support & communication trenches.	
		5.45pm	Enemy sprung a mine in existing Craters at HAIRPIN. Our trenches at left Coy were fallen in. Hostile Machine Gun fire on our digging party from the DUMP. Our Artillery were informed and silenced this machine gun. Except for a few heavy Trench Mortars & Rifle Grenades sent over in Right Coy area the enemy were quiet. Casualties: Other Ranks Killed 'C' Coy 2. Wounded 'C' Coy 2. 'D' Coy 2.	
	20		Enemy intermittently shells trenches at HAIRPIN CRATERS with Heavy Trench Mortars. Otherwise the day was quiet. Our Heavy Artillery retaliated. Casualties: Other Ranks wounded 'C' 2, 'D' Coy 2.	
	21		All day quiet. Casualties: Other Ranks wounded 'C' Coy 1.	
	22		Relieved by 2nd Royal Berkshire Regiment & proceeds to Billets at HOUCHIN. Casualties Other Ranks Wounded D Coy 1.	
HOUCHIN	23		Left Billets in HOUCHIN and proceeds via BRUAY to billets at DIEVAL.	
DIEVAL	24 25		In Billets at DIEVAL.	
	26		Left Billets in DIEVAL and marches via LA THIEULOYE & AVERDOINGT to Billets at GOUY-en-TERNOIS.	
GOUY-en-TERNOIS	27		Left Billets at GOUY-en-TERNOIS marches via HONVAL, REBREUVE & CANTELEUX to Billets at OCCOCHES.	
OCCOCHES	28		Marches from OCCOCHES to Billets at AUTHEUX.	
AUTHEUX	29 30		In Billets at AUTHEUX.	

Army Form C. 2118.

WAR DIARY
or
INTELLIGENCE SUMMARY.
(Erase heading not required.)

Place	Date	Hour	Summary of Events and Information	Remarks and references to Appendices
NAOURS	July 31.		Page 91.	
			Marched from AUTHEUX via FIENVILLERS and CANDAS to Billets at NAOURS.	

CNMarsh. Lieut-Colonel
Comdg 4th (S) Bn. Cameron Highlanders

44th Brigade.
15th Division.

1/7th BATTALION

CAMERON HIGHLANDERS

AUGUST 1 9 1 6

Attached:- Report on Operations 17/18th

Army Form C. 2118.

WAR DIARY
or
INTELLIGENCE SUMMARY.
(Erase heading not required.)

Page 92

Place	Date	Hour	Summary of Events and Information	Remarks and references to Appendices
NAOURS	Aug 1st		In Billets. Cleaning up - Inspecting arms	
"	2nd		In Billets. Practised ditch and rapid firing - Officers practised with Revolver	
"	3rd		In Billets. Draft 3g OR taken on the strength - 1 OR sent to Etaples for dispersal under age. 5/14355 Sgt H.A. REID proceeded to Cadet School for commission	
MIRVAUX	4th		Marched to MIRVAUX via TALMAS, SEPTENVILLE, Reveille 3 am Breakfast 3:20 am Sheet 1/100,000 formed up ready to move off 4.45 am	
LAHOUSSOYE	5th		Marched to LAHOUSSOYE via BEHENCOURT. 1 OR proceeded to ETAPLES for dispersal LENS Sheet AMIENS 1 under age. 1 OR proceeded to ETAPLES for hernia returned to unit 1/100,000	
			1 OR returned from No 4 SCOTTISH GENERAL HOSPITAL	
	6		In Billets & Bivouac. Following officers struck off strength on proceeding to Influenza MAJOR CUNNINGHAM D.S.O wounded 21/7/16 & Lieut MACNIVEN wounded 22/7/16	
			Practised chopping "Strong Post" conception formation Bathing parade in river	
			L'HALLUE. Church Parades Catholics 10.45 am. Presbyterians 6.30 pm	
	7th		In Billets & Bivouac. Bathing Parade in river L'HALLUE	
ALBERT	8th		Marched to Bivouac in field near ALBERT E.7.6	ALBERT Contoured Sheet 1/40,000

O.H.Murphy Cap
Cmdg 7

WAR DIARY or INTELLIGENCE SUMMARY

Army Form C. 2118.

Place	Date	Hour	Summary of Events and Information	Remarks and references to Appendices
			Page 93	
ALBERT	Augr 9th		2n Bivouac - The following orders issued - Bugle calls not to be sounded in any part of this area + whilst the Batt'n is in Bivouac smoke helmets to be worn as a defence against FRICOURT Troops will wear gas helmets in position "F" gas alert. EAST of NORTH and SOUTH line drawn through ALBERT. Troops during daylight must not move in larger bodies than Platoons at 200 yds distance.	
ALBERT	10th		2. Bivouac. Intra-company games.	
ALBERT	11th		2. Bivouac. The Batt'n supplied working parties of 400 O.R. The following instructions issued:- N° 4 Platoon in each Coy to be the Pioneer Platoon. Nos 1,2 & 4 Platoons will be made up to the strength of three full fighting units of 105. N° 3 Platoon will be the weak Platoon. The following officers are taken on the strength from Cadet School. 2nd Lieut. E.D. Hans HOSKEN posted to D Coy 2nd Lieut. E.L.R. DAVIE posted to A Coy 2nd Lieut. J. MACMURRAY posted to C Coy	

O.H. Band Lt Col
7th Cameron High"

Army Form C. 2118.

WAR DIARY
or
INTELLIGENCE SUMMARY.
(Erase heading not required.)

Page 94

Place	Date	Hour	Summary of Events and Information	Remarks and references to Appendices
E.5.6.7.6	Aug 12		Brigade in Division Reserve. Relieved 9th Black Watch in Bivouac at E.5.6.7-6	Attack Map continued Sheet 1/40000
	13		do Divine service at 10 a.m.	do
X.22.a. (Peakwood)	14		Brigade moved into front line. Batt[alio]n formed Brigade Reserve in "C" area. Disposition Headquarters X.22.a Central. C & D Coys in Contalmaison. A & B Coys in X.22.b.	
X.12.a. Peakwood	15		Formed Brigade Reserve in C area. Found working Parties working Highland Trench	Washington Area Map attached B 1/20000
B. Area The Cutting	16		2 O.R. Transferred to tunnelling Coy. 2nd Lieut. J. Mackay wounded. Relieved 9th Black Watch in B. Area - Brigade Support. Disposition Headquarters in the Cutting. C Coy (less 1 Platoon) + D Coy in Bowley Trench. C Coy on the right. D Coy on the left. 1 Platoon C Coy + Kents line in Vivien Keep. A Coy in Contalmaison. B Coy in Cutting Contalmaison X.17.a. Draft of 50 O.R. Received. Casualties nil. Orders received from the Brigade to attack next morning	

2353 Wt. W2344/1454 700,000 5/15 D.D.&L. A.D.S.S./Forms/C. 2118.

Army Form C. 2118.

WAR DIARY
or
INTELLIGENCE SUMMARY.
(Erase heading not required.)

Instructions regarding War Diaries and Intelligence Summaries are contained in F. S. Regs., Part II. and the Staff Manual respectively. Title pages will be prepared in manuscript.

Place	Date	Hour	Summary of Events and Information	Remarks and references to Appendices
A Area (Front line)	Augt. 17th		Page 95	
			Moved up to the attack for details see operation orders and reports in Appendices	Montrepuich area B2h 1/2 gone
			Disposition. Headquarters in Bowlay Trench	
			7/8th K.O.S.B.'s on the right	
			9th Black Watch on the left and in front line	
			8th Seaforths in support.	
			Relieved by 8th Seaforths during the night and early morning A & B Coys	
			in Contalmaison C & D Coys in X 22 b. (C area)	
			Casualties. Officers killed	
			Lieut H. B. Hardman	
			2/Lieut H. B. Borrodie M.C.	
			2/Lieut J. M. Anderson	
			2/Lieut E. C. Mackay	
			Officers died of wounds	
			Lieut J. B. Cameron	
			Officers wounded	
			Capt. H. B. Johnstone 2/Lieut C. R. S. Scott	
			Capt. A. Ogilvy 2/Lieut R. B. Purden	
			Lieut Murchison 2/Lieut b. Mill	
			2/Lieut S. A. Keen 2/Lieut D. Morris	
			2/Lieut C. W. D. Mackay	

(signature) Lt Col

Army Form C. 2118.

WAR DIARY
or
INTELLIGENCE SUMMARY.
(Erase heading not required.)

Place	Date	Hour	Summary of Events and Information	Remarks and references to Appendices
"A" Area (Franvillers)	August 17th		Page 96. Casualties continued - other ranks. Killed A Coy 13 died of wounds A 1 missing believed A Coy 4 killed B. Coy 13 B. 3 B Coy 2 C. Coy 10 C. - C. Coy 2 D Coy 4 D. - D. Coy 1 Total 40 Total 4 Total 9 missing A Coy 2 missing believed wounded A Coy 38 B Coy 2 wounded A Coy 7 B Coy 43 C Coy 2 C Coy 49 D Coy 1 D. Coy 30 Total 7 Total 160	
"C" Area	18th		In Brigade reserve - Reorganizing Batt's Casualties 2 O.R. "D" Coy wounded.	
C Area	19th		In Brigade reserve Re organizing. Found working parties. Casualties killed A Coy 1 wounded D Coy 1. D Coy 1 Total 2	

Army Form C. 2118.

WAR DIARY
or
INTELLIGENCE SUMMARY.
(Erase heading not required.)

Instructions regarding War Diaries and Intelligence Summaries are contained in F. S. Regs., Part II. and the Staff Manual respectively. Title pages will be prepared in manuscript.

Page 97.

Place	Date	Hour	Summary of Events and Information	Remarks and references to Appendices
B. Area	Aug 20		Relieved 8/10th Gordon Highrs in Brigade Support – "B" Battn Area. Reveille 4.30 am. Breakfast 5.30 am. Moved off 6.30 am. Disposition – C Coy less 1 Platoon joined D Coy in Support trench. D. Coy on our left taking on its right with its right on the left of 1 Coy of 8/10th Gordons which remained in Support trench. 1 Platoon C Coy and 1 Lewis Gun in Pillar Keep. A. Coy in Coulotmaison. B Coy in the Cutting. Battery position behind the cutting heavily shelled with gas shells from about 10 p.m. till 2 a.m (21st Aug). No casualties in B.62.	As
B. Area	21		In Brigade Support. Found working parties. Casualties wounded A Coy 1, C Coy 5. Total 6	C/O Lt Col and Lt Cameron, 2ic Capt M. Hyde

2353 Wt. W2544/1454 700,000 5/15 D. D. & L. A.D.S.S./Forms/C. 2118.

Army Form C. 2118.

WAR DIARY
or
INTELLIGENCE SUMMARY.
(Erase heading not required.)

Page 98.

Place	Date	Hour	Summary of Events and Information	Remarks and references to Appendices
A. Area	Aug 12.		Relieved 8/10" Gordon Highlanders in front line – Disposition A Coy 2 Platoons Sniping Trench 2 Platoons Lanca Trench B Coy in Bowden Trench C Coy in Cameron Trench between London Alley and Shosh alley with supports in Highland Trench. D Coy in Cameron Trench between Gordon alley and Munster alley with supports in Butterworth Trench. Headquarters in Bowling Trench. During the night commence construction of 6 strong points 160yds in front of front line – Received draft of 153 O.R. Casualties wounded A Coy 1 died of wounds killed C. Coy 3 B Coy 2 B Coy 1 D Coy 4 C Coy 3 Total 4 D Coy 1 Total 7	do.

C.T.W. Lt Col
Commanding 11th A. & S. Highrs.

WAR DIARY
or
INTELLIGENCE SUMMARY.

Army Form C. 2118.

Place	Date	Hour	Summary of Events and Information	Remarks and references to Appendices
			Page 99	
"A" Area	Aug 23		In front line "A" Batt" area. Heavily shelled during night - 5" of the shining period started previous night made it for occupation. Casualties killed C Coy 2 D Coy 1 & 3rd 3 wounded C Coy 1 Shell shock Coy 2	
Scott's Redoubt	24		In Brigade Reserve. Relieved by 9th Batt" Black Watch and reliere 8th/10th Gordon Highlanders in SCOTTS REDOUBT. Received draft of 105 O.R. The following officers joined the Batt": 2nd Lieut Brown D.M. 2nd Lieut McLean W.J. " Burer J.G. " McPherson R.S.M. " Coventry C.J. " Seattie D.F. " Harriet E.W. " Watt F.D. " Jardine R " Lambert J.L " Zugala A.D.S.	O.K.W. Cunningham Lt Col Comm'g

Army Form C. 2118.

WAR DIARY
or
INTELLIGENCE SUMMARY.
(Erase heading not required.)

Page 100.

Place	Date	Hour	Summary of Events and Information	Remarks and references to Appendices
SCOTTS REDOUBT C. Area	Aug 25 26		2n Brigade Reserve. Found working Parties. Relieved 8/10th Gordon Highlanders in C. Batt. Area Reveille 4.15 am. Breakfast 5 am. C & D Coy in new position by 6.30 am A & B Coys in new position by 7 a.m. Disposition C & D Coy in CONTALMAISON A & B Coy in X 22 b. Found working parties. 2nd LIEUT. J. R STEELE join the Batt.	do
C. Area B. Area	27 28		2n Brigade Reserve. Found working Parties. 2n Brigade Support. Relieved 8/10th GORDON HIGHLANDERS in B. Sub Area Disposition — A Coy in GOURLAY TRENCH B Coy less 1 Platoon in do	M.L. Huf Chief in Command

WAR DIARY
or
INTELLIGENCE SUMMARY.
(Erase heading not required.)

Army Form C. 2118.

Place	Date	Hour	Summary of Events and Information	Remarks and references to Appendices
B Area	Aug 28		Page 101	do
			1 Platoon B Coy sent 1 Lewis Gun to KEEP CONTALMAISON VILLA	
			C Coy in CONTALMAISON	
			D Coy in the CUTTING	
			Garrison for VILLA KEEP moved off at 2.30 a.m.	
			A. B. Coys (less 1 Platoon) to be in new position by 5 a.m.	
			C. D Coys to be in new position by 5-30 a.m.	
			Working Party under LIEUT. ORR continued wiring HIGHLAND TRENCH.	
			Casualties A Coy 1 killed C Coy 1 wounded	
			"7 LIEUT. R.N.B. SEMPLE" joined the Batt'n	
			The following Special Order issued (1274)	
			The Commanding Officer wishes to thank all Officers N.C.O.s and men for the excellent work done by them on the 17th inst. in capturing the allotted portion of the German Trench. They have well upheld the good name of the Cameron Highlanders and he feels sure he can rely on them to do the same in the future.	
			C. J. Willock Lt Col	
			7 Cameron H'rs	

Army Form C. 2118.

WAR DIARY
or
INTELLIGENCE SUMMARY.
(Erase heading not required.)

Page 102

Place	Date	Hour	Summary of Events and Information	Remarks and references to Appendices
B. Area	Augt 28		He greatly deplores the loss of so many good soldiers who can be ill spared at this period of the war — The following wire was received from the G.O.C. 15th Division:— The G.O.C. congratulates you on your fine success The following wire was received "Fourth Army":— Please convey the Army Commanders congratulations to the 15th and 1st Divisions on their successes and the enterprise they are displaying which is invaluable at this stage of the battle —	do
B. Area	29		In Brigade Support Wiring Party under Lieut ORR completed wiring HIGHLAND TRENCH Casualties – C Coy 1 wounded	
Bivouac O.R.1 Trench X.26.d.	30		Brigade moved into Divisional Reserve Relieved by 24th NORTHUMBERLAND Fus.l and occupied bivouac at O.B.1 Trench X.26.d.–	Attack Loos Aug 15

C.F.W.? Cummins? Lt Col. Cmdg 7.

WAR DIARY
or
INTELLIGENCE SUMMARY.

Page 103

Place	Date	Hour	Summary of Events and Information	Remarks and references to Appendices
Bivouac O.B.1 Trench X.2.b.d.	Aug 30th		Extract from London Gazette dated 12.8.16. Temporary Captain N. MacLeod to be Temy Major dated 1st April 1916. 2nd Lieut F.B. Cameron to be Temy Lieut dated 23rd May 1916	
Bivouac O.B.1 Trench X.2.b.d.	31st		In Divisional Reserve. Casualties C Coy 1 wounded D Coy 1 wounded	

Lieut. Col
1st Cameron Highrs

Army Form C. 2118.

WAR DIARY
or
INTELLIGENCE SUMMARY. Appendix
(Erase heading not required.)

Place	Date	Hour	Summary of Events and Information	Remarks and references to Appendices
Albert	Aug 17		Page 104	

Division Orders No. 3 by Lieut Colonel (A.A. Boswell) D.S.O. Commanding 7th (S)
Batt. Cameron Highrs.

Reference 15th Division
Map No 3 a/14 S/16
1/5000.

Wednesday 16th August 1916.

1. The 4th Camerons this will assault the German trench line between the
points S.1.d.4.8. and X.6.a.7.3. on the 17th inst.

2. A, B, & C Coys will form first and second lines. D Coy will be in
reserve.

3. Junction of new trench in the new trench, dug by the ― Battalion,
running from GLOSTER ALLEY to Boyau running BUTTERWORTH TRENCH
and NEW SWITCH about 100 yards parallel to and South German line.

Army Form C. 2118.

WAR DIARY
or
INTELLIGENCE SUMMARY.
(Erase heading not required.)

Appendices

Page 10 E

Assaulting Tactics.

4 (a) First line will consist of the first two Platoons of each of A, B, & C Coys.

Second line will consist of the third Platoon of each of the 3 (above-named) Companies and will follow about 30 yards in rear of first line.

(b) 'D' Coy will be in reserve in BUTTERWORTH TRENCH.

(c) To first fighting 10 of the left Platoon of each of A, B, & C Coys, will form the covering Party under 2/Lt PURDON. This Party will push straight across the German line and take up a position in shell holes as far forward as possible under the Artillery barrage. This Party will be reinforced by 2 Lewis Guns, one on the right & the other on the left.
These two Guns will go over with the second line covering Party.

Page 106

will not withdraw until word is received from the O.C. "A", "B" & "C" Coys.

Memoranda of the first line will form the cleaning party. Live P. Bombs
two Coy. have been issued for dealing with dug outs.

(d) Platoons forming the second line will be the digging parties under:
2/Lt Moir, of "A" Coy., 2/Lt. Black, of "B" Coy. and 2/Lt Scott of "C" Coy.
These Officers will send messages to the R.E. N.C.O.s when they are
ready for the R.E. Personnel to come up. Those digging Platoons
will construct Strong points at about S.18.d.3, S.1.b.11 and X.6.a.9.3.
The following R.E. Personnel will assist each of these Platoons
in constructing the Strong Points:- 1 N.C.O. and 3 men

BLOCKING PARTIES

Double Blocks will be established at about S.1.d.4.8 and X.6.a.9.3
(if necessary) 1 Lewis Gun 10 from B Coy with a Lewis Gun,

Page 107

2/Lt GOUDIE was go over with the second line to establish a double post at about X6a 93 (if necessary) or to bomb the length of the trench. One N.C.O. and three men R.E. will be attached to each of these two parties.

Thirty Mills Grenades and forty rounds double bandolier are issued to each of these two parties.

CARRYING PARTIES

O.C. "D" Company will detail 2/Lt ANDERSON with three fighting teams as carrying parties to the R.Es. R.E. Stores will be brought up when required and dumped in GERMAN SWITCH in central position. Carrying parties will then assist R.E. in consolidating Strong Point.

Two fighting teams of "D" Company will be detailed to carry up S.A.A. Bombs very lights from Dumps to Strong Point. Men required from "D" Company

One fighting team from "D" Company is detailed to carry up

Army Form C. 2118.

WAR DIARY
or
INTELLIGENCE SUMMARY.

(Erase heading not required.)

Instructions regarding War Diaries and Intelligence Summaries are contained in F. S. Regs., Part II. and the Staff Manual respectively. Title pages will be prepared in manuscript.

appendix

Place	Date	Hour	Summary of Events and Information	Remarks and references to Appendices
			Page 10 b	

water in Rebel line to Sheg Point
" " " " " "

DUMPS

R.E. Dump will be formed at X.6.C.8.9.
S.A.A. & Bomb Dump " " X.6.C.8.6 & X.6.C.6.7

each S.A.A. & Bomb Dump containing 12 Boxes S.A.A. and 30 boxes bombs and 2 Boxes Very lights & 10 two gallon tins of water allowing 8 Boxes S.A.A, 20 Boxes bombs and 1 Box Very Lights and 7 tins of water for each of the 3 Sheg Points.

5/ Companies will be in position in Trenches 1/2 an hour before ZERO hour
ZERO HOUR — 8.55 a.m.

6/ A party of 10 men will be detailed by O.C "D" Company to join GLOSTER Sap to German trip.

1577 Wt.W10791/1773 500,000 1/15 D.D.&L. A.D.S.S./Forms/C. 2118.

Army Form C. 2118.

WAR DIARY
or
INTELLIGENCE SUMMARY.
(Erase heading not required.)

Appendix

App 1 og

7. Action by BLACK WATCH

(i) Clear GLOSTER ALLEY and BUTTERWORTH Trench up to Bogan leading to New Switch, & troops by 7 a.m.

(ii) Holding a Party to connect point x.6.a.82. to Serven Line about x.6.a.9.3. This Party will be ready to commence work as soon as the Switch trench has been gained.

(iii) Keep down hostile fire from suspected Snipy Point at x.6.a.93 by Lewis Gun fire from x.6.a.7½. 3½ minutes from ZERO hour.

8. Action by 44th T.M. Battery.

(i) At ZERO hour slowly a barrage on Serven Trench about (S.1.d.5.8)

(ii) At ZERO hour establish an intense bombardment of Serven Trench from about x.6.a.9.½ to a.9.3. This bombardment will cease when the artillery barrage lifts

WAR DIARY
or
INTELLIGENCE SUMMARY.
(Erase heading not required.)

Army Form C. 2118.

Appendix

Page 110

46th T.M. Battery will assist at ZERO hour by bombarding German line from point S.1.d.5.8. eastwards to Railway/ Bombardment to continue to +15 minutes.

9. Action by 44th Machine Gun Coy
(i) To cover the flank of the attack from Point X.6.a.0.5 to the east, and to be ready to take advantage of any target which may present themselves.
(ii) To keep down hostile fire which may come from snipers in shell holes east of GLOSTER ALLEY & S/of German Trench. 46th M.G. Coy will co-operate to the east.

10. Prisoners will be sent to Battalion Headquarters whence they will be sent to GOURLAY TRENCH and handed over to L company of the 8th Seaforths who will escort them to the Corps/Divl. Station at X.28.b.2.6.

WAR DIARY
or
INTELLIGENCE SUMMARY.

Page III

Appendix

11. **Outline of Artillery Action** — 34th Divisional Artillery

  (i) At ZERO hour open an intense barrage 20 yds in front German Front from S.2.a.9.4. to X.6.a.9.3.

  (ii) At this one minute to lift on front of attack to 120 yds and form a barrier round area being consolidated.

  (iii) Similar barrage on rest of German line.

  (iv) Deal with dangerous points in area Corps Artillery.

  Also need cutting in S.2.a. MARTINPUICH Strong Points about X.6.a.2.9 and R.35.G.4.4. with H.A. & Gas Shells. Deal with dangerous points in area.

12. **Medical Arrangements**

  Battalion Aid Post will be situated at junction of O.G.1. with CONTALMAISON/MARTINPUICH Road. Stretcherbearers will not accompany the assaulting line but

Appendix

Page 112

units remained in the quarry SW trench with the services as required

13 Reports made to be forwarded to Battalion Headquarters, position of which not be notified later.

14 Dress Fighting Order. Sufficient food and water for 24 hours units to carry with them.

(sgd) H.B HARDMAN
Lieut & A/Adjt
7th (S) Bn Cameron Highlanders

Army Form C. 2118.

WAR DIARY
or
INTELLIGENCE SUMMARY.
(Erase heading not required.)

Place	Date	Hour	Summary of Events and Information	Remarks and references to Appendices
			Page 113 Appendix	

Appendix

Report to the Brig'. General Commanding the 44th Infantry Brigade by the Officer Commanding the 7th Cameron Highlanders on the attack by the Batt'n on the SWITCH LINE of German Trenches —

1. Assaulting parties left HIGHLAND TRENCH at 8.55 am on the 17th August at the same time as the Artillery Barrage opened. The German line was easily entered. As our men reached the German line a lot of Germans came forward holding up their hands. These were either killed or taken prisoner. The clearing up parties started work and the parties detailed for stopping went forward and started work. A few men went out as a covering party. Digging was carried on till about 10.15 am. By this time the Germans started a bombing attack from the right as there was no officer in the German trench most having been either killed or wounded, the men began to give ground. Captain Moore who was on the right and was with the digging party seeing this came back with Lieut. Orr and organized a bombing attack on the right and formed

Appendix

Page 114   Appendix Continued

a block. Lieut Black was out digging No 2 Strong Point getting heavily sniped by machine gun with clear into the German line and assisted in returning the fire. Officers and deepening the trench. I got word that more bombs were needed in the newly taken trench so formed chains to pass up bombs from the pre-arranged dumps. In the meantime German bombers were used in large numbers. I used two platoons of the 9th Gordon High[rs] who had come up to the hindustan bombs in carrying bombs from Cortal- manor Villa & Buckworth french dumps. These parties were invaluable.

11·45 a.m. About 11·45 a.m. seeing that we were not holding the E.150 N Captain Macrae was trying to collect men to retake this point from the end of Blackline and but he had a difficulty in finding sufficient men and getting sufficient bombs. The Germans had formed a block at the E.150 N so Captain Macrae got the Stokes gun to shoot this point and shortly after the Stokes gun and team were put out of action by by shell fire

1 pm At about 1 pm I with Captain Macrae started to organise two counter attack

WAR DIARY
or
INTELLIGENCE SUMMARY

Army Form C. 2118.

Place	Date	Hour	Summary of Events and Information	Remarks and references to Appendices
Page 115			Appendix continued	
		2.15 pm	I met L' Anderson of the Black Watch and found Martin Ratting and got him to send for another gun and get up more ammunition. The both same time as the team had also been knocked out. At about 2.15 I got word that a Coy of the Seaforth Highlanders had just arrived so I sent for the Coy Commander and he told me he had a weak Coy of about 80 men and they had been carrying sand-bags. So I determined to use two platoons of this Coy for the counter attack. At about 3.50 pm I got word from my left that the Germans were massing on the Warlencourt – Pozières road so informed artillery forward observation officer – the German shell fire were falling pretty heavy by this time. All the arrangements for the counter attack were not completed before 5.50 pm when the two platoons of Seaforth High's about 50 men with a few 7th Camerons men retook the elbow in the even of the elbow gun fire and consolidated the position. I returned with few casualties.	
		5.50 pm		
		6.15 pm	At about 6.15 pm. the Germans opened a heavy on our front line	

WAR DIARY
or
INTELLIGENCE SUMMARY

Page 116

Appendices

8 p.m. with heavy shells until about 8 p.m. then lifted for a bit and then started again.

My Batt⁵ was relieved at about 12.30 a.m. 18ᵗʰ August by the 8ᵗʰ Seaforth Highlanders.

Approximate casualties Officers killed 4 wounded 10 other ranks wounded and missing 240. I should like to notice the following officers for good work Captain Uncome Lieut Orr, Black, Younger, Stein — also Captain Binnie 9ᵗʰ Black Watch for assisting us in consolidating the front line when most of my officers were casualties.

We took 16 prisoners all of the 179ᵗʰ Regiment. We also destroyed two German Machine Guns in the Switch Line.

(Sgd) E. H. Marsh Lt. Col
7ᵗʰ Cameron High⁵

Headquarters
44th S.B.

APPENDIX H³

20ᵗʰ

Attack by 7ᵗʰ Cameron Highlanders on SWITCH LINE

1. Assaulting Parties left HIGHLAND TRENCH at 8.55 a.m. at the same time as the Artillery barrage opened. The German line was easily entered. As our men reached the German line a lot of Germans came forward holding up their hands. These were either killed or taken prisoners. The clearing up party started work, and the parties detailed for digging went forward and started work, a few men went out as a covering party. Digging was carried on until about 10-15 a.m. By this time the Germans started a Bombing Attack from the right, and as there were no Officers in the German Trench, most having been killed or wounded, our men began to give ground. Capt. McCRAE who was on the right, and was out with the digging party, seeing this, came back with 2/Lt ORR and organised a bombing attack to the right and formed a block. 2/Lt. BLACK was out digging No 2 Strong-post. Getting heavily sniped by M.G. fire on right he withdrew into the firing line and assisted in reversing the fire step & deepening the trench. I got word that more Bombs were needed in the newly taken trench so formed chains to pass up Bombs from the pre-arranged dumps. In the meantime German Bombs were used in large numbers. I used two Platoons of the 9ᵗʰ Gordon Highlanders, who had come up to lay Trench boards, in carrying Bombs from CONTALMAISON VILLA to BUTTERWORTH TRENCH dumps. These parties were invaluable.

About 11.45 a.m. seeing that we were not holding the ELBOW, Captain McCrae was trying to collect men to retake this point from the end of GLOSTER SAP, but had difficulty in collecting sufficient men, and getting sufficient Bombs. The Germans had formed

[margin note: This Officer were interesting the Construction of Strong point by]

2

209 x

formed a block at the ELBOW, so Capt. McCrae got the Stokes Gun to strafe this point and shortly after the Stokes Gun and team were put out of action by shell fire. At about 1 p.m. I met Capt. McCrae and re-started to organise the counter-attack. I ~~saw~~ Lieut. Anderson, 9th Black Watch, of the Trench Mortar Battery and got him to send for another gun and get up more ammunition. This took some time as the team had also been knocked ~~into~~ out. At about 2-15 p.m. I got word that a Company of the 8th Seaforth Highlanders had just arrived so I sent for the Company Commander and he told me he had a weak Coy. of about 80 men ~~& they~~ had been carrying sandbags. So I determined to use two Platoons of this Company for the counter-attack. At about 3-50 p.m. I got word from my left that Germans were massing on MARTINPUICH - POZIERES Road, so informed Artillery, F.O.O. The German shell fire was getting pretty heavy by this time. All arrangements for the counter attack were not completed before 5-50 p.m. when the 2 Platoons of 8th Seaforths (about 50 men) with a few 7th Camerons re-took the ELBOW under cover of the Stokes Gun fire, and consolidated the position with very little opposition, and, I understand, few casualties.

At about 6-15 p.m. the Germans opened a very heavy barrage on our front line with heavy shells until about 8 p.m. and then lifted for a bit and then started again. My Battalion was relieved at about 12-30 a.m. on 18th August by the 8th Seaforths. Approximate Casualties. Officers killed four. wounded ten. O.Rs. killed, wounded & missing 240.

I should like to bring to notice the following Officers for good work. Capt. Bateman R.A.M.C. Captain McCrae, 2/Lieuts. Orr, Black, Fraser & Moir, also Captain Binnie, 9th Black Watch for assisting us in consolidating the front line when most of my Officers were casualties. ✱

We took 18 Prisoners of the 179th Regiment. We also destroyed 2 German Machine Guns in the SWITCH LINE.

✱ Also 2/Lieut. Turnbull 8th Seaforths who relieved the SWITCH ELBOW

19/8/16

C/ Smith
LT. COLONEL
COMMDG 7th (SERVICE) Bn. CAMERON HIGHLANDERS

Vol 15
44/15

Q 13

WAR DIARY

OF

7TH (SERVICE) BATTALION CAMERON HIGHLANDERS

FOR

MONTH OF SEPTEMBER 1916.

PAGES 114 to 125 INCLUSIVE

Army Form C. 2118.

WAR DIARY
or
INTELLIGENCE SUMMARY.
(Erase heading not required.)

Instructions regarding War Diaries and Intelligence Summaries are contained in F. S. Regs., Part II. and the Staff Manual respectively. Title pages will be prepared in manuscript.

Place	Date	Hour	Summary of Events and Information	Remarks and references to Appendices
			Page 114	
BIVOUAC O.B.I X.2.b.d.	Sept 1		In Divisional Reserve -	
	2		do. Physical Drill, Handling of Arms under Coy arrangement. R.Q.M.S. Watson proceeded to England for duty as Temp: Q: M: to 11 R WEST SURREY REGIMENT.	
	3.		do. Inspection of Drafts by Brig. General. Church Parade 10 a.m. Baths allotted to Coys. Sgt. Brown promoted C.Q.M.S. vice C.Q.M.S. Wilson. C.Q.M.S. Wilson promoted R.Q.M.S. vice R.Q.M.S. WATSON.	
	4		do. Physical Drill Handling of Arms.	
FRONT LINE RIGHT Bde AREA	5		Batt. relieved the 12th H.L.I and 10th SCOTTISH RIFLES in front line Right Brigade Area ORDER OF RELIEF. B. Coy + 2 Hotchkiss Lewis Guns relieved A. 'D Coy 12th H. L. I. in front line left in SWANSEA TRENCH between the Novel in S.2.C. and NORTHAMPTON TRENCH. 1 Platoon D Coy will relieve 2 Platn of C. Coy 12 H.L.I.	

[signature] Lieut. Major
for Comm. 11th High. L. I.

Army Form C. 2118.

WAR DIARY
or
INTELLIGENCE SUMMARY.
(Erase heading not required.)

Instructions regarding War Diaries and Intelligence Summaries are contained in F. S. Regs., Part II. and the Staff Manual respectively. Title pages will be prepared in manuscript.

Page 115

Place	Date	Hour	Summary of Events and Information	Remarks and references to Appendices
FRONT LINE RIGHT Bde AREA	Sept 5.		in INTERMEDIATE TRENCH. 2. Plat'ns D Coy relieved 2 Plat of C Coy and B Coy 13th H.L.I. in MILL STREET. 1. Plat'n C Coy were in the QUARRY. A Coy with C Coy Lewis guns and 2 H.gun teams have relieved the front Coys 10th SCOTTISH RIFLES. in the firing line RIGHT in BETHEL SAP, CLARKS TRENCH. Strong point. A Coy left to right in NORTH -AMPTON TRENCH C Coy relieved the support Companies 10th SCOTTISH RIFLES with 2 Plat'ns ARGYLE ALLEY and 2 Plat's in CHESTER STREET. ROUTE CONTALMAISON, THE CUTTING, CONTALMAISON and JUTLAND ALLEY TIME B Coy 1 Plat'n D Coy for INTERMEDIATE TRENCH 1 A.M. 5 A.M D Coy (two above Plat's) + H.guns Coy	

Norman Mucked Maj
7th Cameron High

Army Form C. 2118.

WAR DIARY
or
INTELLIGENCE SUMMARY.
(Erase heading not required.)

Instructions regarding War Diaries and Intelligence Summaries are contained in F.S. Regs., Part II. and the Staff Manual respectively. Title pages will be prepared in manuscript.

Page 116.

Place	Date	Hour	Summary of Events and Information	Remarks and references to Appendices
FRONT LINE RIGHT Bde Area	Sept 5		FRONT LINE TIME 2 Plat" C Coy fm ARGYLE ALLEY 1 p.m. 2 Plat" C Coy fm CHESTER STREET 2.30 p.m. A. Coy at 4.45 p.m. All movements at 400 yds interval between Platoons. A. B. Coy did then cooking individually C & D. Coy took up their dinners. Medical Aid Post at Batt" Headquarters. Batt" Headquarters - In the QUARRY	
do	6		FRONT LINE. Killed A Coy 1 O.R. wounded B Coy 4 O.R. B. Coy 1 O.R.	
O.B.1 between S.7.c.2.1 and S.14.a.3.6	7		Batt" moved into position in O.B.1. from S.7.c.2.1. to S.14.a.3.6 (behind BAZENTIN-LE-PETIT WOOD) being relieved by the 6th Batt" SEAFORTH HIGHLANDERS. Disposition from left to right D. B. C (less Plat" J) + A. Coys Moveau Macleod Major 7h Cameron H'rs	

2353 Wt. W2541/1454 700,000 5/15 D.D.&L. A.D.S.S./Forms/C 2118.

Army Form C. 2118.

WAR DIARY
or
INTELLIGENCE SUMMARY.
(Erase heading not required.)

Place	Date	Hour	Summary of Events and Information	Remarks and references to Appendices
O.G.1. between 7.C.2.1 and S.14.a.3.6	Aug 7		Reserve. Disposition 1 Plat D. Coy and 2 Lewis Guns relieved the garrison of the Keep held by D Coy 5th SEAFORTHS Hrs. at about 6. S.7.6.4.8. Platoon marched independently at not less than 400 yds interval. Casualties. Killed A Coy 1. Wounded A Coy 2. B Coy 3. C Coy 5.	
"	8th		Reserve. The following officers were taken on the strength of the Bn. 2 Lieut N. S. SIM G. R. MARTON Casualties Wounded A Coy 3. O.R. B Coy 1. O.R. C Coy 1. O.R. Nominal roll not sent J. Cameron Lt/A	

Army Form C. 2118.

WAR DIARY
or
INTELLIGENCE SUMMARY.

(Erase heading not required.)

Instructions regarding War Diaries and Intelligence
Summaries are contained in F. S. Regs., Part II.
and the Staff Manual respectively. Title pages
will be prepared in manuscript.

Place	Date	Hour	Summary of Events and Information	Remarks and references to Appendices
D.9.1 Wood S7.c.2.1 & S14.a.30 B Coy	Sept 9th		Page 118	
			Brigade Reserve. Battn in Brigade Reserve. Casualties wounded C Coy 1 O.R.	
	10th		Brigade Support The Battn was relieved by B Battn 149th Infantry Bde (6th Northumberland Fusiliers) and B Battn 150th Infantry Bde. The Battn moved into B Ann Disposition A & C Coys in the cutting Contalmaison. D & B Coys in Pearl Alley. Headquarters Peake Wood. Platoons proceeded independently to their new position at not less than 40 yds distances. The Battn relieved the 8/10th Gordon Highlanders in the front line. Disposition A Coy 2 Platoons front line left Connor Trench to Sanderson Trench. Remainder in old Cameron Trench.	
Front Line Sanderson Trench	11th			

Army Form C. 2118.

WAR DIARY
or
INTELLIGENCE SUMMARY.
(Erase heading not required.)

Place	Date	Hour	Summary of Events and Information	Remarks and references to Appendices
FRONT LINE	11		Front line dispositions A Coy 2 Platoons EGG TRENCH & 6th AVENUE C Coy forming line Right 2. Platoons front line & PIONEER TRENCH D Coy 2 Platoons KOYLI Trench 2 Platoons near VILLA WOOD B Coy KOYLI Trench Times A Coy 4.30 am. C Coy 4.45 am D Coy 4.45 am B Coy 5 am. 11 Casualties VILLA WOOD Taken on strength 20 O.R. Casualties wounded 2/Lieut R Tarkin C/2ynd A Coy 1 O.R.	
FRONT LINE	12		Casualties Killed B. 2 O.R. wounded A Coy 2 C. 1 O.R. B Coy 2 C Coy 5 D Coy 3 Norman Munefield Major 7 in Command 7/R	

Army Form C. 2118.

WAR DIARY
or
INTELLIGENCE SUMMARY.
(Erase heading not required.)

Page 120

Place	Date	Hour	Summary of Events and Information	Remarks and references to Appendices
BIVOUAC FROM E.7 Central	Sept 13		RESERVE Relieved by 6/7th ROYAL SCOTS FUSILIERS and proceeded to Bivouacs at E.7 central (just near ALBERT. All movements by Platoon at not less than 100 yds interval. Routes: cutting contal MAISON SCOTS REDOUBT BECOURT WOOD ALBERT ALBERT-AMIENS ROAD. Q.M.S.S. McVAY D Coy Cpl. W.B.K. GLASS A Coy 2/Cpl V.A. TELFER C Coy Pte D.C. WILLIAMS C Coy proceeded to report to Cadet Schools for commissions. Casualties Involuded sick to England B Coy 2 O.R. A Coy 1 O.R. C Coy 1 O.R.	
SHELTER WOOD BIRCH WOOD ROUND WOOD	14		RESERVE The Battn moved into Brigade reserve taking up a position SHELTER WOOD BIRCH WOOD & ROUND WOOD Routes - via ALBERT BECOURT LOZENGE WOOD ROAD all movements by Platoons at 200 yds interval.	
	15		Brigade Reserve	

Norman Murofield Meyer
7th Cameron Btgt

2353 Wt W25:41454 700,000 5/15 D.D.&L. A.D.S.S./Forms/C. 2118.

Army Form C. 2118.

WAR DIARY
or
INTELLIGENCE SUMMARY.
(Erase heading not required.)

Page 121

Place	Date	Hour	Summary of Events and Information	Remarks and references to Appendices
SHELTER WOOD	Sept 16		Brigade Reserve	
	17		do	
KOYLI TRENCH	18		Brigade Support. The 11th Infantry Bde relieved the 43rd Infantry Bde & 46th by 5th in front line came during night of 17th/18th. Disposition: D Coy — HAM TRENCH A Coy — EGG TRENCH C Coy — POST TRENCH and push of SANDERSEN TRENCH B Coy — TANGLE TRENCH. Headqrs Junction of KOYLI TRENCH and WELLA TRENCH <u>Route</u> PEAKEWOOD CONTALMAISON CUTTING QUNTALMAISON PEARL ALLEY Order R, A, D, C, Coys H qrs Each Platoon of B Coy left at 7 p.m. (17 inst) Movements by Platoon at not less than 300 yds interval	Norman Murchford Major 7th Cameron Bgd

WAR DIARY or INTELLIGENCE SUMMARY

Army Form C. 2118.

Place	Date	Hour	Summary of Events and Information	Remarks and references to Appendices
			Page 17"	
BIVOUAC E.O.S. and LAVIEVILLE	19	Bivouac	15th Division relieved by 23rd Division. Battn. relieved by 8th YORKS on night of 18th and morning of 19th, went in Bivouac near ALBERT (E.5.6) afterwards proceeding to Camp at LAVIEVILLE. One of Mine Throwing Coy A.B.C.D Coys Platoons to proceed at 200 yards interval through ALBERT until leading Platoon reaches SOUTH BRIDGE ON railway west of ALBERT when the Brigade closed to 400 yds between Battn. & 10 yds between Coys. The Battn marched in rear of 8th SEAFORTH HSS. + in front of 8/10th Gordons. Brawn down Limbers & other men except transport men also cookers and water carts moved in rear of the Battn. The remainder of transport was brigaded under Bde transport officer. Lewis guns went with their Coys. Headqr guns with D Coy.	
FRANVILLERS	20	Billets	The Battn. moved into Billets in FRANVILLERS. Starting point for the Brigade cross-roads ALBERT-AMIENS ROAD and Mormand Wrocford Ways. 7th Common W.S.P.	

Army Form C. 2118.

WAR DIARY
or
INTELLIGENCE SUMMARY.
(Erase heading not required.)

Page 123

Place	Date	Hour	Summary of Events and Information	Remarks and references to Appendices
FRANVILLERS	20		BILLETS LAVIEVILLE - RIBEMONT ROAD. The Batt: marched in the Rear of the Bge on passing the starting point at 10.20 a.m. Order of March:- Scouts & Cyclists Pipes & Drummers Head Qr Coy "B" "C" "D" "A" Coys HeadQr Lewis Guns Reserve Lewis Gun Teams Transport Battn paraded ready to move off at 9.45 a.m.	
FRANVILLERS	21		BILLETS Cleaning	
	22		" Physical Drill. Bayonet Fighting. Inspection of arms & clothing. Casualties wounded A Coy 1 O.R. C Coy 2 O.R. Draft arrived of 72 O.R.	
	23		" Physical Drill & Bayonet fighting. Divine Service 11 a.m. Norman Macfarlane Major 7th Cameron Highrs	

WAR DIARY
or
INTELLIGENCE SUMMARY.

(Erase heading not required.)

Army Form C. 2118.

Page 124

Place	Date	Hour	Summary of Events and Information	Remarks and references to Appendices
FRANVILLERS	Sept 25		Billets. Physical Drill Coy Training	
	26		" Route March. Coy Training	
	27		" Sighting, wiping & wiring strong points.	
	28		" Musketry 5 rounds deliberate 10 rounds rapid. Continuing those permitted. Completing construction of strong points. The Commander in Chief granted the following awards. Military Cross 2/Lieut to Black 2/Lieut J. Orr. Distinguished Conduct Medal Sergt J. Montgomerie Cpl. J. Drysdale The following were invalided to England 2/Lieut Drew 2/Lieut R.S.M. McPherson 2/Lieut J. McKay	

Norman Mumford Major
7th Cameron High[landers]

WAR DIARY
or
INTELLIGENCE SUMMARY.
(Erase heading not required.)

Army Form C. 2118.

Place	Date	Hour	Summary of Events and Information	Remarks and references to Appendices
FRANVILLERS	Apr 29		Page 125	
		Billets	The following craft taken on strength	
			Lieut R.M. DINWOODIE	
			2/Lieut J McCULLOCH	
			2/Lieut A.C. McELISH	
			2/Lieut D MORRISON	
			16 other ranks	
"	30	Billets	Physical drill Bombing Extended Order Bathing	
		do	do	

Norman Hueston Major
7th Cameron High.

SECRET AND CONFIDENTIAL

ORIGINAL

VOL 16

Q.14

WAR DIARY

– of –

7th (Service) Battalion Cameron Highlanders

For

October 1916

Pages 126 to 138. inclusive

WAR DIARY
or
INTELLIGENCE SUMMARY

Army Form C. 2118.

Place	Date	Hour	Summary of Events and Information	Remarks and references to Appendices
			Page 126	
FRANVILLERS	Oct 1	Billets	Bombing and extended order drill	
	2	"	Divine Service 10 a.m.	
			Bombing and extended order drill	
	3	"	Draft of 8 O.R.	
			Full firing	
			Rate of exchange francs at 5 francs = 3/7³	
			Practicing for Brigade Sports	
	4	"	Brigade sports to be held today cancelled as orders were received to move up the line. Afterwards the move was cancelled. The Bat'n played the 9th Black Watch in the 1ˢᵗ ascn football. Brigade made final and were beaten 1 goal to a corner.	
	5	"	Brigade scheme practicing the attack on a village.	
BECOURT WOOD	6	Bivouac	The Brigade moved up to BECOURT WOOD in order of march 9ᵗʰ	

Maurice Murgood Major

Army Form C. 2118.

WAR DIARY
or
INTELLIGENCE SUMMARY.
(Erase heading not required.)

Place	Date	Hour	Summary of Events and Information	Remarks and references to Appendices
BECOURT WOOD	Oct 6	Bivouac.	127 9th BLACK WATCH GORDON HIGH" SEAFORTH HIGH" 7th CAMERON HIGH" Starting point for the Brigade junction of the ALBERT/AMIENS ROAD and the HEILLY/FRANVILLERS ROAD The Batt" passed the starting point at 2.25 pm The Batt" formed up ready to move off at 1.55 p.m. Order of March Headqrs D.C, B, A Coys Reserve Machine Gun Section and Transport.	
BECOURT WOOD	7	Bivouac.	200 yds being kept between Battns The Batt" remained in Bivouac at BECOURT WOOD news lines round the Cemetery and officers lines on the other side of main road — Movements worked upon	

WAR DIARY
or
INTELLIGENCE SUMMARY.

Page 128

Place	Date	Hour	Summary of Events and Information	Remarks and references to Appendices
CRESCENT ALLEY	Oct 8		Support line relieved the 10th Battⁿ in the support line. The Battⁿ moved off from BECOURT WOOD at 1 p.m. moving by Platoon at 200 yds interval. <u>Disposition</u> 47 Divⁿ on Right. 15th Divⁿ Centre with 44th Bde on right and 45th Bde on left. 8/10th Gordon's Right of firing line. 9th Black Watch left of firing line. 7th Camerons in Support. 8th Seaforths in Reserve. A Coy in O.G.1. B Coy in STARFISH TRENCH C Coy and D Coy (less 1 platoon) in PRUE TRENCH. HEADQRS and 1 Platoon D Coy in CRESCENT ALLEY	
	9		Support line In Bde Support. Casualties killed C Coy 1 O.R. died of wounds C Coy 1 O.R.	

WAR DIARY
or
INTELLIGENCE SUMMARY.

Army Form C. 2118.

Page 129

Place	Date	Hour	Summary of Events and Information	Remarks and references to Appendices
CRESCENT ALLEY	Oct 9		Wounded 2nd Lieut E.L.B. DAVIS A Coy 2 O.R. B Coy 7 O.R. C Coy 16 O.R. D Coy 3 O.R. Accidentally wounded C. Coy 5 O.R.	
do	10th	Support line	in Brigade Support	
Front line	11th	Front line	The Batt'n relieved the 8/10th Gordons on the night of 10/11th in the Front line. Relieve & Disposition as follows. D Coy relieved C/y 8/10th Gordons and 25 men of Black Watch in firing line right. Left of Coy on LE SARS - BAPAUME Rd. B Coy Young line left relieved A & C Coys of BLACK WATCH less 25 men - Right on LESARS - BAPAUME Rd C Coy in Cutting M.16.c relieving Coy 8/10th Gordons - A Coy 2 Platoons in Gun M.22.a relieving 1 Coy 8/10 Gordons 2 Platoons in OG² relieving 8/10th Gordons Norman Hereford Major	

Army Form C. 2118.

WAR DIARY
or
INTELLIGENCE SUMMARY.
(Erase heading not required.)

Page 130

Place	Date	Hour	Summary of Events and Information	Remarks and references to Appendices
FRONT LINE	11 Feb		Front Line Headquarters at M.2.2.a.L.1. Route around alley Spencer Trench 28 Avenue L 0.9.2 thence by Sunken — All movements by Platoons at 200 yds distance — Casualties Wounded in action 2nd Lieut E D HOSKIN A Coy 1, B Coy 6, C Coy 6, D Coy 1, O.R. Shell Shock 2nd Lieut J R STEELE B Coy 4 O.R. Killed in Action B Coy 5 O.R. Invalided to England 2 O.R.	
FRONT LINE	12		Casualties Killed B Coy 1 O.R. Wounded........ Major	

WAR DIARY
or
INTELLIGENCE SUMMARY.

(Erase heading not required.)

Army Form C. 2118.

Place	Date	Hour	Summary of Events and Information	Remarks and references to Appendices
FRONT LINE	Oct 12		Page 131	
FRONT LINE			Casualties. Wounded in action B Coy 6 O.R. Shell shock 1 O.R. Taken in the strength 7 O.R.	
CRESCENT ALLEY	13		Support line. The Battn was relieved in the front line by the 8th SEAFORTH HIGH" and took up the following positions. A Coy in CRESCENT ALLEY between H.Q Coy & PRUE TRENCH B. Coy in PRUE TRENCH right C Coy in O.G.I D Coy in PRUE TRENCH left Battn Headqrs in CRESCENT ALLEY. Casualties Wounded in action. 2 Lieut B. R. Norton A Coy 3 O.R. B Coy 14 O.R.	

Place	Date	Hour	Summary of Events and Information	Remarks and references to Appendices
			Page 132	
CRESCENT ALLEY	Oct 13		Support line. Casualties (continued) Previously reported wounded now died. 1 OR C Coy. Killed in action A Coy 3 OR, B Coy 4 OR, C Coy 1 OR, D Coy 2 OR. Shell Shock D Coy 6 OR	
CONTALMAISON CUTTING	14		Reserve area. The Battn were relieved by the 12th H.L.I. on the night of the 14/15th on being relieved the Battn moved into CONTALMAISON CUTTING, proceeding by platoons at 200 yds interval over CRESCENT ALLEY and CLUMP at High Wood.	

Norman Murchison Major

WAR DIARY or INTELLIGENCE SUMMARY.

Army Form C. 2118.

Page 133

Place	Date	Hour	Summary of Events and Information	Remarks and references to Appendices
CONTALM-AISON CUTTING	Oct 15		Reserve Area - former working parties	
	16		do do	
	17		do do	
	18		do do	
Right Sect'n Front Area	19	C. AREA	The 46th Infantry Brigade relieved the 45 Infantry B'de in the Right Section Front Area. The Batt's relieved the 9th Black Watch. Disposition on Relief A & C Coys relieved 2 Coys 9th Black Watch in the STARFISH TRENCH. A Coy on the Right, C Coy on the Left. B Coy D Coy two two platoons relieved 1/2 Coys in the TANGLE B. Coy on the right 1/2 D. Coy on left. D Coy less 2 Platoons relieved 1/2 Coy in TYNE TRENCH. Headqrs M 33. 0. 4. 4. Order of movement: Companies will move in the following order — Norman MacFarlane	

WAR DIARY or INTELLIGENCE SUMMARY.

Army Form C. 2118.

Page 134

Place	Date	Hour	Summary of Events and Information	Remarks and references to Appendices
Right Sect'n Front Area	Oct 19		E. AREA A.B.C.D Coys Hdqrs. Moved up 200 yds without the leading Platoon of A Coy to lie at the CONTALMAISON VILLA at 4.45 pm where guides will meet them. In Bde nature.	
do A AREA Front Line	20 21		do. A AREA The Batt'n relieved the 8/10th GORDON HIGHLANDER in the FRONT LINE disposition A Coy Front Line Right B.C Coy on the left. B Coy SUNKEN ROAD and TANGLE D Coy O.S. 2 Order of march C.A.B.D Coys Hqrs. Guides met the leading Platoon at Junction of 26th AVENUE and SPENCE TRENCH at 8.30 p.m. Route CRESCENT ALLEY WILLIAM TRENCH SPENCE TRENCH 26 AVENUE. Relieve by guides movement moved up steps	

WAR DIARY
or
INTELLIGENCE SUMMARY.
(Erase heading not required.)

Page 135

Place	Date	Hour	Summary of Events and Information	Remarks and references to Appendices
A AREA FRONT LINE	Oct 21		The Battn worth up two day's rations Batt HQs Casualties A. Coy 1 O.R. wounded	
do	22		In front line Casualties C. Coy 1 O.R.	
B. Area	23	In Support	The Battn were relieved by the 9th Black Watch and moved into "B" Area Disposition A Coy PRUE TRENCH RIGHT B. Coy CRESCENT ALLEY C. Coy PRUE TRENCH Left D Coy O.B.1. Hd Qrs Pru Position to Right of CRESCENT ALLEY Casualties Killed C Coy 3 O.R. Wounded C Coy 2 O.R.	

Army Form C. 2118.

WAR DIARY
or
INTELLIGENCE SUMMARY.
(Erase heading not required.)

Page 136

Place	Date	Hour	Summary of Events and Information	Remarks and references to Appendices
B Area	23	In Support	wounded 1 in A, 1 in B, 1 in C Coys. Shell Shock 1 in B, 2 in C Coy	
Contalmaison Cutting	24	In Reserve	The Battⁿ was relieved by the 12ᵗʰ H.L.I. and proceeded to Contalmaison Cutting. Disposition A.B.C.D. Coy in the Cutting. Head qrs. X.16.D.7.4. Casualties 3 Shell Shock A Coy. Casualties 1 OR D Coy	
do	25	do		
do	26	do		
C Area Starfish Line	27	In Support	The Battⁿ relieved the 10ᵗʰ Scottish Rifles in C Area Starfish Line. Disposition A. C. Coys. Starfish Trench. D Coy. less 2 Platoons Tyne Trench. Nominal hundyard strengh	

WAR DIARY
INTELLIGENCE SUMMARY

Page 137

Place	Date	Hour	Summary of Events and Information	Remarks and references to Appendices
C. AREA	Oct 27		In Support D Coy line & Platoons and B. Coy in TANGLE Headqrs in MARTIN ALLEY. A Coy moved up at 3.30 pm. this Coy followed with 200 yds interval between Platoons. Casualties	
STARFISH LINE			1.O.R. A Coy. 1.O.R. C Coy wounded attached machine gun Coy	
do	28		Casualties 1.O.R. A Coy. 1.O.R. B Coy wounded	
do	29			
FRONT LINE	30		FRONT LINE Battn relieved 10th SCOTTISH RIFLES in A AREA FRONT LINE DISPOSITION B. Coy FRONT LINE LEFT D Coy do RIGHT A Coy SUNKEN ROAD C Coy O.B.1 Headqrs. 26th AVENUE	

Army Form C. 2118.

WAR DIARY
or
INTELLIGENCE SUMMARY.
(Erase heading not required.)

Place	Date	Hour	Summary of Events and Information	Remarks and references to Appendices
			Page 138	
FRONT LINE	Oct 30		FRONT LINE Casualties 1 wounded A. Coy.	
D AREA	31		RESERVE AREA The Battn. was relieved Aug 8/10th Gordon Highs and moved into RESERVE AREA.	
RESERVE			DISPOSITION	
			B/D Coy SWANSEA TRENCH.	
			A Coy O.G.1	
			C Coy GOURLAY TRENCH.	
			Head qr. BAZENTIN-LE-PETIT	
			CASUALTIES.	
			KILLED 3 O.R. B. Coy. 1 O.R. D Coy.	
			WOUNDED 3 O R B. Coy 4 O.R. D Coy	
			SHELL SHOCK 3 OR. D Coy	
			HONOURS.- The under mentioned was awarded the Military	
			MEDAL for bravery in the FIELD	
			S/16536 Sgt D.A. McGILP	
			S/16738 Pte W TRAIN.	
			Norman Murefored Major	
			Commanding 7th Cameron High'rs	

Army Form C. 2118.

WAR DIARY
or
INTELLIGENCE SUMMARY.

(*Erase heading not required.*)

Instructions regarding War Diaries and Intelligence Summaries are contained in F. S. Regs., Part II. and the Staff Manual respectively. Title pages will be prepared in manuscript.

Place	Date	Hour	Summary of Events and Information	Remarks and references to Appendices

2353 Wt W3544/4454 700,000 5/15 D. D. & L. A.D.S.S./Forms/C. 2118.

7th Bn Cameron Highlanders

Nov 1916

Secret & Confidential

Army Form C. 2118.

WAR DIARY
or
INTELLIGENCE SUMMARY.

(Erase heading not required.)

7th (Service) Battalion Cameron Highlanders.—

War Diary

for Period 1st to 30th November inclusive.

pp. 139 to 144 incl.

Army Form C. 2118.

WAR DIARY
or
INTELLIGENCE SUMMARY.
(Erase heading not required.)

Page 139

Place	Date	Hour	Summary of Events and Information	Remarks and references to Appendices
D AREA RESERVE	1916 Nov 1		In Brigade Reserve. Two O.R. transferred to England under age.	OK(?)
BECOURT HILL	2		The Battn on being relieved moved into Camps at BECOURT HILL. R.H.Q., C & A Coys CONTALMAISON SCOTTS REDOUBT BECOURT. B, D Coys H.Qrs BAZENTIN-LE-PETIT CUTTING CONTALMAISON SCOTTS REDOUBT BECOURT. All movement of Platoons at 200 yds interval. All picks, shovels surplus to establishment were handed into RE Dumps at CONTALMAISON.	
do	3		The King was graciously pleased to award the Military Medal for bravery in the field to S/16536 Sjt. D.H. McGIE.P S/16336 Pte W. TRAIN.	
do	4		16 O.R. invalided to ENGLAND sick.	

WAR DIARY
or
INTELLIGENCE SUMMARY.

Army Form C. 2118.

Page 1 No.

Place	Date	Hour	Summary of Events and Information	Remarks and references to Appendices
BRESLE	Nov 5		In Camp. The 11th Infantry Brigade moved to BRESLE relieving 10th Brigade. 4 pm Signal Section 74 Canadians surrendered 3rd Div. Line the Butts parrant du Moulin, Point X Roads F 1 b 7 9 (North of Becourt Wood) at 10 am. Roads 17 3 4 4 – E 1 b a – E 4 c. – E 4 c. 33 – E 3 d 8 7. MAIN ALBERT AMIENS ROAD to CROSS ROADS at D 21 a. Movements of Platoons at 100 yds. interval.	
do	6		In Camp. Cleaning up. – Casualties 1 O.R. accidentally wounded. Lieut. A IRVINE having joined by draft was taken on strength.	
do	7		In Camp. Work as per attached programme. Returned from London Rifle etc. didn't 3rd Nov. 2nd Lieuts K. to Lieuts. T FINDLAY (18th Aug) T ORR (20 Aug)	
do	8		In Camp. Work as per programme. Lieut Munch was granted extension of leave to 10th Nov.	

WAR DIARY
or
INTELLIGENCE SUMMARY

Army Form C. 2118.

Place	Date	Hour	Summary of Events and Information	Remarks and references to Appendices
BRESLE	Nov 9		Page 141	
			In Camp. Work as per programme attached	
			2.Q.M.S. McNAUGHTON was appointed 2nd Lieut & is the 5 Battn.	
			Draft of 21 O.R. taken on strength.	
	10		In Camp. Work as per programme attached.	
			The camp was visited by Lt Col B.O.E.M.C. who expressed himself	CMcW
			as greatly pleased with the appearance of the Battn. and thanked	
			men for the splendid work they, and they not of the 15th Dn.	
			had done.	
	11		In Camp. Work as per programme attached	
	12		do do	
			2nd Lieut E.B. McCUER having joined was posted to C. Coy	
			" J.I. MacDONALD do C. Coy	
			" W.L.MUIR KAY on B. Coy	
			7 SPS having joined were taken on the strength.	

Army Form C. 2118.

WAR DIARY
or
INTELLIGENCE SUMMARY.
(Erase heading not required.)

Page 142

Place	Date	Hour	Summary of Events and Information	Remarks and references to Appendices
BRESLE	Nov 13		In Camp. Work as per attached programme. The following men appointed 2nd Lieuts in 17th Batt LANCASTER FUSILIERS S/14723 A/Cpl W.B.K GLASS S/12878 L/Pvts S. McVAY	CMW
do	14		In Camp. Work as per attached programme. 60 O.R. having joined were taken on the strength.	
do	15		In Camp. Work as per attached programme. The following having received a commission were struck off strength S/11033 Pte W CAIRNEY D Coy LANCASTER FUSILIERS T.F.	
do	16		In Camp. Work as per attached programme. Draft of 4 O.R. was taken on strength. 7 O.R. having been invalided to England were struck off strength 2nd Lieut MURRAY invalided to England is struck off strength. Men had baths.	
do	17		In Camp. Work as per programme attached.	
do	18		In Camp. Work as per programme attached.	
do	19		In Camp. Church parade 11 am.	

Army Form C. 2118.

WAR DIARY
or
INTELLIGENCE SUMMARY.
(Erase heading not required.)

Page 143.

Place	Date	Hour	Summary of Events and Information	Remarks and references to Appendices
BRESLE	Nov 20		In Camp. Work as per programme attached. The Brigade was inspected by Lieut General W.P. Pulteney KCB KCMG commanding III Corps.	
	21		In Camp. Brigade Sports. The Batt won the Championship Cup presented by General Wilkinson C.B. M.V.O.	
			results	
			9th Black Watch 8 Gordons 6 Borders 6 Camerons	
			100 yds 0 8 1	
			Mile 1 5 3	
			Relay 2 5	
			High Jump 3 2.5	
			Putting weight 9	
			Cross Country Race 1 5 3	
			Football 5 3	
			Tug Tow nip 5 8	
			High Jump 2 2 5	
			Points 14 23 14 25	
	22		In Camp. Work per programme. O.C. Coys went Staff-Ride.	

WAR DIARY
or
INTELLIGENCE SUMMARY.
(Erase heading not required.)

Page 1414

Place	Date	Hour	Summary of Events and Information	Remarks and references to Appendices
BRESLE	June 23		In Camp - Work as per programme attached	
	24		In Camp - Work as per programme attached	
	25		In Camp - Church Parade	
	26		Draft of 70 O.R. taken by Strength	
			In Camp. Inspection by G.O.C. 15th Division. 2nd Lt D.J. Smith rejoins from Hospital	OKW
	27		Draft of 8 O.R. taken on Strength	
			In Camp - Work as per programme attached	
	28		In Camp - Work as per programme attached	
	29		In Camp - Companies on circuit runs and races in morning. In afternoon Baggage have special	
	30		In Camp - Companies in an arms' cleaning and races in afternoon cleaning arms and kits	

C Millard Lt Col
Commanding 7'51 Batt Cameron Highlanders

7th (SERVICE) BATTALION CAMERON HIGHLANDERS.

TRAINING PROGRAMME FOR WEEK COMMENCING 7th NOVEMBER 1916.

1st Day (7th November).

7 a.m. to 8 a.m.	— Physical Drill and Officers' Riding School.
9.30 a.m. to 11 a.m.	— Inspection of Arms and Clothing. Close Order Section and Platoon Drill.
11.15 a.m. to 12.30 p.m.	— Handling Arms and Gas Drill. Lewis Gunners, Signallers and Scouts under Instructors.
2 p.m. to 3.30 p.m.	— Bayonet Fighting under Company Officers. N.C.Os. under B.S.M. Specialists under Instructors.

2nd Day. (8th November).

7 a.m. to 8 a.m.	— Physical Drill and Officers' Riding School.
9.30 a.m. to 11 a.m.	— Inspection of Arms and Clothing. Handling of Arms. Rapid Loading. Gas Drill.
11.15 a.m. to 12.30 p.m.	— Platoon Close Order Drill. Lewis Gunners, Signallers and Scouts under Instructors. N.C.Os. under B.S.M.
2 p.m. to 3.30 p.m.	— Bayonet Fighting and Officers' Riding School. Specialists under Instructors.

3rd Day (9th November).

7 a.m. to 8 a.m.	— Physical Drill, Bayonet Fighting and Officers' Riding School.
9.30 a.m. to 12.30 p.m.	— Company Route March (March Discipline).
2 p.m. to 3.30 p.m.	— Gas Drill. Range Finding – Judging Distance. Specialists under Instructors.

4th Day (10th November).

7 a.m. to 8 a.m.	— Physical Drill, Bayonet Fighting and Officers' Riding School.
9.30 a.m. to 11 a.m.	— Inspection of Arms. Platoon Drill. Handling of Arms.
11.15 a.m. to 12.30 p.m. —) 2 p.m. to 3.30 p.m. —)	2 Companies Siting and Construction of Strong Posts. 1 Company on Range. 1 Company Bombing. Specialists under Instructors.

(Continued).

TRAINING PROGRAMME CONTINUED.

5th Day (11th November).

7 a.m. to 8 a.m.	— Physical Drill, Bayonet Fighting and Officers' Riding School.
9 a.m. to 11 a.m.	— Inspection of Arms. Platoon Drill. Rapid Loading. Gas Drill.
11.15 a.m. to 12.30 p.m.) 2 p.m. to 3.30 p.m.)	— 2 Companies Constructing Strong Points and Wiring. 1 Company on Range. 1 Company Bombing. Specialists under Instructors.

6th Day (12th November).

CHURCH PARADE.

7th Day. (13th November).

7 a.m. to 8 a.m.	— Physical Drill, Bayonet Fighting and Officers' Riding School.
9.30 a.m. to 12.30 p.m.	— Company Route March (March Discipline), with Advance Guard.
2 p.m. to 3.30 p.m.	— Gas Drill. Rapid Loading. Handling Arms. Specialists under Instructors. N.C.Os. under R.S.M.

TRAINING AREAS.

Parade Ground	— Field immediately East of Camp.
Bombing Ground.	Near Transport Lines.
Range.	— In hollow West of Camp.

(Signed).   N. McLeod, Major,
Commanding 7th (Service) Bn. Cameron Highrs.

7th (SERVICE) BATTALION CAMERON HIGHLANDERS.

TRAINING PROGRAMME FOR WEEK COMMENCING 12th NOVEMBER 1916.

6th Day. (12th November).

                        CHURCH PARADE.

7th Day. (13th November).

7 a.m. to 8 a.m.	Physical Drill, Bayonet Fighting and Officers' Riding School.
9.30 a.m. to 12.30 p.m.	Company Route March (March Discipline) with Advance Guard.
2 p.m. to 3.30 p.m.	Gas Drill.
	Rapid Loading.
	Handling Arms.
	Specialists under Instructors.
	N.C.Os. under R.S.M.

8th Day (14th November).

7 a.m. to 8 a.m.	Physical Drill and Officers' Riding School.
9.30 a.m. to 11 a.m.	Inspection of Arms and Clothing.
	Close Order Platoon Drill.
	Gas Drill.
11.15 a.m. to 12.30 p.m.	1 Coy. Guard Mounting.
	1 Coy. on Range.
	1 Coy. Constructing and Wiring Strong Points.
	1 Coy. Bombing.
	Lewis Gunners, Signallers, Scouts and Tunnellers under Instructors.
2 p.m. to 3.30 p.m.	1 Coy. Bayonet Fighting.
	1 Coy. Constructing and Wiring Strong Points.
	1 Coy. on Range.
	1 Coy. Bombing.
	Specialists under Instructors.

9th Day. (15th November).

7 a.m. to 8 a.m.	Physical Drill and Officers' Riding School.
9.30 a.m. to 11 a.m.	Inspection of Arms and Clothing.
	Handling of Arms and Platoon Drill.
	Rapid Loading.
	Gas Drill.
11.15 a.m. to 12.30 p.m.	1 Coy. Guard Mounting.
	1 Coy. on Range.
	1 Coy. Constructing Strong Points.
	1 Coy. Bombing.
	Lewis Gunners, Signallers, Scouts and Tunnellers under Instructors.
2 p.m. to 3.30 p.m.	Bayonet Fighting.
	Instruction in Tunnelling.
	Wiring.
	Specialists under Instructors.

                        (Continued).

TRAINING PROGRAMME CONTINUED.

10th Day. (16th November).

7 a.m. to 8 a.m.	- Physical Drill, Bayonet Fighting and Officers' Riding School.
9.30 a.m. to 12.30 p.m.	- Company Route March (March Discipline).
2 p.m. to 3.30 p.m.	- Gas Drill. Range Finding - judging distance. Specialists under Instructors.

11th Day (17th November).

7 a.m. to 8 a.m.	- Physical Drill, Bayonet Fighting and Officers' Riding School.
9.30 a.m. to 11 a.m.	- Inspection of Arms. Gas Drill. Platoon Drill. Handling of Arms.
11.15 a.m. to 12.30 p.m.) 2 p.m. to 3.30 p.m.)	- 1 Coy. Construction of Strong Points. 1 Coy. Assault Course. 1 Coy. on Range. 1 Coy. Bombing. Specialists under Instructors.

12th Day (18th November).

7 a.m. to 8 a.m.	- Physical Drill, Bayonet Fighting and Officers' Riding School.
9.30 a.m. to 11 a.m.	- Inspection of Arms. Platoon Drill. Rapid Loading. Gas Drill.
11.15 a.m. to 12.30 p.m.) 2 p.m. to 3.30 p.m.)	- 1 Coy. Construction of Strong Points and Wiring. 1 Coy. Assault Course. 1 Coy. on Range. 1 Coy. Bombing. Specialists under Instructors.

(Signed). NORMAN McLEOD, Major,
Commanding 7th (Service) Battn. Cameron Highrs.

7th (SERVICE) BATTALION CAMERON HIGHLANDERS.

TRAINING PROGRAMME FOR WEEK COMMENCING 19th NOVEMBER 1916.

13th Day (19th November).

CHURCH PARADE.

14th Day. (20th November).

7 a.m. to 8 a.m.	- Physical Drill.
9.30 a.m. to 12.30 p.m.	- Inspection of Arms and Clothing.
	Companies at Assault Ground.
	Open Order Drill, by Platoons.
2 p.m. to 3.30 p.m.	- Companies on Assault Ground.
	Rapid Loading and Rapid Firing.
	Gas Drill.
	Specialists under Instructors.

15th Day. (21st November).

GAMES.

16th Day. (22nd November).

7 a.m. to 8 a.m.	- Physical Drill.
9.30 a.m. to 12.30 p.m.	- Inspection of Arms.
	Battn. Bombers under Brigade Bombing Officer.
	Range.
	Extended Order Drill, by Companies - Companies practising the Attack.
	Gas Drill.
2 p.m. to 3.30 p.m.	- Range.
	Bombing under Company Instructors.
	Lecture by O.C. Companies - "Care of Feet," etc.
	Specialists under Instructors.
	N.C.Os. under R.S.M.

17th Day. (23rd November).

7 a.m. to 8 a.m.	- Physical Drill and Bayonet Fighting.
9.30 a.m. to 12.30 p.m.	- Battalion Route March.
2 p.m. to 3.30 p.m.	- Gas Drill.
	Bombing.
	Musketry.
	Technical Scheme for Junior Officers of "A" and "B" Companies.
	Specialists under Instructors.

18th Day (24th November).

7 a.m. to 8 a.m.	- Physical Drill.
9.30 a.m. to 12.30 p.m.	- Inspection of Arms.
	1 Coy. Assault Course.
	1 Coy. on Range.
2 p.m. to 3.30 p.m.	- 1 Coy. Bombing.
	1 Coy. Completing and Wiring Strong Points.
	Technical Scheme for Junior Officers of "C" and "D" Companies.
	Specialists under Instructors.

(Continued).

TRAINING PROGRAMME CONTINUED.

14th Day (25th November).

7 a.m. to 8 a.m.	-	Physical Drill and Bayonet Fighting.
9.30 a.m. to 12.30 p.m.	-	Companies Practising the attack in co-operation with Coys. Lewis Guns and Bombers.
12.30 p.m.	-	Camp Inspection by Commanding Officer.

(Signed). C.H. Marsh,
Lieut. Colonel,
Commanding 7th (Service) Batth. Cameron Hrs.

7th (SERVICE) BATTALION CAMERON HIGHLANDERS.

TRAINING PROGRAMME FOR WEEK COMMENCING 26th NOVEMBER 1916.

20th Day (26th November).

11.30 a.m.	-	Church Parade.
2 p.m. to 4 p.m.	-	Wiring Instruction.

21st Day (27th November).

9 a.m.	-	G.O.C's. Inspection.
11 a.m. to 12.30 p.m.	-	Company Drill. Gas Drill.
2 p.m. to 3 p.m.	-	Fire Discipline and Fire Control.
		Bombers under Coy. Instructors.
		Specialists under Instructors.

22nd Day (28th November).

7 a.m. to 8 a.m.	-	Physical Drill.
9.30 a.m. to 12.30 p.m.	-	Inspection of Arms.
		Company Drill. Handling of Arms.
		Extended Order Drill.
		Assault Course.
2 p.m. to 3.30 p.m.	-	Musketry Instruction.
		Bombers under Coy. Instructors.
		Specialists under Instructors.
		1 Coy. Wiring.
		Lecture on "Care of feet".

23rd Day (29th November).

7 a.m. to 8 a.m.	-	Physical Drill.
9.30 a.m. to 12.30 p.m.	-	Battalion in Attack.
2 p.m. to 3.30 p.m.	-	Tactical Scheme for Junior Officers of "A" and "B" Coys.
		Bombing under Coy. Instructors.
		1 Coy. Wiring.
		1 Coy. on Range.

24th Day. (30th November).

7 a.m. to 8 a.m.	-	Physical Drill.
9.30 a.m. to 12.30 p.m.	-	Inspection of Arms.
		Assault Course.
		Battalion Drill.
		Extended Order Drill.
		1 Coy. on Range.
2 p.m. to 3.30 p.m.	-	Bombing under Coy. Instructors.
		Specialists under Instructors.
		1 Coy. on Range.

(Continued).

TRAINING PROGRAMME CONTINUED.

25th Day. (1st December).

7 a.m. to 7.45 a.m.	-	Physical Drill.
9 a.m. to 12.30 p.m.	-	Battalion Route March.
2 p.m. to 3.30 p.m.	-	Bombers under Coy. Instructors.
		1 Coy. Wiring.
		1 Coy. on Range.

26th Day. (2nd December).

7 a.m. to 7.45 a.m.	-	Physical Drill.
9 a.m. to 12.30 p.m.	-	Battalion in Attack and in Defence.
12.30 p.m.	-	Camp Inspection.

(Signed). C.H. MARSH, Lieut. Colonel
Commanding 7th (Service) Battn. Cameron Hrs.

7th Bn Cameron Highlanders

December 1916

Vol 17

WAR DIARY
of
7th (S) Battalion CAMERON HIGHLANDERS
from 1st to 31st December 1916.
№ 145 to 153 incl.

WAR DIARY
INTELLIGENCE SUMMARY

Page 145

Place	Date	Hour	Summary of Events and Information	Remarks and references to Appendices
ALBERT	Dec 1		In Billets. The 44th Infantry Brigade returned. Chr 144th Infantry Brigade in Billets in ALBERT. The 9th CAMERON HIGHLANDERS relieved the 9th BLACK WATCH and puis of Machine guns (through col D.B.C. O.C.) at 9 AM	
"	2		Route LAVIEVILLE MILLENCOURT ALBERT. In Billets – Went as per programme issued	
"	3		Church parades, Cleaning of Billets. "B" Coy went working party.	
"	4		Dil. R. attached to two Battalion in underpinning	
"	5		Work carried programme. Men Bathing	
"	6		In Billets. Route marching (March Discipline) 2 O.R. struck off strength (under age) Draft 3 O.R. taken on strength	

O.K. [signature]

Army Form C. 2118.

WAR DIARY
or
INTELLIGENCE SUMMARY.
(Erase heading not required.)

Page 1 of 6

Place	Date	Hour	Summary of Events and Information	Remarks and references to Appendices
Camp X.23 Central	Dec 7	In Camp	The Batt. relieved the 6/7 R.S.F. in Camp about X.23 Central Road - ALBERT - LA BOISSELLE - CONTALMAISON to Camp order 7 March - H.Q. ., & A, B, D, Coys & G Detachment The Batt followed the 9th SEAFORTH HIGHLANDERS 200yds between Batt.s 100yds between Platoons starting point main ALBERT - BAPAUME ROAD at W 29. B. 7. 5. Time - to pass starting point at 2.30pm first Platoon to be ready to move off at 2.15 pm	ALBERT 1/40000
	8th	do	Batt. on work on position	
	9	do	do Special order issued to Corps Commander thanking Commands India & Belgian on record his great appreciation of the work done by the Troopes on the Roads Railways and tram lines during the last	

Army Form C. 2118.

WAR DIARY
or
INTELLIGENCE SUMMARY.
(Erase heading not required.)

Place	Date	Hour	Summary of Events and Information	Remarks and references to Appendices
Camp nr Y.S Ridge	Aug 9		Page 1407. In camp. Last six weeks in the III Corps area in the reserve position. Ground on the hills rendered the work somewhat of water labour, it was found but that most all angles will render bar exercises. Un work was on these of trenches from to and further to Sart and supper. (4.5 Lb Ap NoD /bars 6.4.5.1.2.46) Ground working parties	
do	10		do	
do	11		do	
do	12		Minor trench and drainage work being carried out. Encampting with "TM.B." at ref 9.E. 2nd Brigade to be relieved by men who have come up as company from 1st Aug to 16 Nov 1916 5 ORs finish off strength wounded to England. Ground working Parties	
do	13		do	

C.J. Willand Capt

Army Form C. 2118.

WAR DIARY
or
INTELLIGENCE SUMMARY.

(Erase heading not required.)

Place	Date	Hour	Summary of Events and Information	Remarks and references to Appendices
Camp X2 Central	Dec 14		Page 148. In Camp. Forward works of line. The following offr. & other ranks reported — S/14710 4/Cpl S.T.R. Black, Pnr, S/2/878 4/Cpl M.A. Burke [?]	
	15		Going into [?] trenches. Pnr accidently self inflicted wound in S/17833 Pnr P. Podmore Park'n going up on ration convoy.	
SHELTER WOOD SCOTS REDOUBT NORTH	16		Major R.W. S.T.B. [?] Rifles was [?] from Hd.Qrs M.B. U.R. Staff of [?] [?] Lieut Burke returned to Bn at Mametz Wood at Shelter Wood Scots Redoubt North. Relief finished H.Q. pres. D.S. B.A.C.18 C & D at [?] ["Coy"?] 1740 W.town 1900hrs [?] served [?]	CR.W.Cam[?]

WAR DIARY
or
INTELLIGENCE SUMMARY

Army Form C. 2118.

(Erase heading not required.)

Place	Date	Hour	Summary of Events and Information	Remarks and references to Appendices
SHELTER WOOD	Aug 16		Page 149	
			Saw 4th Platoon off camp at 2.30pm	
	17		Found working parties	
REDOUBT NORTH			D.Coy + B 63 BR taken over by T.	
			Found working Pties	
	18			
	19		On tech beginning 9.30 a.m. allowed the 4th Plan rate? in the line	
			Thanks to 9th atternoet 3rd S. Lanc & R.W. Inspect in Quests	
			Saw of? trench Hills ABCD E & 2 Stockade 100 yds	
			distance behind Return.	
R.G.D			Route Contemplation	
DROP			same in pleasure during Counts at 1-6 p.m.	
SOUTH			to and working parties	
	20		3 O.R. attack of camp transport to UNC to prepare Bn Hqs	
			2 Lieut Emerson + 2 nd Lieut D bould joined	
			strength mentioned 5 Regulars	

C A Ward

WAR DIARY
or
INTELLIGENCE SUMMARY.

(Erase heading not required.)

Army Form C. 2118.

Place	Date	Hour	Summary of Events and Information	Remarks and references to Appendices
FRONT LINE R6M AVENUE	Feb 21		Front Line The Batt: attacked on 5/2/18 broken through on the right and led C. Coy attempts B Coy in front line S/C and TRENCH MARLENCOURT ALLEY GIBBERT ALLEY etc. A Coy relieved 2 Pl — O.C.1 B Coy relieved A & D Coys in L & R AVENUE D Coy moved into front line near R10 in R M AVENUE Ord of march C.A.C. & H.Q. B.D. Coys with remainder of 100 yds between each in Order about 2 pm Route. A 61 N. 9 to n 5-n 10 north bound from n 26 bm SL 6 to n 5 EAST of MARTINPUICH C. B+J. Coys then struck toward to West of M ARTAPUICH Each Coy drew a Police Van Stages & two B.D. Coys issued supplies in readiness 2.3 drawn from 1 place Everything Carried out without a hitch in arriving thru front & M trenches the bn reached appliance that all in like place and west front 3 p.m. & posts etc.	

Place	Date	Hour	Summary of Events and Information	Remarks and references to Appendices
FRONT LINE	Aug 21		Page 157	
			FRONT LINE BSM in charge of Ruins party from Trench 7 to Chateau Ruins	
R. & A WENTHE	22 23		Some cooks & bakers transferred to FIELD DRIVE CAMP SOUTH	
do			10 O.R. transferred to ALBERT & made subsh.	
do			The following had been relieved into rest:	
			C. Coy relieved B. Coy	
			D. Coy " B "	
			B. Coy " A "	
			A. Coy " — "	
			All arrangements made between Coys relieving & relieved at 8.30 pm	
do	24"		The following for detention fixed also:	
			A. Coy relieved C. Coy	
			C. " " D "	
			D. " " B "	
			B. " " A "	
			All arrangements made between Coys relief started at 8.30 pm	
			Casualties missing 2/Lieut A.C. McLeod + one O.R. Wounded 2/Lieut J.B. W. PIERRALON + 3 O.R.	

WAR DIARY
or
INTELLIGENCE SUMMARY.
(Erase heading not required.)

Army Form C. 2118.

Page 152

Place	Date	Hour	Summary of Events and Information	Remarks and references to Appendices
AcID DROP Rea CAMP So.	25		RESERVE. The Batt. was relieved by the 8th Cdn. Inf. Bn. 3 Coys of reinforcements returned to D. C. D by A " " " " C " " " " B " " " " to return to same and inspect Rectd A.C.I.D. Deck Camp South	
ELZEAR CAMP SOUTH	26		The Bn. remained in Reserve and 92 reinforcements joined. Nos. 4B + 9 + 11 + 12 B. Four Bn. were relieved by R.I. Regt relief occurred to Shelling West N.R Order of March A.B.C.D Hd. Qrs. L.T.M. Ration Regtl Comm Waggon — Transport Looh	
	27	do	Found working Parties	
	28	do	Found working Parties	

Instructions regarding War Diaries and Intelligence Summaries are contained in F. S. Regs., Part II. and the Staff Manual respectively. Title pages will be prepared in manuscript.

WAR DIARY
or
INTELLIGENCE SUMMARY.
(Erase heading not required.)

Page 153

Place	Date	Hour	Summary of Events and Informa[tion]
	Dec		
[illegible]	29		Reserve. – [illegible] working [illegible]. Baths.
[illegible]	30		Reserve. [illegible] working [illegible]. Baths
[illegible]	3[illegible]		Front Line. [illegible] Infantry Div. [illegible] Infa[illegible]
			This Batt. will relieve the 6/7th R.S.F. [illegible]
			C Coy will relieve A. Coy 6/7th R.S.F. Left
			A. Coy – B Coy Right
			B Coy – D Coy Support
			D Coy – C Coy Reserve. Fiers [illegible]
			Order of March C. A. B. D. Coys Hd Qrs.
			Time – 1st Platoon will leave Camp at 3.30 pm 200 yds between Platoons
			Route CONTALMAISON – MARTINPUICH – LE SARS [illegible]
			[illegible]

2353 Wt. W2540454 700,000 5/15 D. D. & L. A.D.S.S./Forms/C. 2118.

7th (S) Batt'n,
The Cameron Highlanders
January, 1917

Q 17

Secret and Confidential

44th Bee - 1st Div

Army Form C. 2118.

WAR DIARY
or
INTELLIGENCE SUMMARY.
(Erase heading not required.)

Vol 19

WAR DIARY.

of

1st (Scottish) Battalion CAMERON HIGHLANDERS

Period from 1st to 31st January (inclusive) 1914.

by 155 to 162 incl

192 / 81

Army Form C. 2118.

WAR DIARY
or
INTELLIGENCE SUMMARY.
(Erase heading not required.)

Page 155

Place	Date	Hour	Summary of Events and Information	Remarks and references to Appendices
FRONT LINE RIGHT SECTION	Jan 1		The 7th CAMERON HIGHLANDERS relieved the 6th/7th R.S.F. in front line on night Dec 31st/Jan 1st. C Coy relieved A Coy R.S.F. Left front A Coy " B " Right front B Coy " D " Support Sunken Road D Coy " C " Reserve FLEERS LINE	193
	2		Order of march C.A.B.D Coys Hd Qrs	
FRONT LINE RIGHT SECTION			D Coy relieved A Coy B Coy relieved C Coy	
"	3		A considerable amount of work was done front were improved walled and intercoms with chalk trench.	

Norman Hugh ? Major

WAR DIARY or INTELLIGENCE SUMMARY

Page 156

194

Place	Date	Hour	Summary of Events and Information	Remarks and references to Appendices
SUPPORT AREA	June 4		This Bn was relieved by 5th SEAFORTH HIGH'rs	
			A Coy moved to PRUE TRENCH	
			B " " STARFISH LINE	
			C " " SEVEN ELMS	
			D " " STARFISH LINE	
		14.0"	SEVEN ELMS	
SUPPORT AREA	5		This Bn found working & carrying parties and dug new communication trench near SPUR TRENCH	
"	6		Ditto Relieved at 6 PM by 8/10 Bn GORDON HIGHLANDERS and proceeded to PIONEER CAMP	
PIONEER CAMP	7		In Camp	
SCOTS REDOUBT NORTH	8		This Bn relieved 10th SCOTTISH RIFLES at SCOTS REDOUBT NORTH	
"	9		In Camp. Dull. Bn found working & carrying parties	
"	10		In Camp	
"	11		In Camp	

Norman Munford Major

Army Form C. 2118.

WAR DIARY
or
INTELLIGENCE SUMMARY.
(Erase heading not required.)

Page 157

Place	Date	Hour	Summary of Events and Information	Remarks and references to Appendices
SCOTS REDOUBT NORTH VILLA CAMP	Jan 12		In Camp. The Bn moved to VILLA CAMP N. than day.	
VILLA CAMP	13		In Camp. Watering Parties supplied	
ACID DROP COPSE	14		The Bn was relieved by 8/10 GORDON HIGHLANDERS and moved into reserve to ACID DROP COPSE	
"	15		In Camp. Found Carrying Parties	
FRONT LINE	16		The Bn relieved 9th BLACK WATCH on night 16/17th between A Coy from line right C Coy from line left B Coy Support & Reserve O.G.1 / Prison DESTREMONT FARM D Coy Reserve in 26th AVENUE	

Norman MacLeod
Major

Army Form C. 2118.

WAR DIARY
or
INTELLIGENCE SUMMARY.
(Erase heading not required.)

Page 158

Place	Date	Hour	Summary of Events and Information	Remarks and references to Appendices
FRONT LINE RIGHT BATT" LEFT SUB-SECTOR	17/1/17		FRONT LINE Wiring & improving Posts.	
	18/1/17		do Inter Coy relief. B. Coy relieved C Coy in the front line left D Coy — A — night On relief C Coy moved into support in O.G.1 as A Coy moved into Reserve in 26th AVENUE	
do	19/1/17		do Continued wiring & improving posts. Enemy shelled SHARK trench about 10 pm. wrecking F SHARK WALK. Casualties killed 1 O.R. wounded Lieut J Dunn. 3 O.R.	
SCOTTS REDOUBT NORTH CAMP	20.1.17		RESERVE The 44th Infantry Coy went into Div" Reserve being relieved by the 46th Infantry Bde. The 7th Cameron Highlanders being relieved by the 12th Batt" HIGHLAND LIGHT INFANTRY A Coy H.L.I relieved A Coy in 26 AVENUE RESERVE B Coy do C Coy in O.G.1 SUPPORT C Coy do D Coy in FRONT LINE RIGHT D Coy do B Coy in FRONT LINE LEFT	

196

Army Form C. 2118.

WAR DIARY
or
INTELLIGENCE SUMMARY.

(Erase heading not required.)

Page 159

Place	Date	Hour	Summary of Events and Information	Remarks and references to Appendices
SCOTTS REDOUBT NORTH CAMP	20/1/17		RESERVE. On relief the 7th Camerons will proceed to SCOTTS REDOUBT NORTH by Platoons marching independently with 25 yds interval. Strength. Draft of 6 OR's taken on strength. 1. O.R. under age proceeding to England & joined 1. O.R. Reporting Cadet School for returning & strength	
do	21/1/17		RESERVE. Found working parties.	
	22/1/17		do. Found working parties. Lt-Colonel D.F.M. CRIGHTON took over command of the Battn from 18/1/17 MAJOR N.B. MACKENZIE (4th CAMERON HIGHRS) attached to this Battn with effect from 14.1.17	
do	23/1/17		Found working parties. Strength 3 ORs having proceeded to England struck off strength do HONOURS. Temp/ Capt. K. MACRAE } MENTIONED IN do A. OGILVIE } DISPATCHES S/14241 SSt J.D. McGILL } 4.1.17	

Norman MacKenzie Major

Army Form C. 2118.

WAR DIARY
or
INTELLIGENCE SUMMARY.
(Erase heading not required.)

Page 160

Place	Date	Hour	Summary of Events and Information	Remarks and references to Appendices
FRONT LINE	24/1/17		FRONT LINE The 4th Infantry Bde relieved the 45th Infantry Bde in the right sector. The 7th Camerons relieved the 6/7 R.S.F. in the left subsector. C Coy 7th Camerons relieved Coy 6/7 R.S.F in left front. A do do Right front B do do Support Sunken Rd D do do Reserve FLERS LINE Order of March C.A.B.D Coys. Head of Lead Platoon 100 dem Camp at 3-45 p.m. 200 yds interval between Platoons Strength: 2 O.R. struck off strength evacuated to England.	
do	25/1/17		Front Line	
do	26/1/17		Front Line D Coy relieved A Coy in Right front. B Coy relieved C Coy in Left front. on relief A Coy moved in Reserve in FLERS line and C Coy into support in SUNKEN ROAD	

Norman Hunsford Major

WAR DIARY
or
INTELLIGENCE SUMMARY.
(Erase heading not required.)

Page 161

Place	Date	Hour	Summary of Events and Information	Remarks and references to Appendices
Front Line	26/9/17		Front Line. Casualties Wounded 2nd Lieut J A Symon + 3 O.R. Burnt Lieut T. Orr M.C. + 4 O.R. Killed 1 O.R. Missing 1 O.R. believed killed in fire.	
do	27/9/17		do	
Support Line	28/9/17		Support Line. The Battn was relieved by the 8th Seaforth High-rs C. Coy 8th S.H. relieved D Coy 7th Cameron's Right Front B. Coy do B Coy do Left Front D Coy do C. Coy do Support, Sunken Rd A Coy do A Coy do Reserve Flers Line on relief A Coy moved into Prue Trench C - Martinpuich B - Starfish Line D - 7 Elms H.Qrs 7 Elms	

WAR DIARY or INTELLIGENCE SUMMARY

Army Form C. 2118.

Page 162

Place	Date	Hour	Summary of Events and Information	Remarks and references to Appendices
SUPPORT LINE 7 ELMS	29/4/17		Casualties killed 8 O.R. Wounded 1 O.R. Missing believed wounded 1 O.R.	
RESERVE PIONEER CAMP	30/4/17		The 7th Cameron High[rs] were relieved in support by the 9th Battn Black Watch. A Coy 7th Cameron relieved by Coy Black Water Prue Trench B. Coy do do STARFISH. C. Coy do MARTINPUICH D. Coy do 7 ELMS. On relief the 7th Cameron High moved into Reserve at PIONEER CAMP.	An Suidhe Arce Coming 7/Cameron High
PIONEER CAMP	1/5/17		RESERVE Cleaning up. Inspection of feet clothing and equipment.	Norman MacGregor Major

7th (S.) Batt'n.,
The Cameron Highlanders
February, 1917

Army Form C. 2118.

WAR DIARY
or
INTELLIGENCE SUMMARY.

(Erase heading not required.)

WAR DIARY

of

1st (Service) Battalion Cameron Highrs.

from 1st to 28th February 1917 incl.

pp. 163 to 168 incl.

Vol 20

201/H

WAR DIARY or INTELLIGENCE SUMMARY

Army Form C. 2118.

Page 163

Place	Date	Hour	Summary of Events and Information	Remarks and references to Appendices
PIONEER CAMP	1/2/17	RESERVE	The 44th Infantry Brigade was relieved on the night of the Feb 7th by the 5th Australian Bde. This Battn. was relieved by 18th Australian Battn. On relief the 7th Camerons moved into BECOURT CAMP. Order of March. B, D, A, B, HQ, Coys: 100 yds between Platoons. Route CONTALMAISON, LOZENGE WOOD. Each man carried a blanket & spare values. Started by 9.30 am	
BECOURT CAMP	2/2/17	CORPS RESERVE	Cleaning ammunition & equipment.	
do	3/2/17	do	Cleaning & collecting bombs. 2 OR struck off strength. 29 OR draft taken on strength	
CONTAY	4/2/17	do	The 4th Bde moved to CONTAY and BRESLE. The 7th CAMERONS moved to CONTAY	
CONTAY	5/2/17	do	Order of March. Scouts Band HQrs D.A.B.C. Coys. The Battn. to Parcels at 11.5 am in rear of 3rd Gordons 200 yds to be maintained between Battns. Route × Roads ALBERT CATHEDRAL × — W 28.C.1.1.	

MILLENCOURT
HENENCOURT

Page 16 b

Place	Date	Hour	Summary of Events and Information	Remarks and references to Appendices
CONTAY	5/2/17	AT REST	Cleaning up, inspecting arms equipment & clothing. Lecture by C.O.	
	6/2/17	do	Training as per programme. Attached Appendix I. Major (T/Lt.Col.) D.E.MM. CRIGHTON CAMERON HIGH'S (from Command 6th CAMERONS) to command 7th Cameron will effect from 1st January. Strength - Draft 9 O.R. taken on strength. 2/Lieut J. DUNN transferred to ENGLAND wounded.	
do	7/2/17	do	Training as per programme. Strength - 15 O.R. struck off strength invalided to England.	
do	8/2/17	do	Training as per programme.	
do	9/2/17	do	3 O.R. struck off strength evacuated.	
do	10/2/17	do	Training as per programme. Strength - the following draft was taken on strength. 2/Lieut A. McNIVEN & 31 O.R.	
do	11/2/17	do	Church Parade.	
do	12/2/17	do	Training as per programme. Lecture to 2 i/c in Command. Struck off strength 1 O.R.	

Army Form C. 2118.

WAR DIARY
or
INTELLIGENCE SUMMARY.
(Erase heading not required.)

Page 165

Place	Date	Hour	Summary of Events and Information	Remarks and references to Appendices
CONTAY	13/7/17	In rest.	Training as per programme attached. Lecture on sanitation to Medical Officer & O.R. strength of Battn proceeded to England	
BEAUVAL	14/7/17	In rest	The 44th Batt. moved to new training area. The 7th Camerons moved to BEAUVAL Starting point E. Coy H.Qrs. Order of March Scouts Band A.B.C.D.E. Coy, HQrs Lewis Guns Transport From Scouts to was cluding point at B. 5th were 400 yds between Battn. Route HERISSART, LE VAL DE MAISON, VERT GALAND FARM Evacuated & strength of strength 6 O.R. Following Officers joined to Strength. 2nd Lieut T.S. DENHOLM R. CHISHOLM J.P. SMITH T.S. RONALDSON	
GAZAINCOURT	15/7/17		The 7th Camerons moved to GEZAINCOURT. Starting point of all Stores. Time 11 a.m. Order of March Scouts Band B.C.D.A.G. HQs L.G.s Transport The Batt" will follow the same orders 400 yds interval between Battn.	

WAR DIARY
or
INTELLIGENCE SUMMARY.

Army Form C. 2118.

Place	Date	Hour	Summary of Events and Information	Remarks and references to Appendices
SEZAINCOURT	15/1/17	Inspect.	Page 166. Inspection of Aeroplanes. Lieut Col. E.H.MARSH. P.S.O. Lieut T. ORR M C and 3 O R. Appointed to temporary Commission & attached Matangh a/c 9 M. T. LUTT pa A SCOTT	
BOUQUE-MAISON	16/1/17	do	The 7th Camerons moved to BOUQUEMAISON Starting point Transport lines 8.10 a.m. 400 yds distance between Batt. Order of March Scouts Band C.D.H.B Co's H.Qs L.S.S. Transport	
CROISETTE	17/1/17	do	The 7th CAMERONS moved to CROISETTE (less 2 Co's 6 FRAMECOURT) Starting point X roads at N end of BOUQUEMAISON Time 7.45 A.M. Order of March Scouts Band D A.B.C. Co, HQs L.S.S Transport. 400 yds between Batt. B. & D. Co's will leave the Column at NUNE and move over MOULIN L'HAILE to main S Pol road to FRAMECOURT	

WAR DIARY
or
INTELLIGENCE SUMMARY.

Army Form C. 2118.

(Erase heading not required.)

Page 167

Place	Date	Hour	Summary of Events and Information	Remarks and references to Appendices
MONCHEAUX	18/9/17	In Rest.	The 7th Cameron moved to MONCHEAUX, Marching point X roads just south of CROISETTE Time 9.15 am. Order of march Bands Band & Coy, H.Q & L.Gs Transport. Rest. - FRAMECOURT P? HOUVIN STATION BONEVILLE. B.v C Coys with 10 in the column at FRAMECOURT at 10.30 am	
do	19/9/17	do	Training as per programme attached. Taken on strength from draft. 2nd Lieut I.A. SINCLAIR + 8 O.R.	
do	20/9/17	do	Training as per programme	
do	21/9/17	do	Training as per programme & attached of strength 16 O.R.	
do	22/9/17	do	Lecture by 2i/c in command Broken Periods of 16 Officers + 545 O.R. moved to Milly with command	
do	23/9/17	do	4 days draft in a working party. Training as per programme	
do	24/9/17	do	Working party on machinery at Milly. The H.A.D. details. Bde moved to new area 2/m 7th CAMERONS moved to MAIZERES	

Army Form C. 2118.

WAR DIARY
or
INTELLIGENCE SUMMARY.
(Erase heading not required.)

Page 168

Place	Date	Hour	Summary of Events and Information	Remarks and references to Appendices
MAISIERES	24/2/17	In Rest.	Order of Church Service ABCD Coy HQ Transport (less working party) Starting point Orderly Room from 11.30 am. Route MONTS-EN-TERNOIS Govy Emerchicourt – Church Febvin 16 O.R.	
"	26/2/17		Church Parade Working Party at MILLY Training of Specialists Working Parties at MILLY	
"	27/2/17		Training of Specialists Working Parties at MILLY Strength – atta. staff of Major N.B. MacKenzie 115 + 37 O.R. taken on strength. 2/Lieut N.S. SIM rejoined from Hospital.	
"	28/2/17		Training of Specialists Working Parties at MILLY	

Appendix No. 1

7th (SERVICE) BATTALION CAMERON HIGHLANDERS.

TRAINING PROGRAMME FOR WEEK COMMENCING 4th FEBRUARY 1917.

CONTAY AREA.

First Day.
5th February.

9.15 a.m. – 12.30 p.m.	Cleaning up.
	Inspection of Arms, Equipment and Clothing.
	Re-organisation of Specialists (Lewis Gunners, Bombers, Signallers and Observers.)
5.30 p.m.	Opening Lecture to Officers by Commanding Officer.

SECOND DAY.
6th February.

7 a.m. – 7.45 a.m.	Physical and Recreation Drill.
9.15 a.m. – 12.30 p.m.	Battalion Parade.
	Squad and Platoon Drill.
	N.C.Os. under B.S.M.
	Bayonet Fighting.
2 p.m. – 3 p.m.	Elementary Musketry Instruction.
	Specialists (Lewis Gunners, Bombers, Signallers and Observers) under qualified instructors.
5.30 p.m.	Lecture to Officers on Musketry by Commanding Officer.

THIRD DAY.
7th February.

7 a.m. – 7.45 a.m.	Physical and Recreation Drill.
9.15 a.m. – 12.30 p.m.	Battalion Parade.
	Squad and Platoon Drill.
	Bayonet Fighting.
	Guard Mounting.
2 p.m. – 3 p.m.	Elementary Musketry Instruction.
	Specialists under qualified instructors.

FOURTH DAY.
8th February.

7 a.m. – 7.45 a.m.	Physical and Recreation Drill.
9.15 a.m. – 12.30 p.m.	Battalion Parade.
	Squad and Platoon Drill.
	Handling of Arms.
	N.C.Os. under B.S.M.
	Elementary Musketry Instruction.
	Inspection of "A" Coy. by the Commanding Officer.
	One Company – Route March.
2 p.m. – 3 p.m.	Lecture on "Preventive measures against Gas"
	Inspection of "B" Coy. by the Commanding Officer.
	Tactical exercise for Officers without troops.
	Specialists under qualified instructors.

(Continued).

TRAINING PROGRAMME CONTD.   - 2 -

FIFTH DAY.
9th February.

    9.30 a.m. - 12.30 p.m.   Route March.
                                 March Discipline.
                                 Inspection of "C" Coy. by the Commanding Officer.
    2 p.m. - 3 p.m.   Lecture on "Preventive measures against trench feet".
                                 Inspection of "D" Coy. by the Commanding Officer.
                                 Rapid Loading.
                                 Specialists under qualified instructors.
    5.30 p.m.   Lecture on Military Law by the Commanding Officer.

SIXTH DAY.
10th February.

    7 a.m. - 7.45 a.m.   Physical and Recreation Drill.
    9.15 a.m. - 12 noon.   Squad and Platoon Drill.
                                 Extended Order Drill.
                                 Guard Mounting.
                                 Rapid Loading.
                                 Bayonet Fighting.
    12 noon.   Inspection of Billets by Commanding Officer.

                                 The afternoon will be devoted to Recreation.

                               (Signed) ARTHUR R. CHAPMAN,
                                        Captain and Adjutant,
                             7th (Service) Bn. Cameron Highlanders.

Appendix No 2

THE 1/4th BATTALION CAMERON HIGHLANDERS

TRAINING PROGRAMME FOR WEEK COMMENCING 18th FEBRUARY 1917.

MONCHEAUX AREA

14th DAY.
18th FEBRUARY.   CHURCH PARADE

15th DAY.
19th FEBRUARY.

9.15a.m. - 12.30p.m.   Physical and Recreation Drill
                                  Bayonet Fighting
                                  Specialists under qualified Instructors.
                                  Company Drill
2p.m. - 3p.m.   N.C.Os. under B.S.M.
                                  Rapid Firing with Dummies
                                  Specialists under Instructors.
                                  Revolver Practice for Officers.
Evening.   Lecture on Attack Formations by Commanding Officer.

16th DAY.
20th FEBRUARY.

9.15a.m. - 12.30p.m.   Physical and Recreation Drill
                                  Company Drill
                                  Specialists under Instructors
                                  Ranges (Rapid Firing)
                                  1 Coy. Route March
2p.m. - 3p.m.   N.C.Os. under B.S.M.
                                  Revolver Practice for Other Ranks.
                                  Specialists under Instructors
                                  Musketry Instruction
                                  Wiring Instruction

17th DAY.
21st FEBRUARY.

9.15a.m. - 12.30p.m.   Route March (3 Coys.) March Discipline.
                                  Specialists under Instructors.
                                  Judging Distances.
2p.m. - 3p.m.   N.C.Os. under B.S.M.
                                  Taping off Strong Points on Compass Bearing
                                  Musketry Instruction
Evening.   Lecture by Second in Command.

18th DAY.
22nd FEBRUARY.

9.15a.m. - 12.30p.m.   Route March (1Coy.)
                                  Physical and Recreation Drill
                                  Company in Attack (2 Coys.)
                                  Bayonet Fighting and Guard Mounting
                                  1 Coy. - Wiring Instruction.
2p.m. - 3p.m.   N.C.Os. under B.S.M.
                                  Tactical Exercise for Officers. Writing of
                                      Orders.
                                  Specialists under Instructors.
                                  Musketry Instruction.

                                  Fire Direction and Fire Control
Evening.   Lecture on Tests of Elementary Training by
                                      Adjutant.

Appendix N° 3

TRAINING PROGRAMME FOR WEEK ENDING 3rd MARCH 1917.

7th BATTALION CAMERON HIGHLANDERS.
(less Working Party of 16 Offrs. & 530 O. Rs. at MILLY

SUNDAY.
25th FEBY.

10 a.m.   CHURCH PARADE.

26th FEBY.
TO
3rd MARCH.

9.15a.m. – 12.30p.m.   Training of Specialists, as
2p.m. – 3 p.m.   follows:-
                            Signallers under Battn. Sig-
                            nalling Officer.
                            Bombing Class under Battn.
                            Bombing Officer.
                            Lewis Gun Detachment under
                            Lewis Gun Officer.

                           All Specialists will daily
                           practice Musketry and Handling
                           of Arms, for one hour.

                           Officers will be instructed in
                           Bombing and Lewis Gun under the
                           respective Instructors.

   In the event of the Working Party at MILLY
returning during the week this programme will be
amended.

                                   (Sd.) G.J.S.LUMSDEN, Lt.& A/Adj.

Index..................................

Q 19

SUBJECT.

7th Cameron Highlanders

No.	Contents.	Date.
	March 1917	

WAR DIARY
or
INTELLIGENCE SUMMARY.

ORIGINAL

War Diary
of
7th (Service) Battalion Cameron Highlanders
for
Month of March 1917
Pages 169 to 182 inclusive
Appendices 1 to 4.

WO 21

WAR DIARY
or
INTELLIGENCE SUMMARY.

(Erase heading not required.)

Army Form C. 2118.

Page 169

Place	Date	Hour	Summary of Events and Information	Remarks and references to Appendices
MIATSIERES	1/3/17		In rest. Training of Specialists. Working Party on railway at MILLY	
do	2/3/17		Training of Specialists. Working Party returned from MILLY Strength 1 O.R. evacuated and struck off.	
	3/3/17		Company training. Fitting the respirators. Divine Service.	
	4/3/17		Training.	
	5/3/17		Training as per attached programme. Strength 1 O.R. evacuated struck off.	
	6/3/17		The "A" Infantry Bde were inspected by the Commander in Chief at Ambrines. The Bde. was drawn up in parade Bivouac Dress fighting Dress. Strength - Draft of 7 O.R. taken on strength.	
	7/3/17		Tactical exercises at Firvilas at LIGNEREUIL. Strength S/14710 A/Sgt. J. CRAWFORD struck off strength on receiving his commission. 9 O.R. struck off being evacuated.	

Norman Mackenzie Major

WAR DIARY
or
INTELLIGENCE SUMMARY.

Army Form C. 2118.

Page 170.

Place	Date	Hour	Summary of Events and Information	Remarks and references to Appendices
MAISIERES	8/3/17	In Rest	Brigade Tactical Exercise at LIGNEREUIL. The Commander in Chief, at his inspection expressed himself as highly pleased with the appearance and steadiness of the Brigade. Divisions that line went to in arrangements to all concerned. Strength 5 O.R. struck off strength. Transport to Inesquières B.Depo.	
—	9/3/17	—	'B' and C Tactical exercises at Trenches at LIGNEREUIL. Strength — Evacuated + struck off strength 3 O.R. Base reporting sick dumping Brigade Drill morning Recreation in afternoon	
—	10/3/17	—	Strength — wounded + struck off strength 2 O.R. Struck P.O.R. taken on strength	
ARRAS	11/3/17	Support	The 11th Inf. Bde. relieved the 15th Inf. Bde. in the I.B. Sector. The 7th Cameronians being C. (Support) Batt". Order of March HQrs A.B.C.D. Coys. 100 yds between by marching DUISANS 7½ yds with the left between Platoons. Route _ PENIN TILLOY HERNAVILLE S.POL - ARRAS ROAD - Head of column to pass Shrine on the PENIN ROAD on outskirts of MAISIERES at 1 p.m. on entering ARRAS Respirators were worn at the "Alert"	

Norman Mungford Major

WAR DIARY
or
INTELLIGENCE SUMMARY.
(Erase heading not required.)

Army Form C. 2118.

Page 17.

Place	Date	Hour	Summary of Events and Information	Remarks and references to Appendices
ARRAS	11/3/17		In Support. A Coy relieved the 5th/6th Gordon Highlanders in the permanent garrison of the CEMETERY DEFENCES. Strength - Evacuated & struck off strength 2. O.R.	
"	12/3/17		In Support in ARRAS.	
"	13/3/17		do	
"	14/3/17		do	
"	15/3/17		Front Line. The Battn relieved the 5th/6th Gordon Highlanders in the Right Sub-section of the 1-3 Sector. D Coy relieved A Coy Gordon High. in front line & Coy " B. Coy do 2 Platoons Support Trench, 1 Platoon in Reserve Trench, 1 Platoon in Billets. A. Coy " D Coy do in Billets near Buff. H.Qrs. B Coy " E Coy do in Billets 78, 79, GRAND PLACE. D Coy 4th/5th Gordon High. relieved A Coy 7th Cameron in the CEMETERY Defences. Relief was carried out in single file to Railway at 75 yds intervals. Strength - Evacuated & struck of strength 16 O.R. Casualties Killed 9 O.R. wounded 16 O.R. died of wounds 5 O.R. Attached for duty with 7th Coy R.E 26 O.R. Norman Winford Major	

WAR DIARY
INTELLIGENCE SUMMARY.
(Erase heading not required.)

Army Form C. 2118.

Place	Date	Hour	Summary of Events and Information	Remarks and references to Appendices
ARRAS	16/3/17		Page 172	
	17/3/17		Front line. Improving & cleaning trenches. B Coy relieved D Coy in front line	
	18/3/17		Front line. Improving & cleaning trenches	
			Front line (1) D. Coy raided the enemy's trenches between the points S.21.a.5.4. — 2½.3 – 0½.5 – 3.5½. Zero hour 2-50 a.m. Captain W.R. Stewart in command. Raid sample in the centre and read shorter on the right.	Sheet 51 S.W.3. 1/10,000
			(2) The 9" + 12 Divisions co-operated at zero hour by simulating raids at points on their divisional fronts.	
			(3) The object of the raid was to establish enemy dispositions and to obtain identifications & information about the enemy.	
			(4) Zero raid lasted for 35 minutes	
			(a) Up to Zero hour the conditions were normal	
			(b) at 2 am hour the 15th Div.ᵗ Artillery assisted by the Corps heavy Artillery and the 9"/12" Divisional Artillery bombarded the enemy's front line & certain points in rear.	

Norman Mumford Major

Place	Date	Hour	Summary of Events and Information	Remarks and references to Appendices
ARRAS	18/3/17		Page 173	

Front line:(4)(a) At Zero plus 2 the artillery will lift from the front to be ridden on to the enemy's support line.

(b) At zero plus 5 a tow barrage will be pushed forward across the area to be raided.

(c) At Zero plus 28 the Infantry will withdraw from the enemy's support line.

(5)(a) From Zero to Zero plus 2 the 44th T.M. Battery will concentrate an intense bombardment on the trenches along W 2.3 W 2.5 W 2.7 to their junction with the enemy's front line.

(b) From Zero plus 2 to Zero plus 35 to maintain a steady rate of fire at points 2.1, 1.17.

(c) At Zero plus 35 to fire rapid fire to O's accepted on the sunken road about G 2.4 & 3.2, and the railway about G 2.6 & 2.6.

6.45 M.G. Coy will co-operate by sweeping the Railway Switch enemy support line S from junction with Plouvain Lane and the FEUCHY SWITCH.

Norman Mumford Meyers

Place	Date	Hour	Summary of Events and Information	Remarks and references to Appendices
ARRAS	18/3/17		Page 172	

Front line (7) The raiding party were in position at 2.35 a.m. lined up along the tapes which had been previously laid out by O.C. D Coy.

(8) The raiding party advanced at Zero phase in two parties each of two Platoons - one push through the Sap - the entrys were about C.24.d.2.3. the other party through the Sap about C.24.d.1.5.

(9) The raiding party was divided as follows:-
Two sections (including rifles bombers and Lewis Gunners) will form a covering party and will push forward on the railway embankment in the neighbourhood of the support line -
1½ platoons will occupy the supported line pushing their own blocks
3 Sections will seize the front line and provide blocks
2 Sections will be employed as moppers-up
1 Section will be held off to support prisoners

10 Arms Skeleton Equipment 120 rounds S.A.A. Bombers 12 Mills Bombs Rifle Bombers 12 N°23 Lewis Gunners 16 drums

Thomas Murphy Major

Army Form C. 2118.

WAR DIARY
or
INTELLIGENCE SUMMARY.
(Erase heading not required.)

Place	Date	Hour	Summary of Events and Information	Remarks and references to Appendices
ARRAS	18/3/17	Front line	Bombing Squad will carry normal equipment with 4 P bombs per squad in addition. Bombing Squads detailed as stoppers up will carry in addition to normal equipment 8 P bombs & Stokes per squad. Remainder of Coy normal bined equipment. Each man of the blocking party will carry 1 pick. 11. The Party in the enemy's support line will withdraw at Zero plus 28 minutes and the whole party will be clear of the enemy's trenches at Zero plus 35— 12. And Post. An advanced and post will be established under the railway about S.24.c.5.4h. our covering wires will be taken to this post. Working crew will be instructed at the Regimental Aid Post about S.23.d.1.5. 13. The remaining Party will return to billets in the Sunken Road via ISLINGTON STREET trench. O.C. A Coy will detail one Officer and 1 N.C.O. will be detailed by O.C. D Coy to be at the rendezvous. Norman Macguod Llwyn	

WAR DIARY
or
INTELLIGENCE SUMMARY.
(Erase heading not required.)

Army Form C. 2118.

Place	Date	Hour	Summary of Events and Information	Remarks and references to Appendices
ARRAS	18/3/17		Page 17 ½.	
			Front line of the battalion 13. ISLINGTON & INTERPRETER ST. trenches to which off men are taking part.	
			2nd Lt. R. LAMBERT and the O.C.S of D Coy to be near Batt. Headqrs who will also check off all men passing up the trench.	
			Both parties will be in position by 3 a.m. The will be proceeded with into of manner of officers and men taking part in the raid.	
			A check will call will be made in the billets. A check will call will be made in the billets.	
		14.	Lieut. McCulloch will attend at Batt. Headqrs at 11.30 p.m. to synchronise watches.	
			O.C. D Coy will detail servt. officer to attend at Batt H.Q. at 12 midnight to synchronise watches.	
		15.	The Prisoners will be escorted from the German lines to our front lines by the section of D Coy detailed for the purpose. O.C. D Coy was responsible that all prisoners so brought in were escorted from the front line to Batt H.Q. from there they will be taken to Bde H.Q.Rs.	

Norman MacArthur Lyon

WAR DIARY
or
INTELLIGENCE SUMMARY.
(Erase heading not required.)

Army Form C. 2118.

Page 179

Place	Date	Hour	Summary of Events and Information	Remarks and references to Appendices
ARRAS	16/3/17		Front Line (17) 2 in. how will be 2.30 am (16) Advanced Batn H.Qrs. will be @ 2.3.a.4,8. The raiding party met with no difficulty in lining along the tap in spite of the fact that a party of about 20 were seen carrying in front of their own strictly before. A machine gun firing opposite the jap was put out of action by a direct hit from a shell. Little difficulty was experienced in getting through the wire and the German trenches were entered without trouble no enemy being encountered. The five which was badly damaged and the Control trench a few yards in rear was very much deepened (5'4"). The party working to the north found 6 dugouts, Wires were heard in all. Altho shells were thrown in - none. Blocks mounting on frames was found in both fire and communication trenches making it difficult to move along - the party working took prisoner 10 dugout. Two much were thrown in by artillery the remainder were attacked with lotchis shells - No dead were seen in the trenches but all dugouts were occupied - a covered dischange gun emplacement was destroyed the gun exploding was seen an identification obtained. The artillery and strokes barrage was very good, effective for infantry upon signal. Thomas Morris Lieut & Major	

WAR DIARY
or
INTELLIGENCE SUMMARY.

Army Form C. 2118.

Page 17B

Place	Date	Hour	Summary of Events and Information	Remarks and references to Appendices
ARRAS	19/3/17	Support	The Battn were relieved in Right Subsector 1-3 Section by 1m 12 H.L.I. B Coy 7th Cameronians will be relieved by A Coy Hd.3 in front line. C do do 2 Platoons in Support trench Redan trench. A do B do in Billets. Ivory Street will be used as an up French. ISLINGTON STREET as a down on relief the Battn will move into billets in ARRAS. At 7.15 pm the Battn will move to HARBARQ. Order of March - H.Q'rs. A.B.C.D Coy. Starting Point - BAUDIMONT GATE. Route - MAINS Pot Rd. CROSS Rd. 49 d.1.6. DUISANS. GOUVES. 100 yds between Coys 75 yds between Platoons	
HARBARQ	20/3/17 21/3/17	Reserve	Cleaning & inspection of clothing & equipment. Training under Coy arrangements. Casualties Killed 1 O.R. during retirement relieve 1 O.R. Wounded 2nd Lieut Sutton + 35 O.R. Died of wounds 2 O.R.	

Norman Burford Wynn

WAR DIARY or INTELLIGENCE SUMMARY

Place	Date	Hour	Summary of Events and Information	Remarks and references to Appendices
HABARQ	21/3/17		Reserve. Strength - Struck off 1 O.R. Kept taken on strength 10 O.R. Special Orders. 18/3/17 The G.O.C. 18 Division wishes to convey his appreciation to all ranks who took part in the morning's raid and his congratulations on the success achieved.	
	19/3/17		Coys Commanders wishes to congratulate all concerned in preparation & execution of successful raid carried out by the 7th Queens. The Commanding Officer wishes to congratulate all ranks on the march of 16 miles from MAISIEMES to ARRAS which was accomplished with no men falling out although carrying full packs.	
	22/3/17	do	Practising attack in open warfare under by arrangements.	
	23/3/17	do	Strength struck off strength 2 O.R. for commission. 2 O.R. transportation. Training under Coy arrangements.	

Norman Mumford Major

Place	Date	Hour	Summary of Events and Information	Remarks and references to Appendices
HABARQ	24/3/17	Reserve	Page 180	
			Practising attack formation in harrowing area. Strength 2nd Lieut G.R. Park joined the Batt'n.	
	25/3/17	,,	Divine Service. Special Order the Commanding Officer wishes to record the bravery & challenged to the following Officers, NCOs & men during the raid on the German Trenches on the night 17/18 March. Capt. W.R. Stewart D.S.O. 2nd Lieuts R.W.S. Scargill, S.R. Nisbitt M. 2/6756 Sgt A Macdonald 5/18641 A/Cpl J Kellar 5/10069 Pte E. McLean Pte 5/16183 W Marron. Strength Draft taken on strength 3 O.R.	
ARRAS	31/3/17	Support	Evacuated, March of strength 6 O.R. The 7th Cameron Highlanders will relieve the 9th Black Watch on completion of relieve the Batt'n will be attached to the 46th Infantry Bde. Starting point cross roads at East of village. Zero 6.30 p.m. Order of March Bomb Squadron Band H Qrs. A.B.C.D Coys. 100 yds between Coys must after reaching own Post Bn 75 yds between Platoons Batt'n will take over north portion front of BLACK WATCH.	

Maurice Murdoch Hughes

WAR DIARY
or
INTELLIGENCE SUMMARY.
(Erase heading not required.)

Army Form C. 2118.

Page 189

Place	Date	Hour	Summary of Events and Information	Remarks and references to Appendices
ARRAS	26/3/17	Support	Strength Draft taken on strength 36 O.R.	
"	27/3/17		Special Order - The Army Commander sends his best congratulations to all ranks of the 46th & 48th Bdes on successful raids carried out by them during the month.	
			Strength taken on strength Draft 2 O.R.	
			Struck off strength wounded 4 O.R. Hospitalisation 2 O.R.	
"	28/3/17		Found working parties	
"	29/3/17		do	
"	30/3/17		do	
			Strength —	
			Casualties wounded in action 4 O.R.	
"	31/3/17		Front Line. The 7th Bde relieved the 46 J. Bde on the right supported of the 1.3 Seets.	
			7th Canadian relieved the 12th H.L.I.	
			A Coy Cameron " D Coy 12 H.L.I. in front line	
			D " " A " " "	
			C " " B " " 3 Plations Support line 1 Reserve line	
			B " " C " " Cemetery Defences	
				in Billets
			Relief to be completed by 10 p.m.	

Norman Muirfield Major

WAR DIARY
INTELLIGENCE SUMMARY

Page 182

Place	Date	Hour	Summary of Events and Information	Remarks and references to Appendices
ARRAS	31/3/17	Front line	Relief carried out in single file by Platoons at 25 yds interval. IVORY trench as up trench, IRISH LANE as down trench.	

B.M. Crutchett Col.

Army Form C. 2118.

WAR DIARY
or
INTELLIGENCE SUMMARY.

(Erase heading not required.)

Instructions regarding War Diaries and Intelligence Summaries are contained in F. S. Regs., Part II. and the Staff Manual respectively. Title pages will be prepared in manuscript.

Place	Date	Hour	Summary of Events and Information	Remarks and references to Appendices
			Appendix	

7th (SERVICE) BATTALION CAMERON HIGHLANDERS.

ORDERS FOR TACTICAL EXERCISE AT TRENCHES AT LIGNEREUIL, ON WEDNESDAY, 7th MARCH 1917.

TUESDAY, 6th March, 1917.

1. The exercise will be carried out by the Battalion.

2. The forenoon will be devoted to the Trenches forming the 1st Objective.
   After lunch the Battalion will move to the Trenches forming the 2nd Objective, and continue the exercise.

3. Companies will parade as strong as possible. Parade States will be rendered to the Battn. Orderly Room by 8.30 a.m. tomorrow.

4. Companies will pass the Starting Point (Main Cross Roads, MAIZIERES) at the following times :-
   "A" COMPANY - 9 A.M.
   "B" COMPANY - 9.5 A.M.
   "C" COMPANY - 9.10 A.M.
   "D" COMPANY - 9.15 A.M.

5. ROUTE :-
   AMBRINES,
   DENIER,
   DENIER & LIGNEREUIL Road,
   to Trenches.

6. Except for Tactical reasons land under Crops will not be crossed.

7. The Battn. Signallers will parade and march in rear of "D" Coy. They will each carry 1 Blue Flag.

8. Haversack rations will be carried.

9. DRESS :- As in Special Order of 4.2.17.

10. Lewis Gun Teams will carry Empty Magazines. All except No. 1s will carry rifles.

(Signed). GEO. J. S. LUMSDEN,
Lieutenant & A/Adjutant,
7th (Service) Bn. Cameron Highlanders.

7th (SERVICE) BN. CAMERON HIGHLANDERS.

ORDERS FOR TACTICAL EXERCISE AT TRENCHES AT LIGNEREUIL, ON FRIDAY, 9th MARCH 1917.

1. The 44th Inf. Bde. will carry out the Tactical Exercise described in the attached, tomorrow, 9th March 1917.

2. 7th Cameron Highrs. will be Support Battalion.

3. 7th Cameron Highrs. will rendezvous at I.10.d.2.7 at 9.45 a.m.
   Companies will march there independently in the following order :-

   "A"
   "B"
   "C"
   "D"
   Hd. Qrs.

at 100 yards intervals between Coys.
   "A" Coy. will pass the Main Cross Roads, MAIZIERES at 8.20 a.m.

4. With reference to para. 12 of the attached, 2nd Lt A.B.S. Legate will attend at Bde. Hd. Qrs. at 9 A.M. to synchronize watches.

   Reports to Battn. Hd. Qrs. which will be :-
   Up will 1st Objective is captured at I.19.c.6.5.
   Between 1st & 2nd Objectives at I.20.a.8.5.

   (Sgd.) GEO. J. S. LUMSDEN,
   Lieutenant and Adjutant,
   7th (Service) Bn. Cameron Highrs.

8.3.17.

COPY
SECRET   Copy No. 10

44th Infantry Brigade Tactical Exercise.
To be held on 9th March 1917.

Reference Sheet 51c. 1/40,000.

1.   The 44th Infantry Brigade (less M.G. Coy.) will attack the trenches
W. and N. of LIGNEREUIL (2 objectives).
        Our front is approximately on the line -
            I.20.c.2.0. to I.20.c.2.6.
        The first objective is approximately on the line -
            I.20.a.10.0 to I.20.a.10.6
        The first objective is (owing to the village of LIGNEREUIL being
out of bounds) represented East of the village approximately on the line
I.22.c.8.3 to I.22.c.8.9
        The second objective is approximately on the line -
            I.23.c.10.5. to I.17.c.9.2.

Right Front Battalion:	8/10th Gordon Highrs.
Left Front Battalion.	9th Black Watch
Support Battalion.	7th Cameron Highrs.
Reserve Battalion.	8th Seaforth Highrs.

        44 T.M. Battery will attach 1 section to each of assaulting and
support battalions.   The remainder of the battery will be in Brigade
Reserve with the Reserve Battalion.

2. POSITIONS OF ASSEMBLY.
        The assaulting battalions will assemble in imaginary jumping off
trenches in one line.

        The Support Battalion will assemble about I.19.d.2.7. in imaginary
trenches.   Its leading wave will follow the rear of the assaulting battalions
at 100 yards distance.

        The Reserve Battalion will assemble about I.19.d.1.3. It will not
move unless ordered except that carriers for A, B, C1, and C2 dumps will
move to their respective positions in rear of the Right Front Battalion.

3.   The attack will be carried out as follows :-
At Zero hour the barrage (represented by the drummers of the leading
battalions) will creep forward from the German front line towards the 1st
objective.

At Zero plus 40 minutes the first objective should be reached - and the
barrage will pause about 300 yards clear of it.

    Zero plus 1 hour 40 mins: The Barrage will creep forward to second
objective.

    Zero plus 2 hours 20 mins: The Second objective should be reached.

- 1 -

7th (SERVICE) BATTALION CAMERON HIGHLANDERS.

TRAINING PROGRAMME FOR WEEK ENDING 10.3.17.

SUNDAY. **4th MARCH.**	CHURCH PARADE. Fitting of Box Respirators and Clothing. Tactical Scheme for Officers of Trenches mentioned in S.S. 20/2/1 d/22. 2. 17.
MONDAY. **5th MARCH.**	Battalion practising Attack, by Companies at Trenches mentioned in S.S. 20/2/1 d/22.2.17. March Discipline. ½ hours drill in use of Box Respirators. (Haversack rations to be carried by troops and consumed on the Training Area.) Dinners on return to Billets.
6 p.m.	Conference of Officers to discuss Training.
TUESDAY. **6th MARCH.**	Battalion at Training Ground (L.14.c.) Attack practised as a Drill. Platoons practising Attack of Strong Points. Bombers and Rifle Grenadiers throwing live Bombs and Grenades, under Brigade Bombing Officer. Lewis Gun Teams under Lewis Gun Officer. Revolver practice for Officers and No. 1s of L.G. Teams. Companies under Army Gymnastic Staff Instructor. Box Respirator Drill. March Discipline. (Haversack rations to be carried by troops and consumed on the Training Area.) Dinners on return to Billets.
6 p.m.	Lecture to Officers on use of the "BAB" Code by Adjutant.
WEDNESDAY. **7th MARCH.**	Battalion at Trenches mentioned in S.S. 20/2/1 d/22.2.17. Box Respirator Drill. March Discipline. (Haversack rations to be carried by troops and consumed on the Training Area.) Dinners on return to Billets.
6 p.m.	Lecture by Commanding Officer on Military Law.
THURSDAY. **8th MARCH.**	
8.45 a.m.- Noon.	Battalion on Training Ground (L.14.c.) Lewis Gunners under Staff Instructors. Bombers and Rifle Grenadiers under Battn. Bombing Officer. Box Respirator Drill. Attack practised as a Drill, by Battalion. March Discipline. Attack on Strong Points.
2 p.m. - 3 p.m.	Musketry. Short Outpost scheme for Junior Officers.

(Continued).

P.T.O.

COPY.

44th Infantry Brigade.
OPERATION REPORT
ON
RAID CARRIED OUT BY THE 7th CAMERON HRS.
ON THE 18th MARCH, 1917.

Copy No.

Previous to the raid a gap had been cut in the enemy's wire about G.24.d.½.4. by the artillery and Medium Trench Mortars. The wire had also been cut about 60 yards South of this point, the gap was not considered sufficient. These gaps had been patrolled several times.

Zero hour was fixed at 2.50 A.M. By 2.30 A.M. one Company of the 7th Cameron Highrs. was in position on a taped line in advance of our front line, facing the enemy's front line from G.24.d.2.3. to 0.5½ This movement was carried out without detection, in spite of the fact that half an hour before a hostile wiring party had been engaged near this point.

At 2.50 A.M. the artillery and Stokes mortar barrage (as laid down in 44th Infantry Brigade Operation Order No. 146, para. 4) began and the raiding Company advanced towards the gap in the wire. Almost simultaneously with the opening of the barrage two hostile machine guns commenced firing - one opposite the gap in the wire about G.24.d.½.4¾. and the other from about Sap W.23.

The machine gun firing from opposite the gap was almost immediately put out of action by a direct hit by a shell.

Little difficulty was encountered in getting through the wire. Apart from the gaps, it is not so thick as it appears. The knife rests, chiefly, proved troublesome.

The raiding Company were able to get into the enemy's trenches without trouble. No Germans were encountered in the trench. By this time a party of 30 or 40 were seen moving over the open towards the Support Line. This party appeared to be almost entirely knocked out by our artillery barrage and some rifle fire from the raiders. (It is thought that is the wiring party referred to).

The fire trench was very badly damaged by our fire. There was only one portion found to be in fair condition - about 20 yards at G.24.d.1.4. The Control trench a few yards in rear was discovered to be a very deep trench - about 10 feet and very broad.

The raiding Company was divided into two parties.

One party after entering the trench at the gap turned Northwards. One dug-out was found between that point and the Railway. Voices were heard: a Stokes shell was thrown in. This party then turned along the Communication Trench which they penetrated as far as d.2¾.6. Five dug-out entrances on the North side of the trench (presumably going under the Railway) were bombed with Stokes shells. Voices were heard in all.

Difficulty was experienced in moving about both fire and communication trench on account of the several wire blocks. These were all mounted on frames. Our men were obliged to get out of the trench at times in order to get past.

(Continued).

7th (SERVICE) BATTALION CAMERON HIGHLANDERS.

ORDERS FOR TACTICAL EXERCISE AT TRENCHES AT LIGNEREUIL, ON MONDAY 5th MARCH 1917.

SUNDAY, 4th MARCH, 1917.

1. The exercise will be carried out by Companies independently.

2. The forenoon will be devoted to the Trenches forming the 1st Objective.
   After lunch the Companies will move to the Trenches forming the 2nd Objective and continue the exercise by Companies independently.

3. Companies will parade as strong as possible. Parade States will be rendered to the Battn. Orderly Room by 8.30 a.m. tomorrow.

4. Companies will pass the Starting Point (Main Cross Roads, MAIZIERES) at the following times :-
   "A" COMPANY   -   9 A.M.
   "B" COMPANY   -   9.15 A.M.
   "C" COMPANY   -   9.30 A.M.
   "D" COMPANY   -   9.45 A.M.

5. ROUTE :-
   MAIZIERES
   DENIER
   DENIER - LIGNEREUIL Road.
   to Trenches.

6. Except for tactical reasons land under Crops will not be crossed.

7. The barrage will be represented by Signallers carrying flags who will accompany each Coy.

8. Haversack rations will be carried.

9. **DRESS.** Fighting Kit as follows :-
   Haversack on shoulder, containing Cap Comforter, Cardigan, Jacket, if in possession, towel, soap, spare oil tin, holdall, iron ration, waterproof sheet; the latter will be carried on top of the haversack, under the flap.
   Mess tin and cover will be slung outside the haversack.
   120 rounds S.A.A.

10. Lewis Gun teams will carry Empty Magazines. All except No. 1 will carry rifles.

(Signed). GEO. H. E. LUMSDEN,
Lieutenant & A/Adjutant,
7th (Service) Bn., Cameron Highlanders.

EX1:— 7th (SERVICE) BATTALION CAMRON HIGHLANDS

SQUADRON OF TRAINING FOR WEEK ENDING 31st MARCH 1917.

DATE	MORNING	AFTERNOON	NIGHT	REMARKS
SUNDAY. 25th March	CHURCH PARADE.			(Coy. & P. Specialists etc.)
MONDAY. 26th March	9.15 a.m. – 12.30 p.m. Squad Training – Squad in extended	2.P.m. – 3.p.m. Musketry, Bayonet Fighting, Wire Cutting, by Coys.	Sub. Conference of Instructors of Training.	The training week is divided at A.B.C. and B.D.C.
TUESDAY. 27th March	9.15 a.m. – 12.30 p.m. Squad Match – Squad Discipline.	2.P.m. – 3.P.m. Musketry & Box Respirator Drill.		
WEDNESDAY. 28th March	9.15 a.m. – 12.30 p.m. Squad Training – Open Warfare and Deployments	Lecture at 2.p.m. to Platoon Commanders & Platoon Sergeants.	2 P.m. Gas.	
THURSDAY. 29th March	9.15 a.m. – 12.30 p.m. Route March – March in Close Formation	2.P.m. – 3.P.m. Musketry and Bayonet Fighting		

Norman Macleod Major.

DATE.	MORNING.	AFTERNOON.	NIGHT.	REMARKS (Kind of Specialists etc.
FRIDAY. 30th March.	9.15 a.m. - 12.30 p.m. Battn. Training - Attack formations, extn. etc.	2 p.m. - 3 p.m. Musketry and Box Respirator Drill.	Marching by compass lecture for officers.	
SATURDAY. 31st March.	9 a.m. - 12 Noon Company training. Box Respirator Drill. Musketry. Bayonet Fighting. 12.15 p.m. Inspection of Billets by the Commanding Officer.	RECREATION.		

(Sd.) GEO. J. SLUMSDEN.
Lieutenant and A/Adjutant,
7th (Service) Bn. Cameron Highrs.

Index..................

Q20 44/15

SUBJECT.

7th Cameron Highlanders.

No.	Contents.	Date.
	April 1917	

SECRET AND CONFIDENTIAL

WAR DIARY — Vol 22

OF
7TH (SERVICE) BATTALION CAMERON HIGHLANDERS

MONTH OF APRIL 1917

PAGES — 182 TO 199

Army Form C. 2118.

WAR DIARY
or
INTELLIGENCE SUMMARY.
(Erase heading not required.)

Page 182

Place	Date	Hour	Summary of Events and Information	Remarks and references to Appendices
ARRAS	1/4/17		FRONT LINE Strength - Wounded 2 O.R. 2nd Lieut D Mori M.C. taken on strength	
do	2/4/17		"	
do	3/4/17		RESERVE. The Battn. were relieved in the front line by the 8/10th Londons on relief the Battn. moved into billets in the Grand Place.	
do	4/4/17		Reserve In billets in Arras	
do	5/4/17		Reserve In billets in Arras	
do	6/4/17		Reserve In billets in Arras	
do	7/4/17		Reserve In billets in Arras	
do	8/4/17	11.30 pm	Support At 11.30 pm the Battn. moved out of billets in the Grand Place over the Scarpe & communication trenches to assembly trench in front of the Cemetery. Battn. Headquarters in cellars in Rue de Douai.	
	9/4/17	3.30 am 5.30 am	" Battn. reported in position ready for attack. (Zero hour) Under intense Barrage the assaulting Battns (8/10th London high on right & 8/10th London on left) supported by the 7th London high attacked the first system of enemy trenches. Wounroumen of 3rd Major

WAR DIARY
or
INTELLIGENCE SUMMARY.

Army Form C. 2118.

Place	Date	Hour	Summary of Events and Information	Remarks and references to Appendices
FRONT LINE			Page 183.	
		Support Bn.	[Black Line] which was gun with slight loss. the Battn then occupied O.G.1. and O.G.2.	
		7.50 a.m.	The attack on the second objective (Blue Line) was covered. The 9th Black Watch on left were held up at the Railway Triangle. This also prevented the 5th & 6th Division from reaching their objective. the Battn were ordered up to support the assaulting D.H.Q. and with the assistance of a tank the Black Watch captured the railway triangle & line from the assembly trench. the casualties with the exception of the Black Watch were not heavy.	
		3 pm	About this time orders were received for the Battn to relieve the 9th Black Watch on the left. The Battn was then scattered in Hensch trench (the French) and Hermies trench & also in several H.Q. Cays to fall back to Hermies trench and reorganise.	
	10/4/17		After reorganisation B & D Coys. moved forward into Hensch trench and two Platoons of Hess Trench to return up Hermies trench	

Norman MacLeod Lieut

WAR DIARY
or
INTELLIGENCE SUMMARY.

(Erase heading not required.)

Army Form C. 2118.

Page 184

Place	Date	Hour	Summary of Events and Information	Remarks and references to Appendices
FRONT LINE	10/4/17	1pm	Instructions A. & B. Coys moved to CROISILLES Finish line Trench. War commenced to consolidate and wire round them. We stood on from when the Battn was ordered to proceed to the East side of FRENY to support the 4/5th London Btn. This move was complete before dark. Orders were received that the Cavalry occupied the town of [illegible] when strong by the Battn on [illegible] [HIGH] and the Battn were to push up the [illegible] Trench commenced behind these previously occupied.	
	11/4/17	12.45 am	Orders were received that the Division was to attack at 5 am on the frontage from the [BERDLING] Munich Trench to a map reference on the South, to the RIVER SCARPE on the North. The 14th Infantry Brigade being in support.	
		3 am	It's am orders were received from Brigade to move from present [ESSAY] points of the Brown line which was up [illegible] to the Quarry [ABBER] at a night point to a co. left front.	

Norman Mayeur Major

Army Form C., 2118.

WAR DIARY
or
INTELLIGENCE SUMMARY.
(Erase heading not required.)

Page 185

Place	Date	Hour	Summary of Events and Information	Remarks and references to Appendices
ARRAS FRONT	11/4/17	4 A.M.	B Coy Right Support D Coy left support. Two more were completed by 4 a.m. A/10 London Regt were on our left & A/Seaforths & A/Black Watch in Support. Orders were received from Bde to move forward and take offensive line running through 1. 22 - 23 - 34	
		11 a.m.	at 11 am companies moved from their position in artillery formation to the attack moving half right for ORANGE Hill. As soon as MG shot was received the Battn became liable to machine gun fire & shrapnel fire which for a time delayed the advance. The Battn then occupied a system of trenches about H. 29 Central. The 8/10 London on the left were also held up by this fire.	
		2.54 p.m.	Orders were received at 2.54 pm from Brigade that a Barrage on our copses was commencing at 2.50 pm and that the Bde was to attack at 3 pm. The Battn advanced from the trenches about 3pm and again came under exceptionally heavy	

Norman Crawford
Major

WAR DIARY
or
INTELLIGENCE SUMMARY.
(Erase heading not required.)

Army Form C. 2118.

Page 186

Place	Date	Hour	Summary of Events and Information	Remarks and references to Appendices
ARRAS FRONT	11/4/17		Machine gun & shrapnel fire but succeeded in reaching a position midway (roughly) between LONE COPSE and MONCHY.	
		4.40 pm	At 4.40 pm intimation was received from Div that an enemy counter attack was expected. Head position and relief of all regiments was ordered. To put the trenches in H.Q Square (infantry & pack horses) in a state of defence shortly afterwards the Bde intimated that a counter attack was no longer expected. Brigade orders were issued that the Bde was to be relieved by a Battn of 50 Bde.	
		7.30 pm	The greater portion of the Battn reached MONCHY. The men of the Batt in and around Monchy were instructed to place themselves under the command of the Colonel of the Essex Yeomanry who was then in charge of the defence of Monchy. Orders were issued to C.O Coys to withdraw from the position held by them and to link up with the 8/10 Gordons and from a line around	

Aubrey Hungerford
Major

WAR DIARY
or
INTELLIGENCE SUMMARY

Army Form C. 2118.

Page 187

Place	Date	Hour	Summary of Events and Information	Remarks and references to Appendices
ARRAS	12/4/17	3.30 am	100 yards in front of the SUNKEN ROAD. This movement was completed without loss and the Battⁿ was relieved by a Coy of the WORCESTER Regiment. The Battⁿ then moved back to HEUDE trench reaching there about 5.30 am and remained there	
		5.30 am	till 3 pm when it moved back into BILLETS in ARRAS. Our casualties during the operations were:—	

Casualties during recent attack:

	Officers	men
A	6	114
B	4	138
C	3	119
D	5	103
H.Q.	5	47
Total	23	521

Casualties:
	Officers	men
	5	55
	2	37
	1	42
	4	41
	—	—
	12	175

Returned:
	Officers	men
	1	59
	2	99
	2	76
	1	64
	5	47
	11	346

| ARRAS | 14/4/17 | | Reason the Field Marshall in Chief awarded the following decorations:— | |

2ⁿᵈ Lieut B.R. MORTON the Military Cross
2ⁿᵈ Lieut R.W.R. SEMPLE the Military Cross

Worren Hungerford
Major

WAR DIARY or INTELLIGENCE SUMMARY

Army Form C. 2118.

Place	Date	Hour	Summary of Events and Information	Remarks and references to Appendices
ARRAS	13/4/17		Reserve. The Corps Commander has awarded the following decorations: S/16641 A/C KELLY J. D. Coy Military Medal S/14089 Pte McLEAN B. D. Coy Military Medal. Page 188	
	14/4/17		Reserve. Casualties killed in action 4 O.R. Wounded 2nd Lieut T.D.G. WATT, 2nd Lieut D. MOIR M.C. and 21 O.R. Missing 1 O.R. Wounded since died of wounds 1 O.R. Struck off strength 2nd Lieut I.A. SINCLAIR invalided 3 O.R. Transportation 15 O.R. evacuated to England. Casualties sustained during operations 9/12th April. Killed 2nd Lieuts P.G. JENKINS, G.R. NORTON M.C., R.W.B. SEMPLE M.C., J.F. SMITH, J.S. RONALDSON and 19 O.R. Wounded Capt G.A.E. DANY Lieut S.E. RUSSELL 2nd Lieuts T.A. SYMON D.M. BROWN J.R. M'MILLAN E.F. FORREST O.T. COVENTRY and 182 O.R.	

Page 189

Place	Date	Hour	Summary of Events and Information	Remarks
ARRAS	10/4/17		Reserve. Casualties - Missing 24 O.R.	
	25/4/17		The Corps Commander has received the following from R/6785 Serjt MacDonald A "D" Co Melting Medal Shard O.R. from the Commander in Chief :-	

"My warmest congratulations on the important success achieved by yesterday. The measure in which the operation was helped was owed not after the greatest such a formidable hostile troops. Please convey to all employed any appreciation the part they are following shown by them."

The Corps Commander has asked the Divisional Comdr to convey his appreciation and thanks to the Officers Warrant Officers & Non-commissioned officers and to the splendid work they have done both in the preparation for and execution of the attack. The Corps Commander is

Norman Mungford Major

Place	Date	Hour	Summary of Events and Information	Remarks and references to Appendices
ARRAS	15/4/17		Page 190	

particularly pushed by the energy employed to eliminate the
the third opposition was captured.
The Divisional Commander feels sure that the previous
acknowledgement of the work of the Division will be heightened
by all. He wishes to add his own thanks to prime & honor
under his command in whatever in which Officers N.C.O. and
men are inspired with so great a determination to do
their duty. The task given to the 15" Division in the Battle of Arras
entailed hard work in preparation and great gallantry in
attack. The difficulty of the operation only inspired
captured all ranks to greater effort and brilliant success
has been achieved.
The crushing defeat of the enemy on April 9 was due to the
discipline, hard work, untiring energy and magnificent
gallantry of all Ranks. Another page of honour has been

Frederick McCracken

Army Form C. 2118.

WAR DIARY
or
INTELLIGENCE SUMMARY.
(Erase heading not required.)

Place	Date	Hour	Summary of Events and Information	Remarks and references to Appendices
ARRAS	15/4/17		Page 191 Report ached to the previous month of the Division. The Division Commander wishes to thank every officer N.C.O. and man and to pick that it is indeed an honour to command the veteran 15th Scottish Division. Strength 6.O.R. Struck off proceeding to munitions etc. Casualties wounded 4 O.R.	
	16/4/17 17/4/17		Draft taken on strength — 35 O.R. 2nd Lieut J. Thomson wounded to England. Casualties reported wounded since end of previous OR. Brigrose Revis struck off proceed on account of wounds. Casualties killed 2 O.R.	
	18/4/17		Practising attack in open warfare — Strength. Captain A.H. McBean evacuated to England with Lieut W.T. Dickson Struck off P.R. & Struck off Strength. Strength taken on strength 77 O.R.	

Monminhumfordlupi

Page 192

Place	Date	Hour	Summary of Events and Information	Remarks and references to Appendices
ARRAS	18/4/17		Rearr Reported missing wounded 5 OR.	
"	19/4/17		do killed 1 OR	
			Practising attack in open warfare Strength 3 O.R. evacuated & struck off	
"	20/4/17		Practising attack in open warfare Strength 31 Off 1 611 taken on strength	
"	21/4/17		Practising attack in open warfare	
"	22/4/17		Found this the Bn. returned 8/Oth Londn Regt taking over the left subsector. Disposition. A coy on the right, D coy on the left of the front line. C coy in Reserve support about N.11.a.2.6. B coy in Reserve, Headquarters around N.11.a.5.2. The B.W.R. left the GRAND PLACE billets at 6.30 p.m. 100 yds interval between platoons. Route Station, S. SAUVEUR, TILLOY, N.15 & 79, N.16.6.18, N.10 & 5.15 and thence by trolley line.	

Nineteen hundred & Seventeen

WAR DIARY or INTELLIGENCE SUMMARY

Page 193

Place	Date	Hour	Summary of Events and Information	Remarks and references to Appendices
ARRAS FRONT LINE	23/4/17		FRONTLINE	
		3.20 am	The 15th Division attacked the enemy lines opposite them the Battn line (Bridge) at 0 in centre to 0.8 centre to north wood in O 8 B (2). The 44th Bde was on the Right & the 45th Bde on the left with the 46 Bde in support. Dividing line between Bdes. Bruhin + enclosure in O in a. Battn was reported in position ready to attack K.G.n etc left A Coy on the right in the front line A trench C Coy in support B. Coy in Reserve 10th in the B. trench. On the right of the Battn were the 9th Seaforths on the left the 11th Argyll & Sutherland High[rs] (45. Bde)	
		4.45 am	Zero hour. Under an intense Barrage the Battn attacked the German line trenches. Although at once the enemy barraged our front line trench & severe machine gun fire came from the strong point on our front & from the high ground on the south of the Scarpe River. The strong point was rushed at the point of the bayonet.	

Norman MacLeod Lt Col

WAR DIARY or INTELLIGENCE SUMMARY

Army Form C. 2118.

Place	Date	Hour	Summary of Events and Information	Remarks and references to Appendices
ARRAS	23/4/17		Page 194	
		FRONT LINE	Our right was then hung up by machine gun fire. Our left in the meantime pushed on to Bullets Trench capturing the south end of it and taking about 40 prisoners. There was also a machine gun about A15 6 93 which was captured. This would be about 5.30 am. During this time all of B Coy with their left & right touching themselves with the centre of the Batt who had been held up by machine gun fire were advanced one push-portugais or post astride the	
		5.30 am		
		5.45 am	SUNKEN ROAD (A1 18 b.9.5). A small party on the right formed up with Capt Morrison & the Black Watch and formed another post on the SUNKEN ROAD. The officers holding the post in Bullet Trench was with the assistance of a few Stokes & Rifle Grenades drove the hun post in to the Cambrai Road forming their posts in the trench. A new Barrage was found under which we were enabled to	
		6.30 am		
		10.30 am		
		12 mid ?		

WAR DIARY
INTELLIGENCE SUMMARY

Page 145

Place	Date	Hour	Summary of Events and Information	Remarks and references to Appendices
ARRAS	23/4/17		pushed forward the post in the SUNKEN Rd forming a new post in a trench about N.3.a.9.6. fortified party of HAMMER TRENCH. Our fire from this post was able to do good work against the enemy forming up in front of GUEMAPPE	
	6 pm		The 4.6th R.B. advanced through us enabling our fire pour to be its advanced post to a point west on the Railway retired from their trenches.	
	24/4/17 2 am		After re-joining the Batt.n moved back to behind the Brown Line about 2 am. (N.15.b.Central) the no. & Des. becoming Supports.	
	25/4/17		The Batt.n relieved the 10th SCOTTISH RIFLES in front line from CAMBRAI Road to about 300 yds SOUTH the Coy from left to right being C. D. B. A. Coys.	
	26/4/17 10.30 pm		The 1.4th R.B. advanced to the attack our objective being CAVALRY FARM and German trenches to the East of it.	

Norman Crawford Maj.

Place	Date	Hour	Summary of Events and Information	Remarks and references to Appendices
ARRAS	2/4/17		Page 19b	
		FRONT LINE	The advance was much on his manner. took wire covered of L Coy on the left B Coy on the right. The second wave D Coy on the left A Coy on the right. The left was to press through the farm leaving moppers up to deal through and advance to the German trench. The right was to incline slightly to the left so as to get in front of the trench. The Black Watch on our right were also to incline to the left so as to support us. On our right the 46 Bn (6th Cameron) were to attack the German trench running from the farm on the North side of the road. The advance reached the German trench without much difficulty. We found the trench though held and at the same time a machine gun opened on them to their left rear coming from the direction to as 2a. The Batt. were too weak to take but had failed to do so. The Batt. was forced to withdraw leaving a strong point on the right.	
		11 pm		Wm Humphrys Major

WAR DIARY
or
INTELLIGENCE SUMMARY.

Army Form C. 2118.

Place	Date	Hour	Summary of Events and Information	Remarks and references to Appendices
ARRAS	28/4/17	12 noon	FRONT LINE of the Seaforth line and another smaller post to the east of the Farm. They remained withdrawn to our support position. About midnight the Seaforths drew in our post in front of the Farm.	
	29/4/17	2 am	About 2 am an order was received to try and re-occupy the position. This taken was given up as a position that the as a Bde on our left had failed to reach their objective. Officers patrols were sent out and then posts formed with three Lewis Guns running from the south east corner of the Farm 150 yds from it. A second post about 100 yds further south & another about 50 yds. the intention being to link up with the Black Watch on our right who were reported to have advanced and made posts there. After the start of the operation however we never again found touch with the Black Watch.	

Norman Humphry?
R. Hugh?

Army Form C. 2118.

WAR DIARY or INTELLIGENCE SUMMARY.

(Erase heading not required.)

Page 198

Place	Date	Hour	Summary of Events and Information	Remarks and references to Appendices
ARRAS	27/4/17	10.30 p.m	At 10.30 p.m. The Battⁿ was relieved by the Seaforth H^{rs}. moving into support in the B Trenches and SUNKEN Trench.	
Support Line	28/4/17		The Battⁿ were relieved from the support line by the A Coy of the 3rd London Regiment at 9.30 p.m. During the day 6 N.C.O.s and men who had been killed in the action were buried. The Battⁿ with others to billets in GRAND PLACE ARRAS. The following tables shows the casualties for this attack —	

	Killed in		Casualties		Came out	
	Officers	men	Officers	men	Officers	men
A Coy	2	124	2	108	-	16
B Coy	2	136	1	83	2	51
C Coy	2	132	2	57	-	43
D Coy	3	129	2	86	-	33
H.R.	4	49	-	1	4	48
Total	13	570	7	369	6	191

Norman Wingford Major

Army Form C. 2118.

WAR DIARY
or
INTELLIGENCE SUMMARY.
(Erase heading not required.)

Instructions regarding War Diaries and Intelligence Summaries are contained in F. S. Regs., Part II. and the Staff Manual respectively. Title pages will be prepared in manuscript.

Place	Date	Hour	Summary of Events and Information	Remarks and references to Appendices
SIMENCOURT	29/9/17	In Rest	Pay day. The Batt'n moved from ARRAS to SIMENCOURT & billeted in barns leaving the GRAND PLACE at 2.45pm. An interval of 500 yds between Batt'ns and 200 yds between Coys. Route Rue ST AUBERT — LIGNEREUIL — DANVILLE — IZEL — BERNEVILLE.	
do	30/9/17	"	Cleaning up. examining equipment. clothing &c.	Demilitaire Lt Col J/Command'g

3.3.17

7th (SERVICE) BATTALION QUEENS OWN CAMERON HIGHLANDERS.

NOTES ON OPERATIONS, 22nd/28th APRIL 1917.

SUNDAY, 22nd APRIL. The Battalion moved out of Billets in ARRAS, and relieved the 8/10th Gordon Highlanders in the Front Line Trenches.

MONDAY, 23rd APRIL. 3.20 A.M. Battalion was reported in position ready to attack - "D" Coy. on the left and "A" Coy. on the right, in the Front Line or "A" Trench. "C" Coy. in Support, "B" Coy. in Reserve; both being in "B" Trench.
On the right of the Battalion was the 8th Seaforth Highrs., and on the left of the Battalion, the 11th Argyll and Sutherland Highrs. (45th Inf. Bde.).
4.45 A.M. (ZERO HOUR). Under an intense Barrage the Battn. attacked the first line German trench, their objective being the BLUE LINE. Almost immediately the Enemy put a Barrage on our Front Line Trenches, falling, if anything, a little short of it. The Enemy at once opened an intense Machine Gun fire from the Strong Point on our immediate front, and also from the high ground south of the RIVER SCARPE. The Strong Point was rushed at the point of the Bayonet and as our men reached it the Germans attempted to surrender but were apparently overwhelmed in the rush.
Our right Company was then badly hung up and suffered very severely by Machine Gun fire coming from a Strong Point on the right, and another Machine Gun to our immediate front on the North side of GUEMAPPE. Our left had, in the meantime, pushed on, reaching the South end of BULLET TRENCH (up to the point when it meets the Road) clearing it of Germans and taking about 40 prisoners. There was also a Machine Gun about this point (N.18.b.9.8.) which was captured. This would be about 5.30 a.m. By this time the Officer found that he was out of touch on his left and right. He started to consolidate his position, placing his Lewis Guns so as to bring enfilade fire along the remainder of the Trench in order to keep down the heads of the Enemy and so enable other troops to advance.
About 5.45 A.M. the centre of the Battalion, which had been held up by a Machine Gun on its front, was able to advance as the Gun had evidently been knocked out.. It got as far as the SUNKEN ROAD (N.18.b.9.5.) without much opposition. Here they came in touch with the Germans lying in shell holes, and as the party was weak and apparently unsupported on either flank, they dug themselves in. This would be about 6.30 a.m. Another small party of the right Company passed on about this time and were joined by Captain Morrison, Black Watch, with one or two men of that Regiment. Captain Morrison took command of the party, which dug themselves in in the SUNKEN ROAD on the right of the others.
10 A.M. An Officer came back from the post on the left in the SUNKEN ROAD, and reported the position, stating that small parties were reforming to the East of GUEMAPPE, and that the left Company was nearly isolated. He was instructed to return and hold his post at all costs. This he did and, with a Lewis Gun, was able, from his position, to break up parties on the East of GUEMAPPE.
10.30 A.M. The Officer who was holding the left post in the SUNKEN ROAD, with the assistance of a few Stokes Mortar Shells and Rifle Grenades, was able to clear the Trench/

Trench northwards up to the Main CAMBRAI ROAD, and with about 12 men found 3 posts in it. There was no serious attempt on the part of the Enemy to retake this part of the Trench.

At 12 p.m. a new Barrage was opened for a fresh attack. The Officer in the Strong Point at N.18.b.9.5 advanced his post as soon as the Barrage commenced, which appeared to be mostly on his right and not of much strength. Finally forming a Strong Point in a trench about N.13.a.2.6, possibly part of HAMMER TRENCH or a little in front of it, where he remained for the rest of the day sniping and using a Lewis Gun.

About 6 p.m. as the 46th Inf. Bde. advanced, the Enemy began to retire from their trenches and many were caught by our Lewis Gun fire. Many others were seen surrendering to the 46th Bde.

TUESDAY. 24th APRIL. About 2 A.M., after re-organizing, the Battalion moved back to behind BROWN LINE.

During these Operations Stokes Mortars were in the Support Line. It was intended that they should be used in the first place against the Strong Point in front of our Front Line, but for some reason they did not come into action. In the attack on the left of BULLET TRENCH the Stokes Shells proved invaluable.

Rifle Grenadiers were with their Companies and assisted greatly in working up BULLET TRENCH.

The party was so small that it could not have taken the trench without the assistance of the Stokes Shells and Rifle Grenades. The enemy practically evacuated the trench when this fire was brought to bear on them.

The Vickers took up position in rear of the Battalion.

TUESDAY. 24th APRIL. The Battalion was in Brigade Support in N.15.b.

WEDNESDAY. 25th APRIL. The Battalion relieved the 10th Scottish Rifles in the Front Line from CAMBRAI ROAD to about 300 yards South.

THURSDAY. 26th APRIL. 10.30 P.M. The Battalion advanced in two waves to the attack, the objective being CAVALRY FARM and the German Trench East of it. The first wave consisted of "C" Coy. on the left and "B" Coy. on the right. The second wave, "D" Coy. on the left and "A" on the right. The plan of attack was "C" and "D" Coys. to attack the Farm, leaving "Moppers Up" to attend to it while the remainder pressed on to the Trench. - The two right Coys. to swing round, inclining to the left so as to attack the German trench more or less in front. It was understood that the Black Watch on the right would also come up and assist in the attack on the right portion of this trench, but they never reached this point. The Farm building was taken without much difficulty but as soon as this was passed, heavy Machine Gun and Rifle fire was met. Several of the enemy were in shell holes. These were dealt with and the advance continued to within 30 yards of the Trench. On the extreme right, however, the trench was nearly entered.

11 p.m. When the Advance got up to the trench it found it strongly held by the enemy who started bombing. At the same time a Machine Gun opened fire from the trench on the left of the CAMBRAI ROAD near the Farm, on our left rear. The result was the line had to withdraw. A Lewis Gun team took up a position on the right of the enemy trench and opened an enfilading fire so as to keep their heads down and assist the withdrawal. The line then withdrew to its original position leaving a post about 50 yards due East of the Farm and the post which had been formed to the right of the enemy trench. This would be about **11.30 p.m.** At **12 midnight** the enemy attacked our post East of the Farm, which had to withdraw.

FRIDAY. 27th APRIL.

2 A.M. An order was received to try and organize a further attack. In going forward to do this it was found that GORDON ALLEY was full of the 9th Gordon Highlanders. ~~It was therefore necessary to advance over the top.~~ It was found that TANK Trench was lightly held by Seaforth Highrs. There were also small parties in many of the shell holes between SHOVEL Trench and the Front Line, taking cover from Machine Gun fire which was searching that ground. An attempt was made to locate the Stokes Mortars which were in some shell holes, in order to bring them up to form a Barrage. These could not be found on account of the very dark night, the difficulty of movement owing to Machine Gun fire, and also because more time could not be spared as it was getting near morning.
The Front Line was found crowded with Seaforths, Gordons, and Camerons. The Gordons and part of the Seaforths were ordered back to their original trenches. Touch was then established with the Battalion on our left. It was found that they had failed to gain their objective (trench on North of Farm). As they did not intend making another attack, and as we could do nothing so long as the enemy held that trench on our flank, it was decided to form a line of posts from the South-east corner of the Farm to try and connect up with the Black Watch on our right. With this in view two Officers patrols were sent out to reconnoitre the position.
These posts were finally established, one about 100 yards south of the Farm and a little East of it. The next about another 100 yards south, and a third about 50 yards further South. During the day the enemy were seen approaching the Farm building but were driven back by Lewis Gun fire from the posts. After this the enemy shelled the Farm and vicinity. These shells and some of our own fell round the posts but only caused one casualty.
10.30 P.M. The Battalion was relieved by the 8th Seaforth Highrs., taking up a position in SHOVEL and "B" Trenches.

In this attack Stokes Mortars were employed to barrage the Farm building. These were situated in shell holes behind the Front Line. The importance of having a Battalion runner who knows their exact position so as to communicate easily was brought out.
Rifle Grenades would have proved useful against the trench but unfortunately there was only one Grenadier left, the others having become casualties.
The /

The Vickers Guns took up their own position behind the Front Line and, I believed, did good work.
It was found very difficult to keep the men together in the darkness, when the ground was so much cut up with shell holes. The Battalion was much disorganised when it reached the enemy line, on this account. It would probably have been less if there had been more Officers and N.C.Os. to lead them.

SATURDAY, 29th APRIL. The Battalion was relieved by "A" Coy., 3rd London Regt. During the day the Battlefield, as far as possible, was cleared of our dead, 64 N.C.Os. and Men being buried.

Norman Macleod
Major,
7th (Service) Bn. Cameron Highlanders.

1.5.17.

Index..................................

Q 21
44/75

SUBJECT.

7th Cameron Highlanders.

No.	Contents.	Date.
	May 1917	

ORIGINAL

WAR DIARY

of

7th (Service) Battalion Cameron Highlanders

Vol 23

Pages 199 to 206 inclusive

For Month of May 1917

WAR DIARY or INTELLIGENCE SUMMARY

Page 199

Place	Date	Hour	Summary of Events and Information	Remarks and references to Appendices
SIMINCOURT	1/5		In Rest. Training under arrangements of the Corps Commander awarded Military Medals to the following:- S/16323 Sgt. R.J. Cameron — A Coy S/15513 A/Cpl. J. Geddes — A Coy S/25532 Sgt. D. Macaulay — B Coy S/13565 Pte. J. Munford — B Coy S/22946 — J.B. Keiller — BC Coy S/19197 Sgt. M. Morrison — D Coy S/14140 Pte. R. Young — D Coy 2nd Lieut. J. MacCulloch assumed command of C Coy.	
	2/5		In Rest. Training under by arrangements. Casualties in operation 23 to 28th April. Killed. Capt. W.R. Stuart M.C. 2nd Lieut Lambert & Lieut H.R.W. Walker 2nd Lieut M.S. Mackay and 79 O.R. Wounded 249 O.R. Missing 42 O.R. Died of wounds 3 O.R. Norman Macfie Major	

Army Form C. 2118.

WAR DIARY
or
INTELLIGENCE SUMMARY.
(Erase heading not required.)

Place	Date	Hour	Summary of Events and Information	Remarks and references to Appendices
SIMMECOURT	3/5/17	In Rest.	Page 200. Batt'n Training demonstration in Rifle Bombing. Strength. Draft taken on strength 93 OR. Wounded men struck off strength 2 - Lieut A MCNIVEN	
	4/5/17	In Rest	Company training. Strength. Evacuated v struck off strength 5 OR.	
	5/5/17	In Rest	Route March. Strength taken on strength. Lieut J.C. Boyd & Lieuts A.W.H. COOPER, J. LAMONT, D.T. MILNE, J.A. SYMON, C. COURTNEY, A. ROSS, T. TELFORD. Struck off strength 4 OR.	
	6/5/17	In Rest.	Church Parades v Baths. Strength evacuated v struck off strength 1 OR. Draft taken on strength 3 OR.	
	7/5/17	In Rest	Company training. Taken on strength 10 OR.	

Norman Munro Major

WAR DIARY
or
INTELLIGENCE SUMMARY.
(Erase heading not required.)

Army Form C. 2118.

Page 201

Place	Date	Hour	Summary of Events and Information	Remarks and references to Appendices
GRAND RULLECOURT	8/5/17	In Rest	The Battn moved to Billets in Grand Rullecourt. Starting point X roads West of SIMENCOURT thus 8.2 a.m. Drew full marching order. Order of March Scouts, Band, HQrs, A, B, C, D Coys. The head of the Battn to be at the junction of Gouvelrigny & A.S. at 7.15am. Arrived at 2.0 pm between Coys	
"	9/5/17	In rest	Battn Training Lieut Colonel Crichton relinquished command of the Battn on 6.5.17	
"	10/5/17	In rest	Battn Training The Field Marshall Commander in Chief awarded the following decorations Lieut T. Findlay Military Cross 3/14241 C.S.M J.D. McRill Distinguished Conduct Medal R/5076 Sgt P. Fleming do	Norman Rutherford Major

WAR DIARY / INTELLIGENCE SUMMARY

Page 202

Place	Date	Hour	Summary of Events and Information	Remarks and references to Appendices
BRAND	10/5/17		In Rest. Strength 3 ORs evacuated and struck off strength	
RUE = COURT	11/5/17		Batn training	
			Strength 16 OR evacuated and struck off	
			11 OR struck taken on strength	
	12/5/17		In Rest. Batn training	
			Strength evacuated & struck off 9 OR.	
			Taken on strength	
			2nd Lieut J Moran R.S.C. Pollock R.J.E. Gibbs	
	13/5/17		In Rest. Church Parade	
	14/5/17		In Rest. Batn training	
			Strength 2nd Lieut Dumville removed from establishment	
	15/5/17		In Rest. Batn training	
	16/5/17		In Rest. Batn training	
	17/5/17		In Rest. Batn training	
			Strength struck off 7 OR	
			2nd Lieut h.E. Lt Key wounded	

Norman Mungford Major

WAR DIARY
or
INTELLIGENCE SUMMARY.

Page 203

Place	Date	Hour	Summary of Events and Information	Remarks and references to Appendices
BRANDT.	18/5/17	In rest	Battn. Training. Strength 3 O.R. taken off.	
RUMBEUCOURT	19/5/17	In rest	Battn. Training. The Corps Commander has awarded Military Medals to S/1817 Cpl. J. Spain, S/2439 Pte. T. L. Bowen, S/16090 Pte. R. Bell, S/16086 " J. McLellan, S/13166 L/Cpl W. Millar, R/15563 L/Cpl. D. Anderson. Struck off strength 1 O.R. Taken on strength 2/Lieuts R. H. Cameron, F. W. Mackay, C. P. R. Scott, T. D. W. McCracken, T. L. C. Jenkins, R. B. Pinder.	
	20/5/17	In rest	Church Parade. Struck off strength 2 O.R. Taken on strength 15 O.R.	

Norman Lunefoot Major

WAR DIARY or INTELLIGENCE SUMMARY

Army Form C. 2118.

Place	Date	Hour	Summary of Events and Information	Remarks and references to Appendices
VACQUERIE La Bouey	21/5/17	In rest.	Page 204. The 15th Div. were transferred to the SIX Corps. The 7th Cameroons moved to VACQUERIE. Starting point junction 26 Curoy Franc Rubbecourt Zuincourt Roads Guns 5.45 a.m. Order of march HdQrs A.B. C & D Coys transport	
ST. GEORGES	22/5/17	In rest.	Church parade of strength 35 O.R. Taken on strength 2nd Lieut J.S. McNab Struck off strength 2nd Lieut J.T. Mutimer invalided as R Christchn P.B. The Battn. moved to St Georges Starting point cross roads a 6 in VACQUERIE Guns 7.30 a.m. Order of march H.Q. R.E.D. A Coys transport Route leneny nail	
do	23/5/17	In rest.	Battn. training Strength taken on 2nd Lieut W Mutimer Later of strength 1 O.R.	

Norman Mulford Lloyd

Army Form C. 2118.

WAR DIARY
or
INTELLIGENCE SUMMARY.
(Erase heading not required.)

Page 205

Place	Date	Hour	Summary of Events and Information	Remarks and references to Appendices
St GEORGE	24/5/17	In Rest	Batt'n Training. Strength recruited & struck off 1 O.R.	
do	25/5/17	In Rest	Batt'n Training. Bathing Strength	
do	26/5/17	In Rest	Major T.L. Cunningham D.S.O. struck off establishment. Church Parade. Struck off strength 1 O.R. Batt'n route march.	
do	27/5/17	In Rest	Strength taken on 1 OR. struck off 1 OR. Church Parade	
do	28/5/17	In Rest	Struck off strength & died R.H. Cameron & 1 O.R. Batt'n Training	
do	29/5/17	In Rest	Batt'n Training Strength struck off & evacuated 2 O.R. taken on strength 1 n O.R.	
do	30/5/17	In Rest	Divisional Training Strength evacuated 1 O.R. taken on strength 1 n O.R.	

Norman Murison Major

WAR DIARY
or
INTELLIGENCE SUMMARY.

Army Form C. 2118.

Place	Date	Hour	Summary of Events and Information	Remarks and references to Appendices
St GEORGE	31/5/17		Page 206. In not. Batt'n training. Strength & appointments. Capt. A. R. Chapman to be Staff Captain 46th Infantry Bde. 27/12-5/17. Honorary Ruchford Major Commanding 7 (S) Batt'n Queens Own Cameron High'rs	

Index..............................

Q 22

SUBJECT.

7th Cameron Highlanders.

No.	Contents.	Date.
	June 1917	

SECRET AND CONFIDENTIAL

ORIGINAL
Vol 24

WAR DIARY

OF
7TH (SERVICE) BATTALION CAMERON HIGHRS

FOR
MONTH OF JUNE 1917

PAGES 207 TO 214 INCLUSIVE

WAR DIARY or INTELLIGENCE SUMMARY

Army Form C. 2118.

Page 207

Place	Date	Hour	Summary of Events and Information	Remarks and references to Appendices
ST. GEORGES	1/6/17		9th Rnft. 44th Inf. Brigade Sports. Battn: won 2 firsts & 3 seconds - prior Silver bugle won by 8/10th Gordons after tie with 8th Seaforths	
do.	2/6/17		9th Rnft. Battn. Training. Close order drill, open order & outpost. Rifle inspection by C.O.	
do.	3/6/17		9th Rnft. Church Parade. Strength — Arrived by draft 14 O.R.	
do.	4/6/17		9th Rnft. Battn. Training. Close order drill, Coy. drill, Outpost. Attack formation & Range practice. Promotions — 2nd Lt. D.F. Suttie to be Temp. Lieut. 21/20-11-16. 2nd Lt. J.A. Symon to be Temp. Lieut. 4/1-3-17 — Casualty - Previously reported wounded, now reported officially killed in action. 10 R. T.A.S. Elliot - 2nd Lt. J.T. Bookless	
do.	5/6/17		9th Rnft. Inspection by G.O.C. 1 Coy. Close Order Drill. 1 Coy. Outpost. 2nd Lt. M.D. Deans & Lt. H.D. Deans Strength - Officers joined 11 O.R. Struck off 2 O.R.	
do.	8/6/17		9th Rnft. Inspection by G.O.C. 15th Div. Signal. (Lights etc.) Runners (Drill, orders) M.G. (Buckets, orders) L.G. (Assembly orders)	A. Jones S. Major

WAR DIARY
or
INTELLIGENCE SUMMARY

Army Form C. 2118.

Place	Date	Hour	Summary of Events and Information	Remarks and references to Appendices
St GEORGES	6/6/17	Cont.	Page 208. Honours & Awards. For acts of gallantry in the Field. The following Crosses: 2nd Lt. W.L. MURRAY 2nd Lt. N.S. SIM 2nd Lt. J.W. GRAHAM. (15th Bn. Routine orders No. 655 4/31.5.17)	
St GEORGES	7/6/17		Strength. Struck off 2nd Lt. E.W. FORREST (invalided to England, wounded) 1 O.R.	
			In Rest. Brigade Exercise. Strength - Taken on 1 O.R.	
St GEORGES	8/6/17		In Rest. Batt" training - Reinforcements. Appointments: Lieut. W.J.S. LUMSDEN is appointed Adjutant with effect from 15.4.17 vice Capt. A.R. CHAPMAN appointed T.O. Staff Capt. 46. Inf. Bde. Strength: Struck off 2nd Lt. A.R. CURRIE - 9 O.R. Taken on 1 O.R.	
St GEORGES	9/6/17		In Rest. Brigade Field Firing Exercise. Strength - Struck off 4 O.R.	
St GEORGES	10/6/17		In Rest. Church Parade. Strength: Taken on - 2nd Lts. J. MILLAR, J.A. MACDONALD, J.A. BEGRIE, T. GIBB & 11 O.R.	

A. Davies, Major

Army Form C. 2118.

WAR DIARY
or
INTELLIGENCE SUMMARY.
(Erase heading not required.)

Place	Date	Hour	Summary of Events and Information	Remarks and references to Appendices
			Page 209.	
St GEORGES	11/6/17	9a.Rest.	Batt. Training - Range practice etc. The undermentioned were mentioned in Despatches 9.4.17 MAJOR M. MACLEOD CAPT. A.R. CHARMAN LIEUT G.J.S. LUMSDEN S/13264 R.Q.M.S. J. WILSON - S/15620 Sergt. T. TORRANCE - S/13184 L/Cpl. A. BELL - S/16137 L/Cpl. J. O'ROURKE - S/13241 Pte. W. Mc INTOSH.	
St GEORGES	12/6/17	9a.Rest.	Batt. training - Range practice etc. Strength - Officers Draft 9 & O.Rs. Strength 41 & O.R.	
St GEORGES	13/6/17	9a.Rest.	Batt. Training Strength - Taken on No.2 Strength 41 & O.Rn.	
St GEORGES	14/6/17	9a.Rest.	Batt. Training. Practising the Attack with Tanks. Casualties. Previously reported Missing, now reported Killed in Action. 4 O.Rs.	
St GEORGES	15/6/17	9a.Rest.	Batt. Training. Strength - Taken on 1 O.R.	

A. Downes Major

WAR DIARY
or
INTELLIGENCE SUMMARY

Army Form C. 2118.

Page 210.

Place	Date	Hour	Summary of Events and Information	Remarks and references to Appendices
ST GEORGES	16/6/17		9ᵗʰ R.I.R. Batt. Training - Inspection of Rifles by C.O. - Recreation. Strength - Taken on 2.0.R. Stand off 2.0.R.	
ST GEORGES	17/6/17		9ᵗʰ R.I.R. Church Parade. Strength joined by Draft 16, 0.R. Stand off 2.0.R.	
ST GEORGES	18/6/17		9ᵗʰ R.I.R. Batt. Training - Rang Practices etc. Special Order by Major General F.W.N. McCRACKEN K.C.B. D.S.O. "9ᵗʰ (Old Brigade) farewell to the 15ᵗʰ (Scottish) Div. I wish to express my heartfelt thanks to all ranks for their continued assistance to me throughout the period of over two years I assumed command. The standard of discipline & training which has enabled the Division to achieve the success already obtained will, I am convinced, lead in the future to still greater success. The maintenance of this standard added to the high morale, general valour, & the Division will inevitably enable them to obtain the final victory before performing to the level of their units, which is already so greatly proud of their fine achievement. I place at all times wanted their movement & will do departmental - I wish them every possible success in the future." Strength. Stand off 4.0.R.	

A. Goodwin
Major

Army Form C. 2118.

WAR DIARY
or
INTELLIGENCE SUMMARY.
(Erase heading not required.)

Place	Date	Hour	Summary of Events and Information	Remarks and references to Appendices
			Page 211	
ST GEORGES	19/6/17	In rest.	Brigade Examines. Strong II - Struck off 3 O.R.s -	
ST GEORGES	20/6/17	In rest.	Batt. Training - Platoon Firing Competition - Strong II - Struck off 1 O.R.	
CROIX	21/6/17	In rest.	The Batt. moved to CROIX, with 1 Coy. at ST RACOURT. Starting point. 200 yds. N.W. of W in WILLEMAN Time 3.15 a.m. - Order of march. H.Q. 'A' 'B' 'C' 'D' Coy. Transport - Route. WILLEMAN - OEUF - ST RACOURT. Approx. Casualties. Temp Lieut. M. MURCHISON to be temp. Capt. 1/3/17 Temp Lieut. G. J. S. LUMSDEN do. do. 25/4/17.	
PERNES	22/6/17	In rest.	The Batt. moved to PERNES. Starting point. - HESDIN ST POL road, close South of R in CROIX. Time 3.15 a.m. Order of march - H.Q. 'B' 'C' 'D' 'A' Coy. Transport - Route - Main ST POL - PERNES road -	

A. Jenkins Major

Army Form C. 2118.

WAR DIARY
or
INTELLIGENCE SUMMARY.
(Erase heading not required.)

Page 212

Place	Date	Hour	Summary of Events and Information	Remarks and references to Appendices
BOURECQ	23/6/17	On parade	The Batt" moved to BOURECQ with 2 Coys. at ECQUEDECQUE. Starting point Batt" Parade Ground at PERNES. Time 9.45 a.m.	
BOURECQ	24/6/17	On parade	Church Parade. Commanded. Major General H.F. THULLIER C.B. C.M.G. assumed command of II. 15th (Scottish) Division 17.6.17. Strength. Taken on 10 O.Rs.	
STEENBECQUE	26/6/17	On parade	The Batt" moved to STEENBECQUE. Starting point. Orderly room BOURECQ. Time 7 a.m. Order of March H.Q. "D" "A" "B" "C" Coys. Transport.	
ST. SYLVESTRE CAPPEL	26/6/17	On parade	The Batt" moved to BISSEAU and S.E. of ST. SYLVESTRE CAPPEL. Starting point 600 yds. E.N.E. of T ⌐ LE HAUT. Time 4.20 a.m. Order of March H.Q. A, B, C, D, Coys. Transport. Strength. 22 O.R. Struck off. Casualties. Died of wounds. 1 O.R.	

A. Jennings Bramly

WAR DIARY
or
INTELLIGENCE SUMMARY

Page 2/3

Place	Date	Hour	Summary of Events and Information	Remarks and references to Appendices
S.T SYLVESTRE CAPPEL	26/6/17	cont.	Results of Inter Platoon Shooting Competition fired on 20.6.17	
			"A" Coy. No.1 Platoon 173 hits = 4.02 hits per minute - Ration + Coy firing -	
			"C" " No.9 " 160 " = 3.80 " " Coy firing	
			"B" " No.6 " 178 " = 3.71 " do	
			"D" " No.16 " 196 " = 3.50 " do	
			Conditions of Competition - 200 yds. No. 3 figure targets appearing for 1 minute. Platoon firing at these at one time. As many shots as could be got off in the time.	
VLAMERTINGHE	27/6/17		In pursuance of Battn. moved into 9th Army Area, Camp about 2.0 miles S.W. of VLAMERTINGHE. Starting Point - Road junction S/8.I 1/4 mile S. of E in S.T SYLVESTRE. Time 4.45 a.m.	
			Order of March. H.Q. "B" "C" "D" "A" Transport - Route. Road junction 3/4 mile N. of the point W in THIEUSHOUK - Four Roads junction 400 yds. W. of T.T.S in "STA" (GEDEWAERSVELDE) - Road junction 400 yds. S.E. of the last E in BEAUVOORDE - POPPERINGHE Grand Place - Cross road 1/2 mile S. of the T in POPPERINGHE.	
			Intervals of 200 yds. between Coys, 9500 yds. between wheels.	

A. Devine

Army Form C. 2118.

WAR DIARY
or
INTELLIGENCE SUMMARY.
(Erase heading not required.)

Page 214.

Place	Date	Hour	Summary of Events and Information	Remarks and references to Appendices
VLAMERTINGHE	28/6/17		In reserve. Special Order. The G.O.C. 15th Div. expressed himself as very pleased with the Grand Griefs of "The Batt." on the Grand. The C.O. desired to add his congratulations to the Officers, N.C.O.s & men on The Grand. In spite of the early start, with one breakfast, the long Grand was completed without any man falling out. Strength – Struck off 5 O.R.	
VLAMERTINGHE	29/6/17		In reserve. Inspection of Arms & Equipment by Coys. Strength – Struck off 4 O.R.	
do.	30/6/17		In reserve. Church Parade. Strength – Taken on 7 O.R. Struck off 2 O.R.	

Norman Macleod
Lt Colonel
Commanding 1st/5th Battalion Cameron Highlanders

Index..................

Min T.   44/15 Q23

SUBJECT.

7th Cameron Highlanders.

No.	Contents.	Date.
	July 1917	

ORIGINAL
Vol 25

SECRET AND CONFIDENTIAL

WAR DIARY
OF
17TH (SERVICE) BATTALION CAMERON HIGHLANDERS

FOR

JULY 1917

Pages 215 to 225 inclusive

Army Form C. 2118.

WAR DIARY
or
INTELLIGENCE SUMMARY.
(Erase heading not required.)

Instructions regarding War Diaries and Intelligence Summaries are contained in F. S. Regs., Part II. and the Staff Manual respectively. Title pages will be prepared in manuscript.

Place	Date	Hour	Summary of Events and Information	Remarks and references to Appendices
VLAMERTINGHE EERIE CAMP.	1/7/17		On Parade - Church Parade - Casualties Killed in action 2 O.Rs.	
			Strength - Taken on 7. O.Rs. Wounded 5 O.Rs.	
IN SUPPORT E. of YPRES MENIN ROAD.	2/7/17		Struck off 2. O.Rs.	
			The Batt" moved into Brigade Support as follows;-	
			'C' Coy. HALF MOON TRENCH.	
			'D' " " in The ECOLE	
			'A' " " in II CONVENT.	
			Hd. Qrs. in II MENIN ROAD (I 9 d. 05. 45)	
			Route. REIGERSBURGH CHATEAU.	
			Order of march 'C' 'D' 'B' H.Q 'A' - Starting point GUARD ROOM at 8 p.m.	
			The Batt" went into the line bee strong with a Coy. Comdt. 9 3 Officers per Coy.	
IN SUPPORT MENIN RD.	3/7/17		Casualties Killed in action 1 O.R.	
do.	4/7/17		do. Died of wounds 1 O.R.	
			do. Wounded 4 O.Rs.	
FRONT LINE DRAGOON FARM.	5/7/17		Front Line. The Batt" relieved The 9th BLACK WATCH in II LEFT SUB-SECTION - RIGHT SECTOR. Casualties Wounded 4 O.R.	
			'C' Coy. relieved 'C' Coy 9th R.W. in FRONT LINE, LEFT.	
			'B' " " 'A' " " " in FRONT LINE, RIGHT.	
			'A' " " 'B' " " " in ST. JAMES TRENCH.	
			'D' " " 'D' " " " in { MILL COTS (1 Platoon) POTINZE REDOUBTS (1 Platoon) POTINZEROAD (dugouts) (2 Platoons) }	
			Hd. Qrs. at DRAGOON FARM.	
			Finding working parties.	

A. Symons Major

WAR DIARY
or
INTELLIGENCE SUMMARY.
(Erase heading not required.)

Army Form C. 2118.

Page 216

Place	Date	Hour	Summary of Events and Information	Remarks and references to Appendices
DRAGOON FARM	5/7/17	Cont. Front Line	Casualties. - Wounded, since died of wounds 1 O.R. Wounded in action. Capt. T.C. BOYD - 2nd LT. T.A. BEGBIE. 5 O.R.	
do	6/7/17	Front Line	Patrols. 1 Officer & 3 O.R. went out on patrol at 12 midnight. Casualties. Wounded in action 2 O.R. Previously reported missing now reported killed in action 1 O.R. Prisoner of War previously reported missing 1 O.R. Strength. Yahn on 1 O.R. (Shown previously wounded) Strength Off. 14 O.R. Honours & Awards. - Distinguished Service Order. Temp. Major NORMAN MACLEOD (Supplement to London Gaz. II. 4.6.17)	
do	7/7/17	Front Line	Patrol. Patrol of 1 Off. & 2 O.R.	
do	8/7/17	Front Line	Patrol. A fighting Patrol of 1 Off. & 10 O.R. with 1 L/G proceeded alright across no man's land to the STABLES. No enemy encount. tried. Casualties. - Killed in action 7 O.R. Wounded in action 16 O.R.	
VLAMERTINGHE EGRIS CAMP.	9/7/17	In Reserve.	The Battn. was relieved by the 13th Batt. ROYAL SCOTS. C Coy. 7th Camerons relieved by "D" Coy. 13th Ry/ S.c. B " A " " A " " D "	

A. Gordons
Major

Army Form C. 2118.

WAR DIARY
or
INTELLIGENCE SUMMARY.
(Erase heading not required.)

Page 217.

Place	Date	Hour	Summary of Events and Information	Remarks and references to Appendices
VLAMERTINGHE EERIE CAMP	9/7/17	Cont.	On Reserve. Orderly Room formed at Infantry Barracks Bⁿ R EERIE CAMP. Casualties. Wounded in action, since died of wounds. 1 O.R. Wounded in Action. 2 O.R. Strength. 1st Lieut. R.H. CAMERON invalided. Sick to England 27.8.17 on ceasing to be Att^d to 4th Bn H^q S^T. Struck off 4 O.R. Appointments. Temp. MAJOR N. MACLEOD D.S.O. to be adjutant whilst commanding a Bn. Lieut 141 w.e.f. 24.6.17 Temp. CAPT. A. IRVING to be A/C Major whilst employed as 2nd in command a/2.1.5.17. Lieut 141. 27.6.17 The undermentioned Temp F^t Lts O/Bn Captain whilst commanding Companies a/21.5.17. Lieut 141. 27.6.17 Lieut. T.C. BOYD Temp Lt. J. McCULLOCH Temp ½Lt W. BLACK M.C.	

A. Ivans
Major

WAR DIARY
or
INTELLIGENCE SUMMARY.
(Erase heading not required.)

Army Form C. 2118.

Page 2118

Place	Date	Hour	Summary of Events and Information	Remarks and references to Appendices
RUBROUCK TRAINING AREA	10/2/17		9⁰ Rgt: - The Batt⁰ moved by Rail & Road & march to the RUBROUCK TRAINING AREA. Starting point: Y.M.C.A. hut in EBRIS CAMP at 12.25 p.m. Route: March to POPERINGHE - Train to ARNEKE - March to LA CLOSHE & environs. Transport moved separately.	
do.	11/2/17		9⁰ Regt: - Training under Company arrangements - Inspection of kit etc.	
do.	12/2/17		9⁰ Regt: - The Batt⁰ marched to LEDERZEELE Training area & practised Signalling. 6 O.R. from Yanks -	
do.	13/2/17		9⁰ Regt: - Batt⁰: Training 2nd Lt. A. FRASER rejoined on 4.7.17 on completion of duty as O.C. 15th Div. Cy. Strength - 2nd Lt. T.A. BEGGS rejoined from hospital (wounded) on 7.7.17 Rejoined from hospital (wounded) 1 O.R. Struck off: 1 O.R.	
do.	14/2/17		9⁰ Regt: - "A" & "C" Coy took part in a Brigade scheme on RUBROUCK TRAINING GROUND. "B" & "D" Coy: Physical Drill, Bayonet fighting under Symnastic Instr. II Strength - Rejoined from hospital 1 O.R. Joined by Draft 8 O.R.	

A. Garrets
Major

Army Form C. 2118.

WAR DIARY
or
INTELLIGENCE SUMMARY.
(Erase heading not required.)

Place	Date	Hour	Summary of Events and Information	Remarks and references to Appendices
RUSBROUCK TRAINING AREA.	15/7/17		Page 219. 9th Batt. Church Parade. Strength - Struck off 1 O.R.	
do.	16/7/17		9th Batt. The Batt. furnished a Brigade scheme on LEDERZEELE training area.	
WINNEZEELE BILLETING AREA.	17/7/17		9th Batt. The Batt. moved by Route March to WINNEZEELE AREA under orders of Bn. 46th Inf. Brigade. Starting point - Road Junction 3/8 Km. of a mile front of II N in ERINGHEM. Time. 7.30 a.m. Order of March. "D" "C" "B" "A" Transport. Route - ESQUELBECQ - WORMHOUDT - billets about ½ mile South of do. in LOOSSHOCK. Casualty - Accidentally wounded 1 O.R. Remained in Action since Wed. of Arrival 1 O.R. Strength. Joined by Draft 46 O.Rs. Struck off. 2 O.Rs.	

A. Jones
Major.

Army Form C. 2118.

WAR DIARY
or
INTELLIGENCE SUMMARY.
(Erase heading not required.)

Page 220.

Place	Date	Hour	Summary of Events and Information	Remarks and references to Appendices
TORONTO CAMP BRANDHOEK	18/7/17	In Reserve.	The Battⁿ. moved to TORONTO CAMP by Route March. Order of March "C" "B" "A" "D" Transport. Time of starting 12.30 a.m. Route - WINNEZEELE - DROGLANDT - WATOU - PODGRINGHE. Halt for breakfast 5.30 a.m. to 7.30 a.m.	
do.	19/7/17	In Reserve.	Cleaning Camp etc. Strength. Strength H 2 O.R.	
do.	20/7/17	In Reserve.	Inspection of Rifles & Gas appliances by Companies.	
CAMP AT H.16.a.5.8.	21/7/17	In Support.	The Battⁿ. moved into Support Camp at H.16.c.5.8. taking over area occupied by 6th. SEAFORTH HIGHRS. Order of March Hd. Qrs. "A" "B" "C" "D". Time of starting 9.30 p.m. Platoons at 200x interval.	

A. Igoenes
Major.

WAR DIARY
or
INTELLIGENCE SUMMARY.

Army Form C. 2118.

Page 221

Place	Date	Hour	Summary of Events and Information	Remarks and references to Appendices
CAMP AT H.16.a.5.8.	22/7/17		In Support. The Battⁿ remained in Support & provided working parties. Casualties. Died of Wounds 1 O.R.	
FRONT LINE Railway Dugout at SOUTH LANE	23/7/17		Front Line. The Battⁿ relieved the 8th Battⁿ SEAFORTH HIGH^{RS}. in the Right Sub Sect^r. 1 Section. Relief was carried out as follows:- 'A' Coy. 7th Cam relieved 'C' Coy. 8th Seaforth in RIGHT FRONT, 'D' " " " 'D' " " " LEFT FRONT, 'B' " " " 'A' " " " SUPPORT (HALF MOON), 'C' " " " 'B' " " " RESERVE (ECOLE). Hd. Qrs. at Dugout under RAILWAY at SOUTH LANE. The following work was taken over:- Clearing Close Support trench, now being camouflaged. Removal of wire from Front Line. Permanent party for pumping water out of Dugout. Strength of Battⁿ. 15 Officers 342 O.R. A Coy. R. Q. A. L. S.S. C.S.C. D M M.G.Sec.	

A. Ignever
Major

WAR DIARY
or
INTELLIGENCE SUMMARY.

Army Form C. 2118.

Place	Date	Hour	Summary of Events and Information	Remarks and references to Appendices
FRONT LINE Railway Wagons at SOUTH LANE	24/7/17	1 A.M.	Front-Line:- The Batt'n retained its position in the line as described in previous day. A Raid on the Enemy's Front-Line System was carried out by 12 O.R. of "A" Coy, under command of 2/Lt. J. MILLER. The raiders proceeded from T.11.b.6.8 following a course parallel to RAILWAY. A prisoner & machine gun were captured, the being found on crew of L.M.G. who bolted. Two men down to face but whistler killed or wounded was not ascertained. Enemy trenches found to be very much battered & wire though battered, difficult to get over. At Zieg, 81-82 holes were excellent. The party returned with one casualty, one man being slightly wounded. Casualties- Wounded in action (2 gassed) 8 OR. Prisoners 1 OR.	
do.	25/7/17		Work in trenches was continued - Officers' Patrol examined enemy wire & reported it badly damaged. Front-Line:- Operation Orders were issued for relief by 8/10 GORDON HIGHRS, but these were subsequently cancelled. Patrol - No man's land was patrolled & Enemy reported any growth - Cancelled. Wounded in action (1 gassed) 11 OR. Killed in action 10 OR. Strength:- Taken on 16/7 O.R. 100 O.R. (by drafts & returned from hospital.) Struck off 10 O.R. Prisoners of War. Prisoners reported Missing 1 OR.	

A. Irvine
Major

Army Form C. 2118.

WAR DIARY
or
INTELLIGENCE SUMMARY.
(Erase heading not required.)

Place	Date	Hour	Summary of Events and Information	Remarks and references to Appendices
FRONT LINE Railway Dugouts & SOUTH LANE	26/7/17		Page 223.	
			Front line. Batt'n retained positions in line as on previous day. Spade or breakers etc. continued. Patrols reported the general conditions. Casualties. Wounded in action 2 O.R.	
do.	27/7/17		Front line. Dispositions as above. Work continued. Casualties. Wounded in action 3 O.R.	
do.	28/7/17		Front line. Dispositions as above. A raid was carried out on enemy's front line system by "D" Coy. + 3 Platoons of "A" Coy. under command of A/Capt. J.L.C. JENKINS.	
		7 P.M.	Raiding party assembled in front line trench at I.5.d.5.5 & I.5.d.2.7.9 at Zero – 15 mins. (6.45 p.m.) – Artillery, Trench Mortars + M.G. opened an intense barrage on enemy lines at Zero (7 p.m.) Raiders left our trenches at same time & followed barrage as closely as possible. Enemy front line system found to be almost obliterated & a number of the enemy who survived the bombardment were killed or taken prisoner. Raiders penetrated as far as support + reserve lines where more prisoners were taken & casualties inflicted. A.M./g. were also taken. Simultaneously with the raid a party of 14 O.R. under 2/Lt. T.A.B. ELLIOT	

A. Greens
Major

WAR DIARY
or
INTELLIGENCE SUMMARY.

Army Form C. 2118.

(Erase heading not required.)

Place	Date	Hour	Summary of Events and Information	Remarks and references to Appendices
FRONT LINE Railway Dugout at SOUTH LANE	28/5/17	7 p.m. (circa)	Page 224 – Personnel from the right of our line to look for anyhow & in Culvert in Railway Embankment. This party handed Culvert & Dugout & took 6 few prisoners. – Bath Party returned at about 7.30 p.m. having inflicted many casualties on Enemy & taken prisoners 1 Officer & 39 O.Rs. with 1 M/G. Our casualties were slight. – Killed 1 O.R. Wounded 2 O.Rs. 2nd Lt. A. FRASER & 6 O.R.	
CAMP AT H.16.d.6.6	29/5/17	9 a.m.	Batt" were relieved by 8/10 R. GORDON HIGHRS & returned to Camp at H.16.d.6.6 Casualties: Killed in Action 2 O.Rs. Wounded in Action 2nd Lt. A.FRASER, T.M.S. ELLIOT & 17 O.Rs. Missing 2 O.Rs. Wounded & prisoners – Batt" remained in Camp & rested. Casualties: Died of Wounds a/Capt T.C. BOYD (21.7.17) Strength Officers 9 O.Rs. Yeomen on Strength 9½ O.Rs. Appointments. Temp 2nd Lt. J.D.W. McCRACKEN to be acting Captain while commanding a Coy. 2.6.17 Temp 2/Lt. N.S. SIM relinquishes acting rank of Captain on ceasing to command a Coy. 18.5.17. Congratulatory message on the Raid received sent by the R.T.T. on 28/5 from 26? were received from G.O.C. 15th Division Brig. Gen. comdg. 44th Infy. Brigade A. Spens Major	

WAR DIARY
or
INTELLIGENCE SUMMARY.
(Erase heading not required.)

Page 225

Place	Date	Hour	Summary of Events and Information	Remarks and references to Appendices

CAMP AT H.16.d.8.8.	30. Z. 17	8 p.m.	For Reasons. The Batt. marched to position of assembly for the attack. Coy. Strength as follows:-
			
			         Officers O.R.
			 A 4 136
			 B 4 133
			 C 4 148
			 D 4 133
			 H.Q. 4 36
			      20 586
			
			 Batt. is in reserve to the 44th Inf. Brigade. Positions of assembly as follows. A Coy. 2 Platoons ARA Dump.
			 3.0 from ARB Dump (THATCH BARN)
			 3.0 from HAUSMON TRENCH.
			 B Coy. ST JAMES TRENCH.
			 C Coy. in HALFMOON (LEFT Brigade boundary - RIGHT WEST LANE).
			 D Coy. HEDGE TRENCH South of WEST LANE.
			 Bttn H.Q. I.10.d.15.55. (SOUTH LANE)
			
			 Route C.J. ...... via "F" track.
				A. Grams Major

WAR DIARY or INTELLIGENCE SUMMARY

Army Form C. 2118.

(Erase heading not required.)

Instructions regarding War Diaries and Intelligence Summaries are contained in F.S. Regs., Part II. and the Staff Manual respectively. Title pages will be prepared in manuscript.

Place	Date	Hour	Summary of Events and Information	Remarks and references to Appendices
T.10.d.5.15 SOUTH LANE	31/2/17	Zero 3.50a.m.	Brigade Reserve. 'A' Coy. found carrying parties. Remainder in assembly position until about 10 a.m. Shortly after Zero hour THATCH BARN dump (ARA) was blown up, carrying arrangements had from Stahl greatly disarranged. it was unsettled. Platoon detailed for ARA dump carrying forward (~ ARA dump) Casualties heavy among carrying parties. Full loads could not be carried owing to muddy nature of ground & heavy shell fire. Workedown from this to light bag. That 9 men carry then easily but below full. Two became casualties. Thus out of the Four Officers & 9 Sergt-Majors with carrying parties became casualties. The Battalion A Coy. moved forward into GERMAN front system 4 came under fairly heavy shell fire.	
		10 a.m.	Hd. Qrs. moved forward L (GERMAN RESERVE LINE)	
		1 p.m. 2 p.m.	Our Platoon went forward under R.E. Officer + constructed Strong Points on BLACK LINE. Shelling found & this heavy & the work had to be abandoned.	
			Our Coy went forward (BLUE LINE where they constructed from Strong Points & returned Time. Casualties: 1 Lieut. Esperance b. wounded & released alive of operations.	

Norman Mackay
Lt. Col. A. Irving
Major
Comm. 1/4th (Cameron High[landers])

A 5834. Wt. W 4973/M 687. 750,000. 8/16. D.D. & L. Ltd. Forms/C.2118/13.

War Diary.

No official details of operations on 31.7.17 are as yet available. The Batt: has been otick in action. War Diary for that date will be forwarded as early as possible —

A. Jerome
Major -
7th Connaught Rngh.
Aug. 2nd 1917.

Index..........................

Q24 44/15

SUBJECT.

7th Cameron Highlanders.

No.	Contents.	Date.
	August 1917	

SECRET
AND
CONFIDENTIAL

44/15

ORIGINAL
Vol 26

WAR DIARY

OF

7TH (SERVICE) BATTALION CAMERON HIGHRS

FOR

MONTH OF AUGUST 1917.

PAGES 227 to 237 INCLUSIVE

WAR DIARY or INTELLIGENCE SUMMARY

Army Form C. 2118.

Page 227

Place	Date	Hour	Summary of Events and Information	Remarks and references to Appendices
GERMAN RESERVE LINE	8/8/17	5 a.m.	In Support. The Bn.[Battalion] moved forward as Bn.[Battalion] in Support - The 8th Seaforth Highrs.[Highlanders] having relieved the 9th Blackwatch & the 9th Rear Water going back into RESERVE. Disposition of Bn.[Battalion] was as follows :— 2 Coys.[Companies] in front consolidating behind NORTH STATION BUILDINGS. 1 Coy. in STRONG POINTS on BLUE LINE. Enemy counter-attacked RIGHT FRONT of the Brigade. M. Coy. Commanded by The Jungle (Major J.A. Symon) seeing Enemy coming over ridge, advanced out his Coy. in front of the Grand Trunk Rd. where it advanced 4 more Enemy. He left Coy. also co-operated with the 9th Gordons - Grand difficulties. They drove the Enemy back & reoccupied the Original Front Line. The enemy A.C. down a friendly heavy barrage on a hill & the trench. They were in. They were also bombarded from by 4/5 for some time in front by many of the enemy killed - many guns of the enemy?	
		3 p.m.	Our RIGHT FLANK being again in the air. The 6th M. Indians were impossible consolidated forming a FLANK DEFENCE down the YPRES-ROULERS railway. Thus 2 Coys. remained in FRONT LINE at night when were relieved by The 8/10th Gordon Highrs.[Highlanders] The Coy. Strong Points & Platoon in FRONT LINE & 3 Platoons in SUPPORT. Remainder of Consolidation Coy. (reduced to 25% OR) was also placed in SUPPORT.	

W. Young
Brigadier

WAR DIARY
or
INTELLIGENCE SUMMARY.
(Erase heading not required.)

Army Form C. 2118.

Place	Date	Hour	Summary of Events and Information	Remarks and references to Appendices
Front line	2/8/17		Page 228. During the next two days the Battalion held the front line, there was considerable shelling anyway and machine gun fire - but not heavy, also there was some casualties from our artillery fire - The Battalion was relieved by two Companies of the MUNSTER REGIMENT. The Battalion then went back to Camps. It has casualties were sustained during relief.	
Camp H. 16.	3/4/17	11.10 P.M.	With reference to questions asked by ARMY HEADQUARTERS:- 1. BARRAGE. As this Battalion was in Reserve we did not suffer from it in its entirety overspent, very little enemy fire was experienced. 2. ASSEMBLY. The assembly was carried out without difficulty, very little enemy fire and gas being experienced. 3 and 4. Does not apply to this Battalion. 5. Each rifle grenadier carried 12 rifle grenades and each Bomber 12 Mills Bombs. No occasion known to use the Mills Bombs. The Rifle grenades might have been useful in the Counter-attack in clearing snipers but unfortunately in the hurry they were left behind. It might be well in future to carry fewer grenades may be - and to concentrate on their power. The wristlets pattern is considered the best method of carrying. 7 and 8. Does not apply to this Battalion. During the Counter attack the firing from the hip was employed. It was believed that it had a good moral effect on the enemy although perhaps not killing many - further practice is required. Men behind the front line be warned not to fire over or between those in front line. Some Casualties were caused by this. 10. S.O.S. was not employed. 11 and 12. Does not apply to this Battalion. Morrow Munsford Lt.Colonel P.M.S.C.	

Page 229.

13. No.
14. No extra water. Rations were drawn from dumps and proved sufficient.
15. The supply of H₂O was quite sufficient. Carriers knew the points certain and had to make more time for companies to identify them?
16. No difficulty was found in keeping direction. Compasses were used for this purpose.
17. When the carrying parties - attack front became apparent to us the men were much scattered out in small bunches. He put up very little resistance cohesion we advanced and was finished until the consolidation. The only shelling was hurried on the ROAD between NORTH STATION BUILDINGS back to about WILD WOOD. There was considerable M/G fire in front & barrage.
18. There was some machine gun fire from the enemy's rear, on to High Ground to the right of the railway.
19. Sniping from the hips and shoulders during the enemy's attack —
20. This does not apply to this Battalion. Although the carrying parties found the tanks going up drew some shell fire. —

[signature]
Lt Colonel

WAR DIARY
or
INTELLIGENCE SUMMARY.

Army Form C. 2118.

Page 230.

Place	Date	Hour	Summary of Events and Information	Remarks and references to Appendices
CAMP H.16.	4/8/17		The following Casualties were sustained by the Battalion during operations 31/7/17 - 3/8/17.	
			Officers Wounded	
			2"Lt. H.S. DEANS. 31/7/17.	
			" T.A. BEGBIE. 1/8/17.	
			" J. MILLER. 1/8/17.	
			" J.W. MACKAY. 1/8/17.	
			" J. MORAN. 1/8/17.	
			"Capt" J.A. SYMON. 1/8/17.	
			2"Lt. J. LAMONT. 3/8/17.	
			Other Ranks.	
			Officially reported killed. 12.	
			Officially reported wounded 205.	
			Missing believed killed. 23.	
			Missing believed wounded. 17.	
			Missing unknown. 23.	
			Died of wounds. 5	
			Total 285	
			Batt" moved to WINNEZEELE N°2 Area by bus, transport by road.— Embussing took place on Road N°H.9a.7.5.— H.8.d.9.6 at 1 P.M. The Battalion marched to the embussing point from Camp H.16.— Details of Batt" in TORONTO CAMP marched via Cross Roads at H.8.a.50.25 and joined the Batt" at Cross Roads H.8.d.7.4.— X Roads transport marched via X Roads H.16.d.11. Road junction H.14.b.5.3.— X Roads H.7.C.45.— POPERINGHE — ABEELE. — STEEVOORDE — under orders of Brigade transport officer. — Head of Column passed X Roads H.7.C.4.5. at 1.30 P.M. The Billeting area allotted to the Batt" at WINNEZEELE — MAP REF: J.10.d.1.5. — in Yards.	
WINNEZEELE In Camp.	5/8/17		The Army Commander expressed his appreciation of the meritorious act of N°294495 Pte. P. G. DOUGAL. A Cpl. in that he voluntarily supplied a quantity of his blood for transfusion, with the object of saving the life of another soldier. —	
			Draft. 36 O.R. joined the Batt".	
			3 O.R. admitted to hospital.	
			2 O.R. under age proceeded to report to O.C. reinforcements ETAPLES	
In Camp.	6/8/17		Battalion inspected by Commanding Officer. Companies exercised in close order drill under Company arrangements — Draft of 23 O.R. arrived and taken on strength; 2 O.R. admitted to hospital. —	

WAR DIARY
or
INTELLIGENCE SUMMARY.
(Erase heading not required.)

Army Form C. 2118.

Page 231.—

Place	Date	Hour	Summary of Events and Information	Remarks and references to Appendices
In Camp.	7/8/17		Training in Physical drill, bayonet fighting, Platoon & Coy. drill.	
In Camp.	8/8/17		The Battn. was inspected by the G.O.C. 15th Division at 9.30 a.m. in three bodies each in close column of Coys. as follows:— 1st Officers and other ranks who took part in the recent operations. 2nd Officers and other ranks who were on details. 3rd The drafts of 36 and 28 which arrived on the 5th and 6th inst. respectively.— The General voiced his high appreciation of the excellent work performed by the Battalion on the recent operations under such adverse circumstances.— The Commanding Officer expressed his appreciation of the good work and splendid bearing of No. 46965 Pte G. ALLAN 'A' Coy. when under a very heavy barrage while he was acting as guide to a relieving Company in the trenches on the 28th July 17.	
In Camp.	9/8/17		Training. 1 O.R. proceeded to report to O.C. 19th I.B.D. being unfit for further duty in the front line. 3 O.R. proceeded to report to O.C. Lovat Scouts. G.H.Q. Troops and will attack to the Battn.	
In Camp.	10/8/17		Training. 1 O.R. proceeded to attend a course for instructors at S.A.S. CAMIERS. 2nd Lt. T.A.S. ELLIOT died of wounds in No. 65 & at No. 46 C.C.S. and 2.O.R. died of wounds received in action.—	
In Camp.	11/8/17		Battn. route march. DRAFTS. The following officers and other ranks arrived and taken on the strength on 10th August— CAPTAIN P. McE. CRAM. Lt. T. ORR. Lt. W. YOUNG. Evacuations 2.O.R. 18.O.R. 10.— other ranks.	
In Camp.	12/8/17		Church parade. 2nd Lt. J.D.W. McCRACKEN admitted to Hospital sick. 1.O.R. taken on strength Draft 97 O.R. arrived and taken on strength.— 2nd Lt J.D.W. McCracken (wounded) rejoined on dates from 5th to 10th & inclusive 17	Norman Murray Lt. Colonel R.N.F.C.

WAR DIARY
or
INTELLIGENCE SUMMARY.
(Erase heading not required.)

Army Form C. 2118.

Page - 232.

Place	Date	Hour	Summary of Events and Information	Remarks and references to Appendices
In Camp	13/8/17		Range practices carried out and Coy. training. 80 O.R. previously reported missing believed wounded in the recent operations; 2 O.R. previously reported missing - no reported wounded in action and 2-O.R. previously reported missing - unknown now officially reported as wounded in action. - Major IRVING admitted to hospital suffering from accidental gun shot wound to left leg, received at Rifle practice on Range 2.	
In Camp	14/8/17		Forenoon devoted to Coy. training. Regimental Sports were held in the afternoon and these were highly successful. "A" Coy. was successful in winning the Tug of war and the big aside football match; the Sergeants team beat the Officers team in the T.o.g. however the Officers were successful in the tug against all comers (Officers) from the Brigade. The Company Championship points were as follows:- "B" Coy - 50. "A" Coy - 26. "C" Coy - 24. "D" Coy - 20. The best all round athlete was Cy. S.M. Keith "B" Coy. - At the close of the Sports prizes were presented to the successful Competitors by BRIGADIER GENERAL F.J. MARSHALL D.S.O. and on the call of Colonel MACLEOD three hearty cheers were given for the Brigadier. The Divisional Band played at intervals during the afternoon and the Massed Pipes and Drums of the Brigade played at the close of the sports. Great credit was due to 2/Lt GIBB and his Committee for arranging and carrying thro' the Programme of Sports. - 1-O.R. struck off the strength and released for mining. N.B. that A. IRVING accidentally wounded 13/8/17. CAPTN P. McF. CRAM. promoted 2/2 in Command on that date vice	

Norman Munford
P. McF. Cram

WAR DIARY
or
INTELLIGENCE SUMMARY.
(Erase heading not required)

Army Form C. 2118.

Page 233.

Place	Date	Hour	Summary of Events and Information	Remarks and references to Appendices
IN CAMP.	15/8/17		Training Cancelled owing to wet weather and condition of ground. 2-O.R. died of wounds received in action. 2-O.R. previously reported missing believe killed now officially reported killed in action. 2-O.R. previously reported missing — unknown now officially reported wounded and taken as prisoner. 1-O.R. rejoined from Hospital after being wounded on the strength. 1-O.R. Evacuated.	
IN CAMP.	16/8/17		Battalion proceeded to Training area "B" and practiced the attack. 1-O.R. proceeded to report to O.C. 19/5 1.B.D. being unfit for further duty in the trenches (O.C. 19/5 1.B.D. N.R. Watou).	
IN CAMP.	17/8/17		The Battn. moved to BRANDHOEK area N°3 by route march at 12-15 P.M. via WATOU. In BRANDHOEK area N°3 ST. JANISTER, BIEZEN and SWITCH ROAD NORTH OF POPERINGHE. WEST of POPERINGHE-PROVEN Road at an interval of 500 yards was manoeuvred between units and east of that road a distance of 200 yards between Companies and between the rear Coy and Transport. 1-O.R. Struck off the Strength; 1 B.O.R. died of wounds; 7 O.R. evacuated.	
BRANDHOEK CAMP.	18/8/17		1-O.R. Struck off the 12th infantry and the 17th inst. respectively were in-reinforced by the commanding Officer. 1-O.R. struck off strength as being unfit for further duty in the trenches. In the afternoon the officers visited TEN ELMS CAMP and studied the Model of the ground over which the 15th Division is to attack in a few days and in the afternoon the officers N.C.O.'s visited the Training Scheme.	
BRANDHOEK CAMP.	19/8/17		The Battalion proceeded to Training Area 17,18, 23 and 24. The 44th and 45th Infantry Brigades practiced the attack simultaneously. The Battn. was on the left of the 44th Brigade and the 8/Seaforths on 2nd right the Goodoms in support and its Blackwatch in reserve. The Battn. assembled as follows:— A Coy. right front each with a frontage of two platoons. B Coy. left front C Coy. in support D Coy. in reserve At 5.30 p.m. the Battn. moved to Bivouac Camp E.17.A.1.9.; order of march H.Q., A, B, C + D Coys. between platoons. Route.— POPERINGHE-YPRES ROAD to GOLDFISH CHATEAU. P.N.S.C.	

A 3584 Wt. W.4973/M687 750,000 9/16 F.D.F.L. Ltd. Forms/C.2118/13

Army Form C. 2118.

WAR DIARY
or
INTELLIGENCE SUMMARY.
(Erase heading not required.)

Page 234.

Place	Date	Hour	Summary of Events and Information	Remarks and references to Appendices
BIVOUAC CAMP. B.17.A.1-9.	20/8/17		The 15th Division was ordered to continue the offensive on Z day. The attack was carried out by the 45th Brigade on the right, the 44th Brigade on the left and the 46th Brigade in reserve. The 8th Div. attacked at the same time on the left of the 15th Div.; the 8th Brigade kept on the left of the 44th Brigade. Of the 44th Brigade, the disposition of the 44 Infantry Brigade was as follows:— 6/Seaforth Highlanders on the right; 7/Cameron Highrs on the left; 8/10 Gordon Highrs in support. The Battn. moved at 6.30 P.M. to relieve the 8th Bath: Worcester Regt at POMMERN REDOUBT on the night of the 20/21 August. At completion of relief the Battn. was disposed as follows:— 2 Platoons of 'A' Coy and 2 Platoons of 'B' Coy. in POMMERN REDOUBT. 2 Platoons of 'A' Coy and 2 Platoons of 'B' Coy. and 'C' & 'D' Coys. in neighbourhood at C.30.a and C.29.b. Battn. H.Q. in POMMERN REDOUBT. Route for Bath. going to POMMERN CASTLE — via REIGERSBERG CHATEAU – NOORTEAK – The remainder of Bath via 'C' Track H.13.C.5.9 — L.7.3 — A.P.b. via YPRES to MENIN GATE thence by POTIJZE ROAD.— The party proceeding front of YPRES moved (A'Coy in front) at 7 P.M.— The remainder of Bath. marched in the following order. 2 Platoons 'A' Coy.— 2 Platoons 'B' Coy.— 'C' Coy.— 'D' Coy.— Movements and by platoons at 100 yards interval.— Half Platoons were provided for Lewis Guns, there moved in front of companies and proceeded as on the WHITE CHATEAU, POTIJZE ROAD.— All details not proceeding to the trenches returned by Platoons at 200 yards intervals to HAPPID CAMP.—	Strength of Bath going into action. Officers: Other Ranks. 15. 450.
POMMERN CASTLE.	21/22/8/17	At ZERO HOUR 4.45 A.M.	on the 22nd the Battn. was disposed as follows:— A Coy. right front. 'B' Coy. left front. 'C' Coy. right support. 'D' Coy. left support. The attack was launched and the Bn. advanced to a line about 200° west of HILL 35. Where owing to heavy machine Gun & Rifle fire from GALLIPOLI FARM + IBERIAN FARM the Bath. was held up.— Further progress could not be made and the Bath. on both flanks were also held up. The ground was held with the cooperation of the 8/10 Gordons. Meanwhile the 9/Gordons constructed a line about 200° west of...	

Norman Murfin Lt/Col
R.M.1.G.

WAR DIARY
or
INTELLIGENCE SUMMARY.

(Erase heading not required.)

Army Form C. 2118.

Page 235.

Place	Date	Hour	Summary of Events and Information	Remarks and references to Appendices
ERIE CAMP.	23/8/17		a trench and strong points immediately in rear of our position. The Battn. maintained these forward position throughout the day and were relieved in the night of the 22/23 August by the 9th Black Watch.	
	23/24/17		The Battn. after relief proceeded to RUPPRECHT FARM, Battn. H.Q. at VERLORENHOEK in support. The Battn. was relieved by the 8/10 GORDONS and proceeded to "ERIE CAMP" which was reached about 6 A.M.	
	25/8/17		Reorganisation of Companies. Under Authority delegated by Field Marshall Commanding-in-chief, the Coy. Commander recommends to the V.C.O.'s and men for gallantry and devotion to duty in action. Bar to Military Medal.	

No. 6765 Serjt. A. MACDONALD. D. Coy.
Military Medal. No. 200334 A/Sergt. M.P. KING 'A' Coy.
22930 Corpl. W. TAYLOR 'D' Coy.
200204 L/Corpl. J. NICOLSON 'D' Coy.
40965. Pte. G. WALLAN 'A' Coy.
44032 L/Corpl. T. SHUMAKER 'C' Coy. H.Q.
8900 Cpl. A. DONEGAN 'D' Coy.
23246. Pte. J. ROSE 'D' Coy.
16391. Pte. J. TULLOCH 'C' Coy.
10501. Sergt. T. MORGAN 'A' Coy.
26863 A/Corpt. W. ROSE. 'D' Coy.

The following are the official casualties sustained by the Battn. during the operations 20/8/17 to 24/8/17. Officers killed in action – nil. 10 wounded in action –

Capt. Revd. W.B.T. BLACK C.F.	22-8-17	A/Captn. J.L.C. JENKINS.	22-8-17
Captn. J. McCULLOCH	do	2/Lt. C.R.G. SCOTT.	do
Lieut. W. YOUNG.	do	J.I. MACDONALD.	do
2/Lt. J.A. SABISTON.	do	R. JARDINE.	do
		C. COURTNEY.	do

Killed in action – 3.
Other Ranks:
Wounded in action – 132.

Maurewd M Colonel
R/Mjr C.

WAR DIARY or INTELLIGENCE SUMMARY

Army Form C. 2118.

Place	Date	Hour	Summary of Events and Information	Remarks and references to Appendices
			Page No 236	
ERIE CAMP.	26/8/17		1 Other rank previously reported wounded now died of wounds. 27 Other ranks evacuated and struck off strength. 1 O.R. returned from hospital & taken on strength. 1 O.R. previously reported missing 28/7/17 now reported killed in action. Church Parade. A draft of 101 other ranks arrived to-day.	
Ditto.	27/8/17		Reorganizing of Coys. and training. 3 O.R. struck off strength. The following official casualties were sustained on dates mentioned as under:— during operations 20–24/7. — Killed in action. 3 O.Ranks " " " " wounded " 2 O.Ranks Previously reported missing from operations 31/7 to 3/8/17 are now officially reported killed 2 O.Ranks wounded 3 O.Ranks. Previously reported wounded since died of wounds 1 O.Rank.	
Ditto.	28/8/17		Training. 3 O.Ranks taken on strength. Lt. TORR. admitted to Hospital sick.— About two hundred shells were dropped [?] during the of Labions 20–24/7. The following are casualties sustained by the Bath. during the of Labions 20–24/7. killed in action 3 other ranks. ⎫ 1 O.R. struck by fragmt. of enemy Died of wounds 1 O.R. ⎬ reported to F/C 11th F.D.B. previously believed killed 13 O.R. ⎭ 1 O.R. taken on strength. " wounded 10 O.R. " missing unknown 35 O.R.	
Ditto.	29/8/17		Training 2 O.R. previously reported missing rejoined and taken on strength.	
Ditto.	30/8/17		The following are further casualties sustained by the Bath. during operations 20/7–24/7. 1 O.R. wounded 1 O.R. missing believed killed 1 O.R. " " wounded 1 O.R. missing unknown. Two O.R. previously reported missing underarm now reported died of wounds.	

Norman Mackrog Wall
Lt Col
D.W.F.C.

WAR DIARY
or
INTELLIGENCE SUMMARY

Army Form C. 2118.

Page 237.

Place	Date	Hour	Summary of Events and Information	Remarks and references to Appendices
"ERIE" Camp	30/7/17		The following are casualties during operations 31/7/17 to 4/8/17:— 1- Other ranks wounded 110. O.R. missing unknown.); 3- O.R. previously reported missing unknown has since reported. Taken on strength one O.R. Augmented old stock of strength. The Battn. moved to WATOU No 2 area and marched off at 2.P.M. in the following order:— H.Q., C. Coy., D. Coy., A. Coy., B. Coy. The route was via Cross Roads G.4.4.4.— Scottish Road — L.9.C. — L.9.C. —	
No 2 AREA WATOU	31/7/17		2nd Lt. J.W. MACKAY died of wounds on 20.8. 1. O.R. previously reported missing unknown now officially wounded. 5. O.R. evacuated. The following draft were inspected by the C.O. on arrival and were taken on the strength. 2nd Lt E. CAMERON. 145 Other Ranks. Reorganisation of Coy's and inspection of Battn. by Commanding Officer who addressed the Battn. and awarded the Military Medal to N° 4032 L/Corp. T. SHUMACKER. C Coy. H.Q.— General Sir H. de P. GOUGH. K.C.B. K.C.V.O. Commanding 5th Army now in command of the 15th Division on leaving his army asked that he parted with great regret. The reputation of the Division has been earned on many battlefields and has never stood higher than now. He wishes it all good fortune and many further successes in the future. "Will ye come back again". On the 30th Aug't the Battn. which arrived at WATOU were inspected by the General when he expressed to the Commanding Officer his high appreciation of the work of the Battn. in the recent operations.—	

Norman Muirhead D/Lt Col
Commanding 7th Battn Cameron Highrs.

P.W.P.C

Index..............

Mis F

Q 25

SUBJECT.

7th Cameron Highlanders.

No.	Contents.	Date.
	September 1917	

ORIGINAL)
COPY) Vol 27

7TH (SERVICE) BATTALION CAMERON HIGHLANDERS

WAR DIARY

FOR ABOVE UNIT

PAGES 238 TO 243 INCLUSIVE

MONTH OF SEPTEMBER 1917.

SECRET
AND
CONFIDENTIAL

Army Form C. 2118.

WAR DIARY
or
INTELLIGENCE SUMMARY.
(Erase heading not required.)

Instructions regarding War Diaries and Intelligence Summaries are contained in F.S. Regs., Part II. and the Staff Manual respectively. Title pages will be prepared in manuscript.

Page 238.

Place	Date	Hour	Summary of Events and Information	Remarks and references to Appendices
WATOU No 2 AREA.	1/9/17		The 114th Infantry Brigade entrained at CAESTRE and detrained at ARRAS. The Bath. moved at 7 A.M. by ride — Cross Roads K 36 a 0.4 — GODEWAERSVELDE — KEMELHOF — CAESTRE RAILWAY STATION. The Bath. entrained at 2.5 P.M. and arrived ARRAS at 9 P.M. and marched to Billets at MONTENESCOURT which was reached about 1 A.M. on the 2nd current.	
MONTENESCOURT.	2/9/17		BATTALION in rest and refitting area.	
Ditto.	3/9/17		Coy training. 5 Other ranks arrive ask dept on 3rd Aug 1917. 10 other ranks proceed.	
Ditto.	4/9/17		Coy training. wounded during operations 31/7/17 — 3/8/17 now officially reported returned to hospital sick. The following Officers have been awarded decorations as stated below for acts of Gallantry and devotion to duty in action:— Distinguished Service Order a/Captain J.A. SYMON. Military Cross a/Captain J.L.C. JENKINS. 2/Lt. R. JARDINE. 2/Lt. J. MILLER. 2/Lt. R.B. PURDON. Captain A.C. BATESTAIN. R.A.M.C.	
D. Ho.	5/9/17		Coy training. 5 Other ranks previously reported missing believed killed now officially reported killed.	
Ditto.	6/9/17		Coy Training. 61 Other ranks evacuated and struck off strength by draft on 3/9/17 and were taken on the strength. Lt. T. ORR. M.C. admitted to Hospital 26.8.17. 10. 2 O'clock off strength.	
Ditto.	7/9/17		The 114th Inf. Bgde relieved the 46th Infantry Brigade in Divisional Reserve on the Batt. moved off at 3.45 P.M. Route 4.2.C.2.4 — St Pol — ARRAS ROAD — BLANGY PARK (G 24 6.3.G.) PONT — ST NICOLAS and relieved the 10/11 H.L.I. at BLANGY PARK (G 24 6.3.G.) During the march 200 yards was maintained between Coys and 400 yards between Battalions — 2 Other ranks previously reported wounded during operations 20-24/7/17 now died of wounds 22/4.5/17.	

Norman Mitchell Lt Colonel

Place	Date	Hour	Summary of Events and Information	Remarks and references to Appendices
BLANGY PARK	8/9/17		Page 239.	
			BATTALION training and improving Camp.	
Ditto	9/9/17		Church Parade. The following Officers relinquished the acting rank of Captain on ceasing to Command Companies:- Lt J.A. SYMON. D.S.O. 1.8.17. 2nd Lt D.W. McCRACKEN 10.8.17 Lt TIORR. M.C. was evacuated to ENGLAND on 30/7/17. 2nd Lt Fisher on ceasing from Hospital.	
Dk Ho.	10/9/17		Coy. training. Lewis gun teams carried on Range Practices on Range at H.17.a.3.6.	
Dk Ho.	11/9/17		Thousand and Range Practices on 30 yard Range at Rifle Camp. 2nd Lt R.S.D. Pollock returned from duty as a Town Major of YPRES on 1.9.17. 2 other ranks admitted to strength on attachment to Hospital.	
Dk Ho.	12/9/17		Coy. training and Range Practices at the MOST RANGE, ARRAS. No. 8/1035 Pte J. SPENCE has been awarded the MILITARY MEDAL for gallantry in the field.	
Dk Ho.	13/9/17		Coy. training and Rifle Practice on 30 yard range at Rifle Camp.	
Dk Ho.	14/9/17		The 44th Infantry Brigade relieves the 45th Infantry Brigade on the G/2007 of the 15th Divisional front on the night of 14/15 Sept 1917. The Battn relieve the 11th A.&S. Highlrs on the right sector of the Divisional front. The Battn were disposed as follows:- "C" Coy. Right front - Two platoons in front line and two platoons in Support. "D" Coy. Left front - Two platoons in the front line, one platoon in Reserve and one platoon in Belgona Trench (NORTH). "B" Coy. Right reserve } in LANCER AVENUE "A" Coy. Left reserve } 1 Lewis gun post & 1 N.C.O. and 12 men were found from the left Coy in Roosebeke. Headquarters were in JOHNSTONE AVENUE about H.30.d.1.a. The Battn. Norman Mumford W.Lt Col	

WAR DIARY or INTELLIGENCE SUMMARY

Army Form C. 2118.

Page 240.

Place	Date	Hour	Summary of Events and Information	Remarks and references to Appendices
BLANGY PARK	14/9/17		The Battn. moved off from BLANGY PARK at 7 P.M. and entrained at Station B.304 at H.19.c.5.9. and detrained at H.23.b.5.2. Two Coys went by Light Railway at 15 minutes interval.	
IN TRENCHES.	15-22/9		On the night of 15-18/19 Septr. the two Coys in the front line changed over with the two Coys in reserve on LUNDA LANE. On this evening of the 19th the enemy bombarded the front line vigorously, communication trenches held by the Battn. for about 1½ hours from 6.20 P.M. and again for a short period at 8.10 P.M. but the retaliation by our Artillery prevented any action by the enemy infantry. Considerable work was carried out while in the line, namely: — construction of new cubby holes, repairing Lewis gun two new cook houses, construction of new cubby holes, repairing Lewis gun emplacements, and nucleus communication trenches, furnishing work parties to the trembling Cays. in the construction of munitions dumps in NEUFORT Reserve trenches. —	

Casualties sustained during the tour:—
Other Ranks   Killed — 4 ; wounded — 6.

Killed — 1 by shell while in town, were in the line.

The following Officers arrived and date mentioned:—

2 Lt. J. Finlay.   16.9.17.
2 Lt. M.N. MacLeod.   do.
2 Lt. L. MacLeod   do.
2 Lt. R.M. Murray   do.
2 Lt. W.R. Bayne   do.
2 Lt. P.F. Prentice.   do.
2 Lt. A.R. MacDonald   do. 9/17
2 Lt. R.A.M. McCrostie   17/9/17

Captain A. Blaikie.   17.9.17.
2 Lt. H.L. Parker.   20-9-17
2 Lt. J. McMurray.   20-9-17
2 Lt. G.S. Gemmel.   20-9-17.
2 Lt. P. Austin.   do.
2 Lt. W.F. Grieve.   do.
2 Lt. A.N. Blair.   do
2 Lt. N. MacLeod.   do
2 Lt. R.C. Mitchell.   do

2nd Lt. J.D.W. McCracken returned from Hospital on the 18-9-17.
2 Other Ranks struck off strength on 16-9-17 on Transfer to 216 Employment Coy.
1 O.R. previously reported missing, now officially reported killed on 20-24/7/8.
82 Other Ranks arrived by draft on the 14th September and were taken on the strength.—

Norman Murray Lt Colonel

Army Form C. 2118.

WAR DIARY
or
INTELLIGENCE SUMMARY.
(Erase heading not required.)

Place	Date	Hour	Summary of Events and Information	Remarks and references to Appendices
MIDDLESEX CAMP.	23/9/17	Page 24/1.	The Battalion was relieved on the night of 22/23 Sept: by the 8th Bn. Seaforth High[lander]s and proceeded to MIDDLESEX CAMP at G.17.d.80.95. near ARRAS. The Bn. in Brigade Reserve. The Officers with Batt'n are noted as under at this date.— HEAD-QUARTERS. LIEUTENANT COLONEL N. MACLEOD. D.S.O.— IN COMMAND. CAPTAIN P. McF. CRAM. — 2ND IN COMMAND. ⟶ " " G. J. S. LUMSDEN. — ADJUTANT. 2ND LT A.B.S. LEGATE. — ASST ADJUTANT. Do N.S. SIM M.C — INTELLIGENCE. "A" Coy.— CAPTN A. BLAIKIE. — COY. COMMANDER. 2ND LT J.S. McNAB. 2ND LT J.T. BUCKLESS. 2ND " A.R. MACDONALD. 2ND LT N. MACLEOD. 2ND LT S.S. GEMMELL. 2ND LT W.A. BAYNE.S. 2ND LT R.F. PRENTICE. "B" Coy. 2ND LT E.J.G. GIBB. — Coy. COMMANDER. 2ND LT J.G. TELFORD. 2ND LT A.M. ROSS. 2ND LT J.A. DONALD. 2ND LT J. McMURRAY. 2ND LT J.D.W. McCRACKEN. 2ND LT J.N. FINLAY. 2ND LT M.N. McINDEOR. "C" Coy. CAPTN J.C. FRASER — COY. COMMANDER. 2ND LT J.W. GRAHAM. M.C. 2ND LT E. CAMERON. 2ND LT W. MUIRHEAD. 2ND LT E.O. HOSKEN. 2ND LT A.N. BLAIR. 2ND LT W.F. BLAIR. 2ND LT L. MACLEOD. "D" Coy. 2ND LT D.T. MILNE. — COY. COMMANDER. 2ND LT R.B. PURDON. M.C. 2ND LT R.S.D. POLLOCK. 2ND LT T. G'ODEN. 2ND LT R.C. MITCHELL. 2ND L.T H.P. PARKER. 2ND LT R.W. MURRAY. 2ND LT P. AUSTIN. TRANSPORT OFFICER. LT J.H. MAUCHLIN.	

Norman Macleod Lt Colonel

WAR DIARY
or
INTELLIGENCE SUMMARY.
(Erase heading not required.)

Army Form C. 2118.

Page No. 242.—

Place	Date	Hour	Summary of Events and Information	Remarks and references to Appendices
MIDDLESEX CAMP.	24/9/17. 25/9/17.		The day was devoted to cleaning up and inspections under Company arrangements.— 1.O.R. taken on strength as from 30/8/17.— Coy. training. The following is an extract from List No. 152 Appointments, Commissions &c d/8/9/17. Temporary Major T.L. CUNNINGHAM N. MACLEOD. D.S.O. to be Second-in-Command, vice Temporary Major T.L. CUNNINGHAM. D.S.O. 9/11/16.— Authority XVII Corps A/19/39 - 13/9/17 4th Infantry Brigade S.C. 6/56.— 1 other rank previously reported as a prisoner of war is now reported as having died on 26/6/17.— LANGENSALA.— 5. O.R. arrived by draft and taken on strength.— Lt. & Qr. Mr. W.D. LISTER is borne on the authorized establishment of the 5th Army Infantry School and is accordingly struck off the strength.— 8. O.R. struck off the strength.—	
A.140.	26/9/17.		Coy. training.— Under Authority 44th Brigade S.C. 6/101, 15 Bn. A/25/1600, XVII Corps. A. 19/40 Capt. P. McF. CRAM. 4th Bn. to be acting Major whilst employed as 2nd in COMMAND of 7th CAMERON HIGH'RS d/28/8/17. Capt. A. IRVING. SEAFORTH HRS relinquishes the acting rank of Major on ceasing to be employed as Actg. in Command of the 7th CAMERON HRS dated 13/8/17. Authority 44th Brigade S.C. 6/101/15-Bin. A/25/1600. XVII CORPS. A/19/40.—	
Ditto.	27/9/17.		Coy. Training. 1 other rank previously reported missing believe killed during quarter 20-24/8/17 now officially reported killed.— 1 other rank. previously, missing believed wounded, admitted to many Officially killed. 1 - O.R. previously reported missing (unknown) ditto now officially killed.— 3. O.R. evacuated and struck off strength. 42. O.R. arrived by draft on the 25/9 and are taken on strength.— Norman Macleod Lt Colonel	

Army Form C. 2118.

WAR DIARY
or
INTELLIGENCE SUMMARY.
(Erase heading not required.)

Instructions regarding War Diaries and Intelligence Summaries are contained in F.S. Regs., Part II. and the Staff Manual respectively. Title pages will be prepared in manuscript.

Page No. 243.

Places	Date	Hour	Summary of Events and Information	Remarks and references to Appendices
MIDDLESEX CAMP.	28/9/17		Company Training:- 6 Other Ranks previously reported missing believed killed during operations 20-24/9/17 now officially reported killed.	
Ditto	29/9/17		2nd Lt H.S. JEANS is struck off the strength. 1 Other Rank previously reported missing during operations 31-7/17 — 3.8.17 now officially killed.	
Ditto	30/9/17		Church Parade. The following N.C.O.'s and men have been awarded the Military Medal for acts of Gallantry in the Field:- R/6983 L/Sergt. C. Smith. 'C' Coy. S/14297 Corporal A. Simpson. 'B' Coy. S/43231 L/Corpoal J. Foray K. 'C' Coy. S/35/1820 Ditto J. Anderson. 'B' Coy. 1 Other rank struck off the strength.	

Norman Mugford
Lt Colonel
Comdg. 7. P.O. Cameron Highrs.

Index..................

Q26

SUBJECT.

7th Cameron Highlanders.

No.	Contents.	Date.
	October 1917	

Army Form C. 2118.

WAR DIARY
or
INTELLIGENCE SUMMARY.
(Erase heading not required.)

Secret :
Confidential.
War Diary.
— of —
7th (Service) Battalion Cameron Highlanders.

From 1st October 1917. To 31st October 1917.

Pages 244 to 248

Army Form C. 2118.

WAR DIARY
or
INTELLIGENCE SUMMARY.
(Erase heading not required.)

Place	Date	Hour	Summary of Events and Information	Remarks and references to Appendices
			Page No. 244.	
MIDDLESEX CAMP	1.10.17		The 44th Infantry Brigade was relieved by the 46th Infantry Brigade in the Left Sector of the Divisional front on the night of the 1st/2nd October 1917. The Battalion was relieved by the 10/13th Scottish Rifles and moved into BARROSA CAMP at 2 p.m.	
BARROSA CAMP	2.10.17		Rifle practice was carried out by "D" Coy. at the MOAT RANGE, ARRAS. Lewis Gun practice by Hd. Coy. who also carried out at Rgs. Regts. The Remainder of the Battalion at Coy. Training and Wiring.	
DO.	3.10.17		250 Other Ranks arrived by draft and were taken on the Strength on this date. Company Training according to programme.	
DO.	4.10.17		2nd Lt. M.B. RENNIE, LONDON REGIMENT arrived by draft on this date and also 2 other ranks and were taken on the Strength. Company Training according to programme. The following officers have been awarded decorations for gallantry in the field MILITARY CROSS : 2nd Lt. J.T. BOOKLESS 4" CAMERON HIGHLANDERS " 2nd Lt. J.I. MACDONALD 7" ARGYLL & SUTHERLAND HRS. On this date the following officers arrived by draft and were taken on the Strength. Lt. A.J. EASTWOOD LONDON REGIMENT "Lt. R. SMITH DITTO	
DO.	5.10.17		Company Training according to programme. 6 other ranks struck off Strength. 2nd Lieut. A.CHISHOLM and 1st Lieut G.S. Gunj joined the Battn. on this date and were taken on the Strength.	
DO.	8.10.17		Company Training and Tactical exercises. 10 other ranks taken on Strength and 6 other ranks struck off Strength.	

Norman Macleod Lt Col

Army Form C. 2118.

WAR DIARY
or
INTELLIGENCE SUMMARY.
(Erase heading not required.)

PAGE No. 245.

Place	Date	Hour	Summary of Events and Information	Remarks and references to Appendices
BARROSA CAMP	7.10.17		CHURCH PARADE.	
DO.	8.10.17		Platoons practised the attack in conjunction with Sections of 44" T.M.B. Lecture in by Officers, Corporals and up. Coys. on attack formations. 1 Other rank admitted as Killed in action on 17.8.17. 2 other ranks struck off strength.	
DO. and IN THE TRENCHES.	9.10.17		Company Training as per programme. The 44" Infantry Brigade relieved the 45" Infantry Brigade in the Right Sector MONCHY on the 9th October. The Battalion relieved the 13" Royal Scots in the Right Sector as follows. "D" Coy. 7" Cameron Hrs. relieved "C" Coy. Royal Scots Right Front. "C" Coy. do. do. "B" Coy Left Front. "B" Coy. do. do. "D" Coy Support. "A" Coy. do. do. "A" Coy Reserve. "B" Coy. 7" Cameron Hrs. provided the Garrison of "G" Post consisting of 1 Officer, 1 Platoon with Lewis Gun Section. Companies moved from BARROSA CAMP by Platoons at 5 minutes interval in the following order:- "D" Coy. The first Platoon of "D" Coy. moved off from Camp at 1.15 p.m. "C" " "B" " "H.Q." "A" "	
IN THE TRENCHES FROM	9.10.17 to 17.10.17		On the 14" October in conjunction with a Raid carried out by the Division on our Right the Batt. sent out two Patrols each consisting of an Officer and 4 other ranks. No.1 Patrol under 2/Lt. A. Chisholm left the right Coy. area at No. 6 Post. No. 1 Island with instructions to raid the enemy's front line through the gap at I.32.d.03.00. Left the Left Coy. area at I.32.C.20.45. No.2 Patrol under 2/Lt. E.A. Hoskin with the Gap at I.32.C.20.45 and entered the enemy's front line through the Gap at I.32.C.20.45.	

Norman MacLeod Lt Col

Army Form C. 2118.

WAR DIARY
or
INTELLIGENCE SUMMARY.
(Erase heading not required.)

Instructions regarding War Diaries and Intelligence Summaries are contained in F.S. Regs., Part II. and the Staff Manual respectively. Title pages will be prepared in manuscript.

Place	Date	Hour	Summary of Events and Information	Remarks and references to Appendices
IN THE TRENCHES	From 9.10.17		PAGE NO. 246	
			The object of the Patrols was to bring back any identification or material in the immediate vicinity of the points at which they struck the Enemy's Front Line. They were not to search the Enemy's Trenches if identification was not obtainable at the points of entry.	
			The two Patrols left our Front Line at 2.00. + 12 minutes and instructions to return not later than 2 + 27 minutes. No Enemy was encountered and each man was armed with Rifle with 10 rounds in magazine and also two Bombs.	
			The Battalion on the Left also sent out two similar Patrols.	
			At 2.45 minutes and again at 2.4.10 minutes the 44" T.M.B. fired 10 rounds rapid on each of the above points.	
			No. 3 Special Coy. R.E. discharged Thermite from 2 h. 2.4.10 minutes on the Trenches opposite on Front.	
			The Lewis Guns kept up a harassing fire on T.32. c.l.d. Squares.	
	17.10.17		No. 1 Patrol suffered casualties in crossing "No man's Land" when the Officer leading the Patrol was mortally wounded. Only one man of this Patrol returned to our Lines without gaining any information.	
			No. 2 Patrol was observed to enter the enemy Trench but none of this half returned to our Line.	
			The following casualties were sustained in this raiding Patrols.	
			KILLED 2nd Lt. A. CHISHOLM	
			MISSING 2" Lt. E.D. HOSKIN	
			All the members of the raiding Patrols were Volunteers.	
			MISSING 43/22 Y.S.L. W. OSWALD "C" Coy.
			22738 L/Cpl T. BRYCE C
			28153 L/Cpl A. DINNIDDIE C
			30441 Pte. J. EDWARDS C
			40010 4Cpl F. MACDONALD C
			13916 Pte. J. DEVER C
			40505 W. McPHERSON C
			During the Tour of duty in the Trenches the Batt. also sustained the following casualties in addition to the above i.e. Killed 1 other ranks. Wounded 6 other ranks.	
			Our 101st Battalion relief was carried out by the 1st Seaforth Bn. on this date the Battalion being relieved by No. 13 Coy. 3rd Seaforth Highlanders as follows. A. Coy. SEAFORTH HIGH."
			A. Coy.
			B "
			C "

[signature]

WAR DIARY
or
INTELLIGENCE SUMMARY.

Army Form C. 2118.

Place	Date	Hour	Summary of Events and Information	Remarks and references to Appendices
			PAGE 247.	
IN THE TRENCHES	17.10.17		On relief Companies proceeded independently to RIFLE CAMP by Platoons as to avoid undue Contusion Platoons	
RIFLE CAMP	18.10.17	15.00 p	The day was devoted to cleaning of arms, clothing and Equipment and Inspections.	
do			Rifle Practice was carried out on Rifle Camp musketry Range.	
			2nd Lt. N.S. SIM M.C. proceeded to the United Kingdom for Special Duty on 10.10.17 and was accordingly struck off the strength.	
			CAPT. A. BLAIKIE proceeded to join the 14" LONDON REGT. on the 10.10.17 and was also struck off the strength.	
			The Commanding Officer Inspected Schoolroom walls Resultant results of "A" Coy. at the Third Army Musketry Camp and congratulated them on the results obtained.	
			Rapid Firing Competition	
			1st Prize. 7" Cameron Hrs.	
			2" " 7" Cameron Hrs.	
				Recruits L.S.
				33. 3
				31. 8
				Answers:
			Knock out Competition (teams of 4 per section)	Patrol Competition
			1st Prize 7" Cameron Hrs.	2nd Prize 7" Cameron Hrs.
			2nd " 7" " do.	
			Snapshooting Competition (teams of 6 per section)	
			2nd Prize 7" Cameron Hrs.	
			At the XVII Corps Boxing Competition No. R/7673 Pimd. E. DAVIES "C" Coy. and S/26073 Pte. D. TAIT "D" Coy. were both Knocked out in bouts. These men were the only ones of the Battalion who took part.	
			Company Training "B" Coy. Carried out Rifle Practice at the Rifle Range.	
			CHURCH PARADE 27 other Ranks arrived by draft - 2 other ranks struck off strength on this date Lt. Baldwin Rejoined the 5/10" Gordon Highlanders in Suffolk, the 5/10" Gordon Hr. Lt. Army the Baldwin in Rejoin. "A" Coy of the 7" Gordon Highlanders return to "B" Coy of the 5/10" Gordon Hrs on the Company to from completion of JOHNSON AVENUE and took over all working Parties Found by that Company after relief of "E" Suffolk throw Leverton relief "C" Coy of the Battn was relieved by "C" Coy of the Gordons at in this present location	
do.	20.10.17			
do.	21.10.17		to RIFLE CAMP. HEAD QUARTERS, "B", "D" Coys.	
				Norman MacLeod Lt. Col.

Army Form C. 2118.

WAR DIARY
or
INTELLIGENCE SUMMARY.
(Erase heading not required.)

PAGE 248

Place	Date	Hour	Summary of Events and Information	Remarks and references to Appendices
RIFLE CAMP	22.10.17		All indifferent shots of "B" & "C" Coys. on Rifle Range under instruction. Camp fatigues improving Camp.	
DO.	23.10.17		Camp fatigues and Company Training. 3 other ranks struck off strength.	
DO.	24.10.17		Camp fatigues and Company Training. 1 O.R. wounded in action on the 21.10.17 & 3.8.17 now officially killed in action. 1 other rank previously reported missing during operations 31.7.17 & 3.8.17 now officially killed in action.	
DO.	25.10.17		2 other ranks struck off strength. The 46" INFANTRY BRIGADE was relieved by the 46" Rifle Scotch Brigade of the Division front on the night of this and the following night. Details of Battns. [?] "A" Coy.) was relieved by the 12" Bn. H.L.I. "A" Coy of the 7" Cameron Hrs was relieved in HAPPY VALLEY by "B" Coy of the 10" Bn. S.R. The Battn. (less "A" Coy.) 2nd Rifle Camp at 2 p.m. and proceeded to Battn. by Companies at 5 minutes interval in the following order Headquarters Coy "B", "C", "D" details of "A" & "D" Coys. on completion of Relief "A" & "D" Coys proceeded to OIL WORKS ARRAS	
OIL WORKS ARRAS	26.10.17		"A" and three of "B" Coy. who were in Nissen huts in Happy Valley - in billets attached to principal remainder of Battn. bivouac at BUTTE-de-TIR and Rifle Range on the MOAT RANGE	
DO.	27.10.17		Company Training at BUTTE-de-TIR. 3 other ranks struck off strength 2 other ranks admitted to diff. & taken on Strength. 2" Lieut. J.F. BOOKLESS M.C. was evacuated to England - Sick on the 17.10.17 and struck off Strength	
DO.	28.10.17		CHURCH PARADE.	
DO.	29.10.17		Coy. practicing on show front in conjunction with Lt "Trench Mortar Battery and machine gun exercises on the drill and fire movement. 14 other ranks of the A.I.S. Hus. Transferred to the 11" Bn. A.I.S. Hus on the 28/10/17.	
DO.	30.10.17		3 other ranks struck off strength. The Battalion carried out Rifle Practice at Ranges H. 7. d. 7. 8. 5 Sleepclick under instructors. The following officers joined the Unit on the 25.10.17 and are taken on the Strength. 2"/Lieut. A. BANKS, "C" Coy, 2"Lieut J. McINTOSH "B" Coy at BUTTE-DE-TIR	
DO.	31.10.17		Training at BUTTE-DE-TIR 6 other ranks struck off strength.	

Index..................   train B (2)

SUBJECT.

Q 27

7th Cameron Highlanders.

No.	Contents.	Date.
	November 1917	

CONFIDENTIAL

Vol 29

War Diary
of
7th (S) Bn Cameron Highrs.

For the Month of

November 1917.

Army Form C. 2118.

WAR DIARY
or
INTELLIGENCE SUMMARY.
(Erase heading not required.)

Instructions regarding War Diaries and Intelligence Summaries are contained in F.S. Regs., Part II. and the Staff Manual respectively. Title pages will be prepared in manuscript.

Page No 249.

Place	Date	Hour	Summary of Events and Information	Remarks and references to Appendices
OIL WORKS. ARRAS.	1/11/17		Coys. at BUTTE-DE-TIR Bayonet fighting in assault course, also close order drill. Classes under instruction in Signalling, Lewis Guns, Rifle Grenades and musketry. 3 Other ranks arrived in draft & 1 other rank struck of Strength.	
DITTO.	2/11/17		THE 44TH INFANTRY BRIGADE relieved the 45TH INFANTRY BRIGADE IN THE LEFT SECTION of the Divisional front on the 2nd Nov. and the night of 2/3rd Nov/17. The Battn: relieved three Companies of the 11th A. & S. Highrs. and one Company of the 6/7th Royal Scots Fusiliers and formed the Right front Sector of the Brigade Sector:— "D" Coy. 7th CAMERON HIGHrs. relieved "D" Coy. 11th A. & S. HIGHrs. on Right front. "C" Coy. Ditto. ditto "B" Coy. on Left front. "B" Coy. Ditto. ditto "A" Coy. on Support. "A" Coy. Ditto. ditto "C" Coy. in Support. 6/7th Royal Scots Fusiliers in Reserve. There was no big fatigues from Q Branch to A.10 Siding and Trench Ect. by Platoons at 4 minutes interval to Company area. "K.R." "A" and "B" Companies entrained at 2 R.M. and "C" & "D" Companies entrained at the Ramel place at 6 P.M. Details of the Battn: were accommodated at 45, 49, 65 and 74 Rue St. MAURICE.	
IN THE TRENCHES	3rd/11 4th/11 5th/17 6th/17		On the 6th Nov. an internal relief in the Battn. took place:— "B" Coy. was relieved by "C" Coy. On relief "D" Coy. became support Coy. in WELFORD RESERVE, "D" Coy. became Reserve Coy. "A" Coy. was relieved by "D" Coy. Right front. in LANCER LANE.	
IN THE TRENCHES	7th/11 8th/11 9th/17 10		On the 10th November there was an inter Battalion relief of the 44th Brigade. The Battn. were relieved by the 8th Battn. Seaforth Highrs. as follows:—	

Norman MacLeod
Lt Col

WAR DIARY or INTELLIGENCE SUMMARY

Army Form C. 2118.

Page No 250.

Place	Date	Hour	Summary of Events and Information	Remarks and references to Appendices
IN THE TRENCHES.	10/11/17		"A" Coy 7th Camerons was relieved by 13th Coy 8th Seaforth Highrs. "B" ditto ditto by "A" Coy 8th ditto. "C" ditto ditto by "C" Coy ditto. "D" ditto ditto by "D" Coy ditto. Companies on relief proceeded to RIFLE CAMP independently. — An interval of 5 minutes between platoons who maintained both in the Trenches and on the road. — The Battalion details rejoined the Battn. at RIFLE CAMP. The movement was taken later.	
RIFLE CAMP.	11/11/17		CHURCH PARADE. 2nd Lt. R.A. PROVEN arrived by draft on the strength. 4 other ranks taken on strength. and 21 other ranks who arrived by draft taken on strength. 10 other ranks returned to strength. 5 other ranks were exchanged for a similar number with the 6th Battn Cameron Highrs. During 12 hours in the line 3 other ranks were wounded. —	
RIFLE CAMP.	12/11/17		Battn. in BRIGADE RESERVE. Supplying Coys. and clearing H.Q. to other ranks struck off strength other ranks who arrived by draft on 11/11/17 were taken on strength.	
Ditto.	13/11/17		Norice Sawing Saunders under instruction and parades under Company arrangements. Carrying out Camp improvements. — MAJOR B.J.T.B. COULSON, KING'S OWN SCOTTISH BORDERERS arrived on the 3-11-17 and was attached to Battalion Headquarters. — 2nd LT. R.W. MURRAY was evacuated to the UNITED KINGDOM, sick on the 3-11-17 and to attack of the Strength. — 2 other ranks taken on strength. 2 O.Rs wounded in action on 12-11-17. The Battalion relieved the 8/10th GORDON HIGHrs. as support Battn. to the 44th BRIGADE on the	
Ditto.	14/11/17		date. "A" Coy 7th CAMERON Highrs relieved "D" Coy 8/10 GORDON HIGHrs. in the RAILWAY CUTTING "C" Coy. ditto "C" Coy. ditto in the EMBANKMENT AT BRIGADE H.Q. "B" Coy. ditto "B" Coy. ditto in LANCER LANE leaving K.L. MINES. "D" Coy. ditto "A" Coy. ditto in STIRLING CAMP. "H.Q. Coy." relieved "H.Q. Coy." Coys. left RIFLE CAMP in the following order:- "B" Coy.] by Platoons at 4 minutes interval. The first platoon "B" Coy. left the Camp "A" Coy.] at 1-15 P.M. — Details were accommodated in the old Divisional H.Q. "C" Coy.] "H.Q. Coy."] Camp and moved off at 2-30 P.M. — "D" Coy.]	

Norman Macpherson Lt. Col.

WAR DIARY or INTELLIGENCE SUMMARY

Army Form C. 2118.

PAGE Nº 251.

Place	Date	Hour	Summary of Events and Information	Remarks and references to Appendices
NEAR FAMPOUX IN TRENCHES.	14/11/17 to 18/11/17		Battalion in Support to 44th Brigade. 5 other ranks struck off strength. The 147th INFANTRY BRIGADE was relieved in the LEFT SECTION of the DIVISIONAL FRONT on the 17th NOVT. 2nd Lt. CAMERON HIGHRS was relieved by the 12th H.L.I. to support Battalion as follows:— "A" Coy. 7th CAMERON HIGHRS was relieved by "D" Coy. 12th H.L.I. Companies billeted at present Bivouacs. "B" Coy. do do do Platoons at 4 minutes notice to Coys. "C" Coy. do do do PLACE ST CROIX, ARRAS. "D" Coy. do do do	
OIL WORKS. ARRAS.	19/11/17		Coy. Parades as per Training Programme. 2nd Lt. A.M. ROSS evacuated to ENGLAND on 9-11-17. 1 o/r struck and wounded of strength 2 other ranks struck off strength. — 1 other rank killed in action on 15-11-17.—	
Ditto.	20/11/17		Coy. Parades as per Training Programme. 4 other ranks arrived by draft and were taken on strength on the 14th, 15th, and 19th respectively. 8 other ranks evacuated and struck off strength. A warning order was received in this date stating that in the event of the enemy attacking on the Divisional Front and the Battalion being ordered forward from ARRAS, the Battn. to be ready to move on 15 minutes notice Coys. to proceed by the routes reconnoitred by O.C. Companies to the following areas:— "A" Coy. in the Rest. corner of LANCER AVENUE from H.38.c.7.7 to H.36.c.4.9½. "B" Coy. from H.36.c.4.9½. to the junction of LANCER AVENUE and LONE AVENUE H.36.a.4.3. "C" Coy. from H.36.a.4.3. to H.36.a.20.75. "D" Coy. from H.36.a.20.75. to H.30.c.10.25. Battn. H.Q. to be at Machine Gun Headquarters at H.35.b.44. The 8/10th GORDON HIGHRS to be on our left and the 8th Batt. Seaforth Highrs in support.	
Ditto.	21/11/17		Coys. Carried out Range Practices as Butte de TIR and struck on the assault course there.— 4 other ranks evacuated and struck off strength.—	
Ditto.	22/11/17		Coy. Training at BUTTE de TIR and Inspection by Commanding Officer.	
Ditto.	23/11/17		Coy. Training at BUTTE de TIR.— 2 other ranks struck off strength.—	
Ditto.	24/11/17		Coy. Training at BUTTE de TIR.—	

WAR DIARY or INTELLIGENCE SUMMARY

PAGE No. 252.

Place	Date	Hour	Summary of Events and Information	Remarks and references to Appendices
OIL WORKS - ARRAS.	25/11/17		CHURCH Parades. 2 other ranks struck off strength.	
Ditto.	26/11/17		The 144th INFANTRY BRIGADE relieved the 45th INFANTRY BRIGADE in the Right Sector of the Divisional Front on this date. The Battn. relieved the 6/7 Battn. ROYAL SCOTS FUSILIERS at WILDERNESS CAMP on Reserve. Coys and Companies proceeded on the 's Hounng order from Billets by Platoons at four minutes interval. 'A' Coy, 'B' Coy, 'C' Coy, 'D' Coy and H.Q.Coy. First platoon of 'A' Coy left Billets at 2 P.M. 3 other ranks evacuated and struck off strength.	
WILDERNESS CAMP.	27/11/17		The Battn. in Reserve to Brigade. Parades under Coy. Arrangements. Lieut. A.J. EASTWOOD admitted to hospital on the 26.10.17.	
DITTO.	28/11/17		The Battn. in Reserve to the Brigade. Parades under Coy. arrangements. The Battn. was relieved on this date by the 1st Battn. EAST LANCASHIRE REGT. and on relief the Battn. proceeded to the OIL WORKS, ARRAS. Companies marched by Platoons at 4 minutes interval in the following order. 'A' Coy, 'B' Coy, 'C' Coy, 'D' Coy and H.Q.s Coy.	
OIL WORKS.	29/11/17		Coy. Training and training of specialists.	
DITTO.	30/11/17		5 other ranks struck off strength. 1 other rank taken on attached. 1 other rank previously reported missing 31/7/17 - 3/8/17 is now officially killed in action.	

P.M. & C.

[signature]
Lt. Col.
Comdg. 7th Queen's Own Royal West Kent Regt.

Index...............

SUBJECT.

7th Cameron Highlanders.

Q 28

No.	Contents.	Date.
	December 1917.	

Army Form C. 2118.

WAR DIARY
or
INTELLIGENCE SUMMARY.
(Erase heading not required.)

Secret & Confidential

War Diary —

7th (Service) Battalion Cameron Highlanders

1/12/14 to 31/12/14.

Pages 253 to 256.

WAR DIARY or INTELLIGENCE SUMMARY

Army Form C. 2118.

Place	Date	Hour	Summary of Events and Information	Remarks and references to Appendices
OIL WORKS - ARRAS.	1/12/17		The 44th INFANTRY BRIGADE relieved the 45th INFANTRY BRIGADE in the left Section of the Divisional Front on this date. The 7th Cameron Highrs relieved the 13th Bn. Royal Scots as Right Front Battn. and the disposition of the Battn. was as follows:— "A" Coy. 7th Cameron Highrs relieved "A" Coy. 13th Royal Scots Right Front "B" Coy. 7th Cameron Highrs " "C" Coy. " ditto Left Front "D" Coy. 7th Cameron Highrs " "B" Coy. " ditto in Support "C" Coy. 7th Cameron Highrs " "D" Coy. " ditto in Reserve. Companies proceeded to the trenches in the following order "A","B","D","C" and H.Qrs. by the following route:— ATHIES - CANAL BANK (keeping on the North bank all the way) - Mine-ment east of North Pont Gd Line between maps F.29a56 G. and H. was by platoons? at 5 minutes interval. The Recony Coy. furnished a party of 1 N.C.O and 20 other ranks at FAMPOUX and relieved the Waler Guard of the 13th Royal Scots there. 2 other ranks struck of the Battn. strength. Batn. H.Qrs. were in CADIZ RESERVE (H.12.d.75.13)
IN THE TRENCHES	8/12/17		An inter-Coy. relief in the Battn. was carried out on this date. "C" Coy. relieved "A" Coy. - Right Front } on relief "B" Company became support Coy. "D" Coy. relieved "B" Coy. - Left Front } and "A" Company Reserve Coy. The relief was commenced at 1.30 A.M. and completed by dawn - patrols and work parties were carried on without interruption.
Ditto. —	13/12/17		The Battn. was relieved by the 8/10th Gordon Highrs. Sub. Restion on this date. "A" Coy. 7th Cameron Highrs was relieved by "B" Coy. 8/10th GORDON HIGHrs "B" " ditto " "D" Coy. ditto "C" " ditto " "A" Coy. ditto "D" " ditto " "C" Coy. ditto On relief the 7th Cameron Highrs became support Battn. and Companies occupied the area held by the corresponding Coys. of the 8/10 Gordon Highrs Warren Lingford Lt Col

WAR DIARY or INTELLIGENCE SUMMARY

PAGE No. 254.

Place	Date	Hour	Summary of Events and Information	Remarks
IN THE TRENCHES.	13/12/17. 15/12/17		Batt. H.Q. were located off the Rankin Road at H.H.C.7.9. 27 other ranks struck off the strength.— MAJOR B.J.B. COULSON proceeded to join the 18th Welsh Regt and is struck off the strength.— 2 other ranks taken on the strength.— No. S/23888 Pte JOHN H. RITCHIE IN RECOGNITION of his gallant conduct in saving a comrade from drowning near ARRAS on the 8th September 1917 has been awarded the Testimonial on Parchment of the Society of the Royal Humane Society.— LIEUT. A.J. EASTWOOD, LONDON SCOTTISH (attached) has been invalided to ENGLAND sick on the 2-12-17 and is struck off the strength.— 1 other rank previously reported missing now reported — Prisoner of War in Germany. The undermentioned appointed Temporary Lieuts. 1-7-17 2/Lt E. CAMERON. 2 Lt W. BLACK. M.C. (30.7.17) do R.A.M. McCROSTIE. do J.D.N. McCRACKEN. do R.B. PURDON. M.C.	
IN THE TRENCHES Support Batt.	17/8/17/12/17		The 46th Infantry Brigade relieved the 44th Infantry Brigade in the left Sector 15th Divisional front on the 17th/18th Dec. — The Brigade on relief became Brigade in Divisional Reserve. The 7th Cameron Hirs were relieved by the 10th Scottish Rifles, as support Batt. On relief the 7th Cameron Hirs proceeded to the ECOLE DES JEUNES FILLES, ARRAS. The Coys of the Battn. were relieved by the corresponding Coys of the 10th Scottish Rifles. On relief the Coys proceeded independently by Platoons at 100 yards interval via— CAM VALLEY, BLANGY LOCK, RUE DE DOUAI and ARRAS STATION.— 15 other ranks struck off strength. 2 other ranks taken on the strength.— 7 other ranks wounded in action on dates between 5—14 Dec 1917.— During the tour in the Trenches considerable work was performed in revetting and generally Trenches and erecting wire entanglements in advance of front support etc. lines.	
ECOLE DES JEUNES FILLES. ARRAS.	19/12/17		An R.E. N.C.O. lecturing equipment and inspections. 1 other rank taken on strength.—	Norman Murray Hy Lt Col

WAR DIARY or INTELLIGENCE SUMMARY

Army Form C. 2118.

Page No. 255.

Place	Date	Hour	Summary of Events and Information	Remarks and references to Appendices
ECOLE DES JEUNES FILLES. ARRAS.	20/12/17		For all ranks not on working parties parades in Platoon & Close order drill and carried out on BUTTE DE TIR. Brigade Commander offered his appreciation of the manner in which all ranks have worked under the trying conditions imposed by the recent tour in the line. He considered that the improvement in the condition of the trenches, but from the point of view of defence and cleanliness was most marked and will repay the amount of labour expended. 1919 other ranks arrived by draft on the 17th December and were taken on the strength from that date. Operation Order No. 92 of Feb. 17/12/17 states: Reports indicate that the Enemy may resume the offensive on a wider or narrower part of the Western Front. The following action will be taken by 7th TR. Bn:— (1) All Companies while the 4th Brigade is in Divisional Reserve will "Stand to" 6 Stand Down" during the period of "Stand to" the men will wear fighting order. Haversack containing iron ration & on back and extra Bottle full. (3) Each Company will have a store of ammunition sufficient to equip the men & the Company to the following scale. 220 Rounds S.A.A.; 1 Bombing & R/G Squads Sections with Rifle Grenades. (4) On receipt of orders the men will at once be equipped & the whole Battalion ready to move in half an hour.	
Ditto	21/12/17		Companies occupied the Musketry Range for Rifle practice and Platoon stores under which it was carried out in private grounds at Bellets. Specialist parades organised by units instructors. Capt. G.J.S. LUMSDEN admitted to hospital on the 18th and evacuated to England & sent to England.	
Ditto	22/12/17		Company training at BUTTE DE TIR and at Bellets. 1 other rank taken on the strength. 30 other ranks struck off the strength.	
Ditto	23/12/17		The 44th Infantry Brigade relieved the 45th Infantry Brigade in the Right Sector of the front on this date. The 7th Canadian M.G. Bn. relieved the 11th A.M.G. Bn in Brigade Reserve in the trenches in and about the CORPS LINE. Companies proceeded in the following order on the movement of 9 at 8 A.M. "D" — "A" — "B" — "C" and H.Q. Coy. The	

Norman Murdoch Wile

Army Form C. 2118.

WAR DIARY
or
INTELLIGENCE SUMMARY.
(Erase heading not required.)

Page No. 256.

Place	Date	Hour	Summary of Events and Information	Remarks and references to Appendices
IN THE TRENCHES	27/12/17 To 31/12/17		The route was via Rue Douai – Beaupy Lock – Caen Valley and entrance to line by Cnets Trench. Headquarters were in Pudding Trench (H.16.b.7.5). Whole Batt. in reserve. Various work parties were furnished. The Batt. relieved the 8th Seaforth Highrs on this date on the Right Section of the Divisional front. "B" Coy. 1st Camerons relieved "C" Coy. 8th Seaforth Hghrs on right front. "C" Coy. ditto "D" Coy. ditto in centre. "D" Coy. ditto "B" Coy. ditto on left front. "A" Coy. ditto "A" Coy. ditto in support in BEDFORD RESERVE. The Batt. moved off at 4.15 P.M. in the following order: "D" "B" "C" "A" + H.Q. Coy. "D" Coy. proceeded via FAMPOUX LOCK – TRIPLE AROH; "B" "C" "A" + H.Q. Coys. via FAMPOUX LOCK – CHINSTRAP to MEDICAL AID POST. The closing weeks of the year & the opening of the next year were spent in the Trenches the weather being of the most wintry description.	
	8/1/18			Norman Murgray Lt. Col. Comm'g. 1st Cameron Highrs

7th Bn Cameron Highlanders

Jan - Feb 1918

SECRET AND "CONFIDENTIAL"

War Diary

7th. (Service) Battalion Cameron Highlanders

From 1st January 1918. To 31st January 1918.

VOLUME 31
Pages 257 to 260.

WAR DIARY
OR
INTELLIGENCE SUMMARY.

(Erase heading not required.)

Army Form C. 2118.

Page 257

Place	Date	Hour	Summary of Events and Information	Remarks and references to Appendices
THE TRENCHES	1/1/18 & 2/1/18		The 44th Infantry Brigade was relieved by the 2nd Guards Brigade in the Right Section of the Divisional Front on the night of the 2nd–3rd January 1918, and the Division became in reserve to the Corps. The 1st Cameron Hgrs. were relieved in the Right Sub Section by the 3rd Grenadier Guards. Companies were relieved as follows:— "B" Coy. 1st Cameron Hgrs. by No. 2 Coy. 3rd Grenadier Guards Right Front. "C" Coy. Ditto by No. 4 Coy. Ditto Centre Front.} The extracted front of 3rd Bn "D" Coy. Ditto by No. 3 Coy. Ditto Left Front } were relieved on the night "A" Coy. Ditto by No. 1 Coy. Ditto Support. } of the 2/3 January. Guides for the relieving platoons, Company HQrs Batln. Headqrs the Medical Aid post proceeded to Junction of INVERNESS AVENUE and ROAD (H 22.a.8.4.) to meet the 3rd Bn Grenadier Guards at the following times:— "D" Coy. 5 P.M. "D" Coy. and Headqrs Coy. and Medical aid post at 7.30 P.M. A.R.R.C. on relief proceeded by Route to Billets in ECOLE DES JEUNES FILLES and the remainder. 2 Battalion returned to Billets by — them on light Railway, and arrived in Billets by 1.30 A.M. on the 3rd January. Casualties 1 Officer During the tour in the Trenches severe frost and snow was experienced. other ranks killed.	XVII
ECOLE DES JEUNES FILLES	3/1/18		The day was devoted to cleaning clothing and equipment. Inspections under Coy. Arrangements. Company Drill parade. Inspections. Specialists paraded under instructors. — 57 other ranks arrived by	
Ditto	4/1/18		charge on types dress. Range was carried out. 13 other ranks struck off strength and 2 2.R. Musketry practices on the Range. 2nd Lt. P. DRUMMOND, LONDON REGT arrived by draft. taken on strength.	
Ditto	5/1/18		30 other ranks wounded in action 16 other ranks arrived by draft taken on the strength.	
Ditto	6/1/18		4/1/18 and taken on the strength. Church Parade. 2nd Lt. T.S. DENHOLM arrived by draft on the 5/1/18 and taken on the strength. —	

Norman Murray Lt. Col.

Army Form C. 2118.

WAR DIARY
or
INTELLIGENCE SUMMARY.
(Erase heading not required.)

Page 258

Place	Date	Hour	Summary of Events and Information	Remarks and references to Appendices
ECOLE DES JEUNES FILLES.	7/1/18		All Companies carried out Section & Platoon training and Range Practices. Specialists under instructors.—	
DITTO.	8/1/18		LIEUT. W. BLACK. M.C. has been accepted as an observer on probation for duty with the ROYAL FLYING CORPS and is struck off strength.— 2 other ranks taken on the strength having arrived by draft. 6 other ranks struck off strength.— Companies carried out Section & Platoon training in extended order drill, handling of arms, physical and bayonet fighting & bombing. Specialists under instructors.— 2 other ranks arrived by draft & taken on strength.— 10 other ranks struck off strength.—	
DITTO.	9/1/18		Companies carried out Section & Platoon training and Rifle Practices on the Range.— 40 other ranks taken on strength & 5 struck off strength.—	
Ditto.	10/1/18		Ditto ditto and Rifle practices on the range. 1 other rank taken on strength, 10 struck off strength.—	
Ditto.	11/1/18		Companies carried out Section & Platoon training.— 1 other rank struck off strength.—	
Ditto.	12/1/18		Companies carried out Section & Platoon Training; Lewis Gunners range practices. The Commanding Officer inspected all Companies.—	
Ditto.	13/1/18		Church Parade.— 1 other rank taken on strength and 2 other ranks struck off strength.—	
Ditto.	14/1/18		Company Training and Rifle Practices on the range. Specialists under instructors.— 3 other ranks taken on strength and 2 other ranks struck off strength.—	
Ditto.	15/1/18		The Battn. were inspected on this date by the G.O.C. 15th Division on the BUTTE DE TER Parade Ground. 3 other ranks struck off strength. The Field Firing Practice fixed for this date was cancelled owing to the inclement weather.—	
Ditto.	16/1/18		Companies carried out Lewis Gun and Rifle practice at the Divisional Ranges.— 1 other rank struck off strength & 1 other rank taken on strength.— Bombers proceeded to Belmoral Camp for practice in Live firing.—	
Ditto.	17/1/18		Companies carried out Companies Specialists under instructors.— 20 other ranks taken on strength and total Route march struck off strength.— 20 other ranks taken on strength and total Route march by Companies. Specialists under instructors.— The Officers of the Battn. were entertained to dinner after which a concert was held. During the P.t 10 January the Battn. the Commanding Officer addressed the Troops and gave a short review of the proceedings the Commanding Officer addressed the Troops and gave a short review of the opening days of the Battn. during the past year and the few historians of the Battn. had upon the Regiment. He wished all the men that the year of Rest in the year before us. On the evenings of these dates the men were entertained by a visit to the Theatre in Arras where the "Jocks" performed the programme "Robinson Crusoe".	

Norman Murray

Army Form C. 2118.

WAR DIARY
or
INTELLIGENCE SUMMARY.
(Erase heading not required.)

Page 25-9.

Place	Date	Hour	Summary of Events and Information	Remarks and references to Appendices
ECOLE DES JEUNES FILLES	18/8.		Companies on Rifle Range at BUTTE DE TIR and practicing the attack. Broken parties made for Scouts	
Ditto.	19/8.		Gunners at BUTTE DE TIR Range. All specialists under instruction. 5 other ranks struck off strength. The Commanding officer inspected Companies on the Gunnery Ground at BUTTE DE TIR. Company Drill & Platoon practicing the attack. 2 other ranks taken on strength.	
Ditto.	20/8.		Church Parade. Major E. C. GRIEVE rejoined by draft on the 16.1.18 and is taken on the strength. 3 other ranks struck off strength.	
Ditto.	21/8.		Company Training. – Lewis Gunners on Divisional Range. – 6 other ranks struck off strength. 4 other ranks rejoined by draft to-day and are taken on the strength. LIEUT R.A. PROVEN proceeded to report to M/G Training Centre, GRANTHAM on the 18. and is struck off strength.	
Ditto.	22/8.		The Battalion reconnoitred the position for practising the attack east of ST NICOLAS, during the afternoon. In the evening the Battalion moved out of BILLETS to the position of assembly as at Belgrade exercise, in the event of attack by the enemy north or South of THE SCARPE. 12 other ranks struck off strength.	
Ditto.	23/8.		The Battalion carried out the scheme as laid down in Division Order 97 in practising the attack. – 5 other ranks struck off strength. No 5/15565 PTE J. MACLEOD has been awarded a bar to Military Medal.	
Ditto.	24/8.		Companies practicing the attack. Specialists under instruction. 3 other ranks struck off strength; 2 other ranks taken on strength.	
Ditto.	25/8.		Platoon Rifle Competitions were carried out on the Divisional Range in connection with the Army Rifle Association Competitions. – 3 other rank struck off strength and 10 other ranks taken on strength.	
Ditto.	26/8.		A Brigade exercise under Divisional arrangements was carried out on the Cole Battle field north of ACHICOURT. The Cameron H'lders & 2/10 Gordon H'lders carried out the attack with the 9th & 13th Black Watch in Support & Reinforce in reserve.	
Ditto.	27/8.		Church Parade. 3 other ranks joined by draft & are taken on the strength.	

Norman Munro(?)

Army Form C. 2118.

WAR DIARY
or
INTELLIGENCE SUMMARY.
(Erase heading not required.)

Instructions regarding War Diaries and Intelligence Summaries are contained in F.S. Regs., Part II. and the Staff Manual respectively. Title pages will be prepared in manuscript.

Place	Date	Hour	Summary of Events and Information	Remarks and references to Appendices
ECOLE DES JEUNES FILLES.	28/8 to 29/8.		Page 260. Coy. Training. Specialists under instructors. 1 Other rank taken on strength.— The Battn. Carried out a Field exercise practicing the Attack. The undermentioned have been mentioned in despatches, extract from London GAZETTE Suppt d/21.12.17. Lt. Col. MACLEOD. D.S.O. Lt. J. A. SYMON. D.S.O. Lt. J. H. MAUCHLIN.	
Ditto.	30/8.		5 other ranks struck off strength.— Companies carried out Rifle practices at the BUTTE DE TIR. Specialists under instructors. 4 other ranks taken on the strength; 1 other rank struck off strength.—	
Ditto.	31/8.		Companies carried out Rifle practice at the Divisional Range; also two gymnors on new Range. The Battalion has greatly benefited by the period of intensive training it has undergone during the past month.	

Munford Lt Col
Comdg 4 Cameron Highlanders

2/9/18

Vol 32

Q 30

War Diary
of
7th (Service) Battalion Cameron Highlanders.
Pages Nos 261, 262, + 263

for month of February, 1918.

Secret + Confidential.

WAR DIARY
INTELLIGENCE SUMMARY

Army Form C. 2118.

Page No 261

Place	Date	Hour	Summary of Events and Information	Remarks and references to Appendices
ECOLE DES JEUNES FILLES	1/2/18		Company parades in Gas drill, Physical & Bayonet fighting; also companies practising the attack. Lewis Gunners under Lewis Gun Officer and Signallers under Signalling Officer. A tactical scheme by the Commanding Officer for Junior Officers was held. North East of ARRAS.	
Ditto	2/2/18		3 other ranks arrived by draft on 3/8 January and taken on strength. Companies paraded on the square ECOLE DES JEUNES FILLES and were inspected by the Commanding Officer. Companies carried out practice for the Brigade Platoon Competition on the Surround Range. 2nd Lieut. A.B.S. LEGATE proceeded to ENGLAND on the 31-1-18 for a 6mm Tr of duty and is accordingly struck off strength. 1 other rank taken on strength.	
Ditto	3/2/18		Church Parades.	
Ditto	4/2/18		44th Bde Platoon competition – Lewis Gun competition. Bathing parades & Kit inspections. 30 O.R. taken on strength. 30 O.R. evacuated and struck off strength.	
Ditto	5/2/18		Inspection by M.O. Battalion moved up to front line trenches and relieved 1st Batt Duke of Wellingtons regiment and part of 2nd Batt Essex Regiment in accordance with issued Operation order. Battalion moved off at 4pm and relief complete at 11pm. Disposition A company right, front, B company left front, C company reserve, D company support. 20 O.R. struck off strength.	
IN THE TRENCHES	8/2/18		BELGIAN CROIX DE GUERRE awarded to R/3871 R.S.M. W. VASS & S/13264 R.Q.M.S. J.P.W. WILSON. Readjustment of Brigade front on night of 8/9 February. A coy relieved by D coy 8" Seaforth Highlanders. B coy " " C coy 11" Argyll & Sutherland Highrs C coy " " 6/7 Platoon 13" Bn Royal Scots D coy " " 2 Platoons 11 A.77th Sutherland Highrs 1 Coy and 2 coy 8" Seaforth Highrs. On relief Battalion became Reserve Battalion in BOIS des BOEUFS camp.	
BOIS des BOEUFS CAMP	10/2/18		Church Parades. 115 O.R. struck off strength. 20 O.R. reported Killed in action 5/2/18. 5 O.R. reported wounded in action various dates. B rolls no 3170 of 20/7 Entry of CAPT G.J.S. LUMSDEN wounded and struck off strength cancelled.	

R. W. H. Orann Major
Commanding 7/8 Cameron High[landers]

WAR DIARY or INTELLIGENCE SUMMARY

Army Form C. 2118.

Page No 262

Place	Date	Hour	Summary of Events and Information	Remarks and references to Appendices
BOIS des BDEUFS Camp	11/2/18	-	Battalion moved up to support area in accordance with operation order No 104. A Coy relieved D/10 Gordon Highrs B " " C " " D " "	
IN THE TRENCHES	17/2/18	-	Relief started at 4pm and completed at 7.30pm. Battalion relieved 9/10 Gordon Highrs in front line. Dispositions D Coy Right front, C Coy Left front, B Coy Right support, A Coy Left support. Relief started 5.40pm and completed at 7.30pm	
Ditto	20/2/18	-	An inter-company relief took place. A Coy relieved C Coy LEFT FRONT. B Coy relieved D Coy RIGHT FRONT. D Company became right support company. C Company became Left support coy. 2nd Lts A.R. MacDONALD and 258 O.R. of A Company raided the enemys trenches at 3.30 AM. At 3.30pm the artillery opened a barrage on the enemys front line. At 3.10 + 2 the artillery lifted and the raiding party dashed forward into the enemys trench. At 3.10 + 7 the party withdrew were all back to their own front line at 3.30 + 10. There was no German in the enemys trench but 2 men were found in a B sap head. 1 was killed and 3 brought back as prisoner. Our casualties Nil.	
Ditto	23/2/18	-	On night of 23rd/24th battalion was relieved by 8' Seaforth Highlanders battalion in BOIS des BDEUFS camp. A Company relieved by C Coy 8' Seaforth Highrs B " " B " " C " " A " "	
BOIS DES BDEUFS Camp	25/2/18	-	Bathing parades. 41 OR Wounded and struck off strength. 2 OR taken on strength.	
"	26/2/18	-	Congratulations were received from the Corps Commander and Brigadier on the successful raid of 23/2/18. Lt Tuffman RNI Stoy Lt J. AITKENHEAD taken on strength. 1 OR taken on Strength.	

P.M.H. Cran Lt Col
Commanding 7 Camerons?

WAR DIARY
or
INTELLIGENCE SUMMARY.

Page No 263.—

Place	Date	Hour	Summary of Events and Information	Remarks and references to Appendices
Bois des Boeufs Camp	27/2/18	—	Extract from Supplement to London Gazette dated 1-1-18 shows Capt. G.J.S. LUMSDEN as having been awarded the MILITARY CROSS. 1.O.R struck off strength. Tempy Lieutenant R.B. PURDON M.C. to be acting captain. 7/2 2/Lieut J.S. McIVAB relinquishes acting rank of captain. - 15 O.R signalled for official purposes as having died on various dates. 1 other reported missing	
Ditto	28/2/18	—	Gas appliances inspected. 1OR reported wounded in action. 1.O.R struck off strength. 27 O.R Taken on Strength.	
Ditto				

P.M.F. Cameron Major
Commanding 7/ Cameron H'rs

44th Brigade.

15th Division.

7th BATTALION

CAMERON HIGHLANERRS

MARCH 1918

Appendices attached.

    1. Map shewing dispositions.
    2.   do.   do.
    3. Reports from individuals on fighting of 28th March.

Additional appx.   Award by Royal Humane Society. Map sent by Officer of Bn showing positions held on R. Scarpe.

pages 264 to 267

WAR DIARY
of
7th (S) Bn. CAMERON HIGHRS
for the month of
MARCH 1918

WAR DIARY or INTELLIGENCE SUMMARY

Army Form C. 2118.

Page N° 264.

Place	Date	Hour	Summary of Events and Information	Remarks and references to Appendices
BOIS DES BOEUFS.	1st March 1918 to		On this date the Battn. relieved the 8/10th Gordon Highrs. and the comm. support Posn. and was disposed as follows:- "A" Coy. 1 Platoon in can strongpoint "B" C.D. E work Coy. H.Qrs. in LES FOSSES FARM. "B" Coy. - 3 Platoons in LES FOSSES FARM with 1 Platoon in BROWN LINE. "C" Coy. BROWN LINE L/R. "D" Coy. BROWN LINE Right. "D" Coy. and 1 Platoon of "B" Coy. moved across country on their way from time to come into their Kine at 5-40 P.M. "A" & "B" Coys and 1 Platoon of "B" Coy. moved by and road route in Artillery formation in the order "A" "B" moving off as a to base over the BROWN LINE at 6-5.P.M. — 10th. moved strength of Brown Line. The Battn. was relieved in the support area by the 8th SEAFORTH HIGHRS and a return relieved	
IN SUPPORT. IN THE TRENCHES.	7th March 1918		On this date the Battn. was in the front area:- A Coy. 8/10th GORDON HIGHRS. Left support. B Coy. 7th Cameron H/rs relieved "A" 8/10 Gordon H/rs. Left support. C Coy. ditto "B" ditto. Right support. D Coy. ditto "C" ditto. Left front. ditto "D" ditto. Right front. An inter-company relief was carried out on the Battn. on the 10th March "A" Coy relieved "C" Coy who on relief became left support Company. "B" Coy. was relieved by "D" Coy who on relief became Left support Coy.	
IN RESERVE BOIS DES BOEUFS.	13/3/18 14		The 8th Seaforth Highrs relieved the 7th Cameron H/rs. in the front area and the Battn. proceeded to BOIS DES BOEUFS and became Reserve Battn. Decorations to the undermentioned have been awarded:- MILITARY CROSS. 2nd Lt A.R. MACDONALD. MILITARY MEDAL. S/10391 L/Sergt. W MACKAY 240 S/20054 2 L/Corporal J STUDDART 240 S/11016 Pte H. FINLAY. The following officers have been evacuated to England sick on the dates mentioned and are accordingly struck off strength. 2nd Lt H.L. PARKER 22.2.18 } Struck off strength. 2nd Lt J. McINTOSH. 11.3.18 } & the under taken on strength. 2nd Lt J.W GRAHAM M.C. proceeded on 3-3-18 to United Kingdom for Gratuitous Leave & duty & Norman Macpherson X Lt Col	

2nd Lt H.L. PARKER 22.2.18
2nd Lt J. McINTOSH 11.3.18

A5834 Wt.W4973/M687 750,000 8/16 D.D.&L. Ltd. Forms/C.2118/13.

WAR DIARY
or
INTELLIGENCE SUMMARY.

(Erase heading not required.)

Army Form C. 2118.

Page No 265.

Place	Date	Hour	Summary of Events and Information	Remarks and references to Appendices
BOIS DES BOEUFS.	15.3.18		Battalion in Reserve. 38 other ranks evacuated and struck off the strength. — 18 other ranks absorbed into the establishment of the 15th Bn. Machine Gun Company on the 11.3.18 and are according[ly] struck off strength. — The following Casualties occurred in action on the dates mentioned. — 2 other ranks killed on 11th & 12th March; Died of wounds 1 other rank 28/2/18; Wounded in action 1 on 15/3. 1 on 23/2/18; 1 on 27/2/18; 9 on 9/3/18; 12 on 10/3; 3 on 11/3/18; 1 on 12/3/18; 12 on 13/3/18. —	# other rank is taken on to strength.
DITTO.	16.3.18		Battn: in Reserve. 3 other ranks struck off strength. 1 other rank died of wounds.	
	17.3.18		Ditto. Church Parades. 10 other ranks struck off strength. —	
	18.3.18		Ditto. Company training. 2 other ranks struck off strength. —	
DITTO.	19.3.18		The Battalion relieved the 8/10th GORDON HIGHrs on the Evening of this date and became Support Batt. The Battn: was disposed as follows:— "C" Coy. with 1 platoon in each strong point 'B' 'C' 'D' and 'E'. "D" Coy. with 3 platoons in APPLE and PEAR TRENCH near 'E' Strong point. "B" Coy. with 2 platoons N.12.C. and 2 platoons immediately north of FOSSES FARM with H.Qrs. in Cave N.12.C.S.2. "A" Coy. with 4 platoons in N.12.C. H.Qrs. along with "B" Coy. 7 other ranks struck off strength. — 41 other ranks arrived by draft on the 18th inst: and are taken on the strength. —	
IN THE TRENCHES	20.3 21/16 22/16		Battalion in support with H.Ears at LES FOSSES FARM off the CAMBRAI ROAD.— On the afternoon of the 22nd 2ND LT. S. S. GEMMELL was killed during hostile bombardment. —	
DITTO.	22/23/18		The Battn: was ordered to withdraw to the Army Line in N.7a and b. The withdrawal was covered by "D" Coy. who occupied Fork, Spade and Gordon Trenches — special attention being paid to the flank defences of Gordon Avenue. At this stage 1 Coy. of the 8/10 GORDON HIGHrs occupied front system of Trenches with orders to hold the line until forced back. This Coy. withdrew thro' "D" Coy. of the 7th Cameron HIGHrs from this point "D" Coy. fought a rear guard action to 16 Prov: line and passed thro' the 8th Seaforth HIGHrs holding this line and rejoined the Battalion. Before withdrawing O.C. "D" Coy. destroyed the Old Headquarters dugout at Crossroads under the Cambrai Road. The Electric lighting plant in LES FOSSES FARM was also rendered useless.—	

Norman Hereford Lt Col

Army Form C.2118.

WAR DIARY
or
INTELLIGENCE SUMMARY.
(Erase heading not required.)

Instructions regarding War Diaries and Intelligence Summaries are contained in F.S. Regs., Part II. and the Staff Manual respectively. Title pages will be prepared in manuscript.

Page No. 266.

Place	Date	Hour	Summary of Events and Information	Remarks and references to Appendices
IN THE TRENCHES.	23/3/18		The withdrawal of the Batt. to this new position was carried out in good order and with few Casualties.	
	24 & 25.3.18		On the afternoon of this date the Batt. moved forward from the Army Line in Support to the 8th Seaforth Highrs. with their right on N.F.C.80. and their left on the Brown line, following in line of the awaited trench behind the new line. This line was held with 2 Coys. in front and 2 Coys. in support. Batt. Hqrs. were at SHAMROCK CORNER (Trench system anyout).	
	25/26/3/18		On the night of 25/26, the 7th Cameron Highrs. were relieved by the 5/10 Gordon Highrs and the Batt. moved forward and relieved the 8th Seaforth Highrs. in the front line. The disposition of the Bn. was as follows :— A Coy. Left Front. B Coy. Left Support. C Coy. Right Front. D Coy. Right Support. 11 Batt. Headqrs in N.P.C.85. ||Batt. strength taken on strength having arrived by drafts of 6 1 other rank on 26th March and 37 other ranks on return from hosp. & 25th March inclusive — on the 25th March; 16 other ranks struck off strength, 24 and 27 being indecisive. 7 other ranks killed in action between 24 and 27 March indecisive. 2nd Lt. T. GIDDEN wounded in action (acc.) on 8.3.18. 30 O.R. ranks wounded in action between 21st and 27 March indecisive. 3 other ranks died of wounds	8, 26, 27/78
	27/28/3/18		On the night of 27/28 there was an inter-company relief. D Coy. relieved A Coy. Left front. B Coy. relieved C Coy. Right front. On relief "A" & "C" Coys. became Right & Left support Coys. respectively.	
	28/3/18		About 3 A.M. on the 28th. The enemy opened an intense bombardment on the front line and immediate support Coys. lasting about a time slackened and went on the front line heavier than ever. At once lines. This barrage was very heavy. The Barrage came back on the front line and apparently to the Brown line. The enemy infantry were advancing in enemy Aeroplane came over and apparently period when the enemy infantry were almost immediately the enemy again got down a very observed men in the front line as almost immediately the enemy again got down a very heavy barrage. Heavy casualties were sustained during the Bombardment particularly on "D" Coy front. About 7 P.M. enemy infantry attacked and gained a footing in the front trenches and commenced to work round the left flank in considerable numbers — to avoid being cut off the remainder of "D" Coy with drew by squads under covering fire to a trench in rear of the Brown line. Here the Line held up the German attack until about 1.30. P.M.; heavy Casualties being inflicted on the enemy. About this period the enemy and the line was then withdrawn to the Army Line in front of TILLOY, which was reached about 3 P.M. —	

Unmemmbered 2nd/Col.

A 5834 Wt. W4973/M687. 750,000. 8/16 D.D. & L. Ltd. Forms/C.2118/13.

Army Form C. 2118.

WAR DIARY
or
INTELLIGENCE SUMMARY.
(Erase heading not required.)

Place	Date	Hour	Summary of Events and Information	Remarks and references to Appendices
IN THE TRENCHES	28/29/3/18		Page No. 267. About midnight the Battalion was withdrawn from the action and proceeded via ARRAS, DAINVILLE to WANQUETIN. The Casualties sustained by the Battalion during the Battle were as follows:- OFFICERS: KILLED (28.3.18) 2ND LT. W. MURHEAD. 2ND LT. H. R. RENNIE. (LONDON SCOTTISH) 2ND LT. J. S. DENHOLM. 2ND LT. J. N. FINLAY. (LONDON SCOTTISH) WOUNDED AND MISSING. (28.3.18) 2/LT. J. A. DONALD. 2/LT. A. R. McDONALD. M.C. 2/LT. N. J. GRIEVE. WOUNDED: (LT. E.J.G. GIBBS (remaining at duty). 2ND LT. J. McMURRAY. 26.3.18 (2ND LT. M. R. McINDEOR (LONDON SCOTTISH) WOUNDED (BELIEVED P. of W.) 2ND LT. L. MACLEOD. MISSING: G.A/CAPTN. D. I. MILNE. 2/LT. R. DRUMMOND. (LONDON SCOTTISH) D.C.M. 2/LT. J. S. MACNAB. 2/LT. R. SMITH (LONDON SCOTTISH) CAPT. A. C. BATEMAN. R.A.M.C. M.C.	
WANQUETIN	30/3/18		The Battalion proceeded to ARRAS and were billeted in Cellars at PETITE PLACE where the details of the Bath. rejoined from the 15th Division Provisional Bath. The 4th Infantry Brigade was located in PETITE PLACE in Divisional Reserve.	
ARRAS	31/3/18		The 4th Infantry Brigade relieved the 45th Infantry Brigade in the line near TILLOY. The 7th Bn. Cameron High'rs. being in reserve. The Casualties to other ranks on the 28th were as follows. Killed in action. 1. M.Y.D. 2 Wounded in action. 71. Missing believed killed. 6. Wounded & believed P of W. 22. do believed 28 Wounded & Missing. 28. P of W. 28 Wounded remaining at duty. 1. Missing unknown 2/3 Total 372.	

Report on operations of 7th Cameron Highlanders for MARCH 22nd to April 29th 1918

Army Form C. 2118.

WAR DIARY or INTELLIGENCE SUMMARY.
(Erase heading not required.)

Instructions regarding War Diaries and Intelligence Summaries are contained in F. S. Regs., Part II. and the Staff Manual respectively. Title pages will be prepared in manuscript.

Page No. 1.

Place	Date	Hour	Summary of Events and Information	Remarks and references to Appendices
LES FOSSES FARM.	22/3/18	8 p.m.	Battalion received orders to withdraw from the support area to the Army Line. The battalion was then disposed as follows. A.Coy:- Trench running S. from LES FOSSES FARM. B Coy:- 2 Platoons LES FOSSES FARM, 2 Platoons in old Gun pits about 300 yards S.E. of LES FOSSES FARM. C.Coy:- Strong points B.C.D.E. D Coy. 1 Platoon GORDON AVENUE, 3 platoons APPLE TRENCH. Batt. H.Q. LES FOSSES FARM. All bombs, S.A.A. and other Trench Stores, with the exception of a few gun belts were immediately carried back from the Trenches and Strong points and dumped at Batt. H.Q. Motor lorries and limbers came up and all Stores were loaded and cleared from the Battalion area by 2 a.m. – 22/4/18.	See map Appendix 1.
–do–	23/3/18	1 a.m.	By this time the 8th/10th GORDON HIGHRS. had withdrawn from the front line. The 7th CAMERON HIGHRS. then started to withdraw less 1 company (D) left as a rearguard in SPADE and FORK TRENCHES.	–do–
ARMY LINE.		6 a.m.	The battalion less D. Coy. was in position in the Army Line disposed as follows. A Coy:- from N7.d.O.O. to N7.b.5.5. – B Coy N7.b.5.5. to N.1.d. 4.7 – C Coy in old German trenches behind B coy.	
OLD SUPPORT LINE.		7.30 a.m.	The enemy put down a fairly heavy barrage on our old front and support lines and CAPT. MILNE (O/C D Coy) saw large numbers of the enemy working up GORDON AVENUE and round in rear of the Hawk guard which he had formed on his right. He ordered his company to withdraw. This was carried out with the loss of all casualty who was too badly wounded to be brought back. The company retired fighting and CAPT MILNE waited until the whole of his company was clear. He then withdrew himself, giving orders to the R.E. officer at LES FOSSES FARM to blow the mine under the CAMBRAI ROAD and to destroy the Electric plant at the farm.	–do–
SUPPORT AREA.		10.30 am	D Company reported themselves in position in old German trenches behind A. Coy. (N7.1.a.O. & N7.b.5.5.)	
		11. am.	8th SEAFORTH HIGHRS who were then holding MINORCA and NOVA SCOTIA trenches received orders to move forward in support to the 8th SEAFORTH HIGHRS.	
		1.30 p.m.	The battalion was in position in support disposed as follows. A Coy:- SWITCH LINE from N8.C.8.O. to N9.d.O.4. – B Coy:- SWITCH LINE from N9.d.O.4. to junction with NOVA SCOTIA TR. N10.C.85.75. C Coy:- Old 45 Bde H.Qrs and Shell holes behind B Coy. – D Coy:- Old Trenches and Shell holes behind A Coy. – Batt. H.Q. at SHAMROCK CORNER N8.d.S.8. Casualties 4 wounded.	
–do–	24/3/18		Casualties 3 O.R. Killed. 9 O.R. wounded.	

Norman Mcleod Lieut Col.
Commdg 7th (S) Battn Cameron Highlanders.

Army Form C. 2118.

WAR DIARY
or
INTELLIGENCE SUMMARY.
(Erase heading not required.)

Page No. 2

Place	Date	Hour	Summary of Events and Information	Remarks and references to Appendices
FRONT LINE	25/26/3/18	9.30 pm	On the night of the 25/26 the Battalion was relieved by the 8/10' GORDON HIGHRS in support and relieved the 8" SEAFORTH HIGHRS in the front line. Dispositions:— A Coy Left Front. MINORCA TRENCH from junction with CAMBRAI road to N.11.c.0.6.— C. Coy:— Right Front. MINORCA Trench from N.11.C.0.6 to junction with MACKENZIE TRENCH.— D. Coy:— Left Support NOVA SCOTIA TRENCH from N.4.C.7.4 to N.10.a.8.1.— B Coy:— Right Support NOVA SCOTIA TRENCH from N.10.a.8.1 to N.16.A.9.5. Battn HQ:— old 45. Bde Hqr N.9.c.9.8. Forward Battn HQ:— old 44. Bde HQ. N.10.d.4.7.	See map. Appendix 1.
—do—	26/3/18		During the night 26/27 patrols were out constantly. On the left patrols got out 800 yards and were unable to get into touch with the enemy. On the right the enemy were found to be occupying strongly the sunken road at in N.11.C. Casualties 2 O.R. wounded 1 O.R. N.Y.D.	
—do—	27/3/18		During the day the enemy shelled our front and support lines along an entire front with 5.9's. Particular attention was paid to the CAMBRAI ROAD. Casualties Nil. During the last three days the trenches were improved and the wire repaired. Patrols were out constantly but reported no unusual activity.	
—do—	28/3/18	2 am	On the night 27/28 an intr Company Relief took place. D Company relieved A company on left Front. B Company relieved C. Coy on Right Front. Casualties 5 OR Killed, 20R wounded, 1 OR N.Y.D. A small party of the enemy was seen in front of our wire on the right of the left company. This is how no doubt that their intention was to find the gaps and to cut wire. They were dispersed with rifle and Lewis gun fire. This party did not exceed 15 men. Word was sent to the O/C company to send out a patrol to find out if any of the wounded enemy were wounded. The result of this patrol was never reported.	
		3.15 am	The enemy opened a barrage on the front line using gas shells on the left company's front South of the CAMBRAI road. This lasted about ½ hour. The barrage then moved on to the back areas moving forward to the front line again. About	
		4 am	The barrage on the front line having become less, the officer on duty patrolled the whole left Coy front up to the CAMBRAI road and saw that everyone was "standing to" returning to the right of the Coy.	

Norman Hurley ?
Lieut Col
Commdg 7'(S) Batt" Cameron High"

Army Form C. 2118.

Page No. 3

WAR DIARY
or
INTELLIGENCE SUMMARY.
(Erase heading not required.)

Place	Date	Hour	Summary of Events and Information	Remarks and references to Appendices
FRONT LINE	28/3/18	4 a.m.	There were a good many casualties. The barrage was again put down on the front line. The N.C.O. who was on duty (the officer on duty was killed) states that he tried again to patrol the right but found the trenches flattened and the ground like a ploughed field. He found nearly everyone killed or buried.	See map Appendix 2.
		5.15 a.m.	The enemy again put down a very heavy T.M. barrage on the left which probably killed any men left in that portion of the trench south of the CAMBRAI ROAD. At the same time the enemy could be seen jumping from shell hole to shell hole in front of LES FOSSES FARM. The S.O.S. was then fired & Rapid fire was opened on the enemy. On the centre of the line held by the Batt^n the enemy were about 100 yards away in front of the wire. The men still say they could have held them. Suddenly it was seen that the enemy were working around our left flank near By was attempted to form a flank defence but found to be impossible. The front line had then to fall back rapidly to prevent itself being surrounded. By this time most of the officers had become casualties. It quickly did the enemy come round the flank that the signallers and others of the advanced H.Q. (the old Adv Bde H.Q.) were not able to get out in time to escape. The extreme right of the battalion was also heavily shelled along with the left of the 3rd Divis^n. Here the enemy also broke through. From the Batt^n H.Q. we could see the line on our right retiring then on our own men withdrawing. The officer on the night threw back a platoon to try and form a flank defence, but again the enemy got round the flank forcing him to retire. The retreat was carried out in an orderly fashion covering fire being kept up with Lewis Guns rifles. The men at no time were out of hand, which says a lot for them inasmuch as nearly all the officers had become casualties, and it was the first time that many of the men had been in the trenches being new recruits. At no time was the shelling so heavy on the centre as it was on the flanks. I believe that the men on the flanks were completely wiped out. This seems to be proved by the fact that no officer or man belonging to the 3 platoons on the left or the platoon on the night have come back, and only one out of the next two platoons. In other (words

Norman Wickford Lieut Col.
comm^dg 7(S) Batt^n Cameron Highlanders.

Place	Date	Hour	Summary of Events and Information	Remarks and references to Appendices
FRONT LINE	28/3/18		only 7 men returned out of 6 platoons. Even before the last barrage there were very few of them left. The smoke and dust were such however that no one could see more than a few yards. What happened NORTH of the CAMBRAI ROAD it is impossible to say as the road at that point is sunk and, judging from the conduct of those who did come back, if any remained they must have fought to the last.	See Map Appendix 2
		8.15am	By this time the line had retired to the SHOTEL line and a line running North. There was no difficulty in getting the men to stop, only a few wounded men going back. There could not have been more than 3 officers and 150 O.R. who became mixed up with the 6" CAMERONS and the 8/10" GORDONS who were holding this line. The officers + NCOs at once began to collect their men. Capt WOOD was in charge of the 8/10 GORDONS. He was detailed to collect ammunition and to get it distributed along the line so it contained none. This was successfully done, partly from the dump at SHAMROCK CORNER & partly from the old trenches.	
		8.30am	In consultation with CAPT WOOD of the 8/10 GORDONS it was decided to make a counter attack & to retake the BROWN LINE. We sent messages both by pigeon and by power buzzer asking for an artillery barrage at 9.30am to support the counter attack. Evidently these messages never got through. We held back the counter attack till 10.30am so as we were constantly expecting the barrage and	Appendix 3.
		10.30am	did not wish to go forward in case we ran into it. About this time I received a message (copy attacked) from O/C A Coy. 6" CAMERONS who were on my left stating that his flank was in the air and that the enemy were as far as FEUCHY CHAPEL cross roads on his left and rear. I instructed him to form a flank defence and try to get in touch with his left and to hold on for all he was worth. I went along the 6" CAMERON front and found that it was strongly held. I also found 3 Vickers guns in this trench on top of the hill which I instructed to N.P.C.O.2) be disposed to swing round and support the flanks if necessary. I then saw CAPT WOOD and told him of the situation on the left and that I had decided to give up the idea of a counter attack until we saw how the situation developed. Capt. Wood also agreed to	

Norman Murgatroyd Lieut Col.
Commdg 7" (S) Batt" Cameron Highlanders.

WAR DIARY
or
INTELLIGENCE SUMMARY.
(Erase heading not required.)

Army Form C. 2118.

Page No. 5

Place	Date	Hour	Summary of Events and Information	Remarks and references to Appendices
FRONT LINE	28/3/16 29/3/16	10.30am to 1.30pm	to take one of his Companies and to put them into the strong points so as to thin out our front line and get greater depth. This was satisfactorily carried out. As the line was well organised and I felt I could be of no further use in the front line, I withdrew my M. Guns as previously instructed to the HQ of the 8/10 GORDON HIGHRS. As soon as I arrived I received an order for the line to withdraw to the army lines and I sent forward instructions accordingly, withdrawing to the HQ of the 8th SEAFORTH HIGHRS. What remained of its Battn was withdrawn to the old trenches near by, with the exception of one officer and a few men who had attached themselves to the 8/10 GORDON HIGHRS and remained with them in front of the enemy lines until the 8/10 GORDONS were relieved. This party killed many of the enemy in the afternoon by sniping and Lewis Gun fire. The batt. also was then withdrawn to WANQUETIN at 1am on the 29/3/16.	
		11 pm	To sum up, the enemy successfully annihilated by barrage fire our right and left flanks and tried to surround those who were left in the centre. All the officers of the front Coys having been either killed or wounded the line was methodically withdrawn under the N.C.Os. The support Coys had the same experience. No one returned from the platoons on the flanks and out of the four companies only one officer and about 100 or returned to the switch line. The men at all times were well in hand and showed a good fighting spirit. The rapid fire which was brought to bear on the enemy and afterwards the sniping must have caused him heavy casualties. Early in the attack the enemy brought up a light gun and pack animals were seen coming up with it. He also mounted several M.Gs which caused several casualties when the line was withdrawn from the switch line. The total casualties were Officers. 3 Killed 3 Wounded 10 missing O.R. 1 Killed 72 Wounded 299 missing	

Norman Mucford
Lieut Col.
Commdg 7 (S) Battn Cameron Highlanders

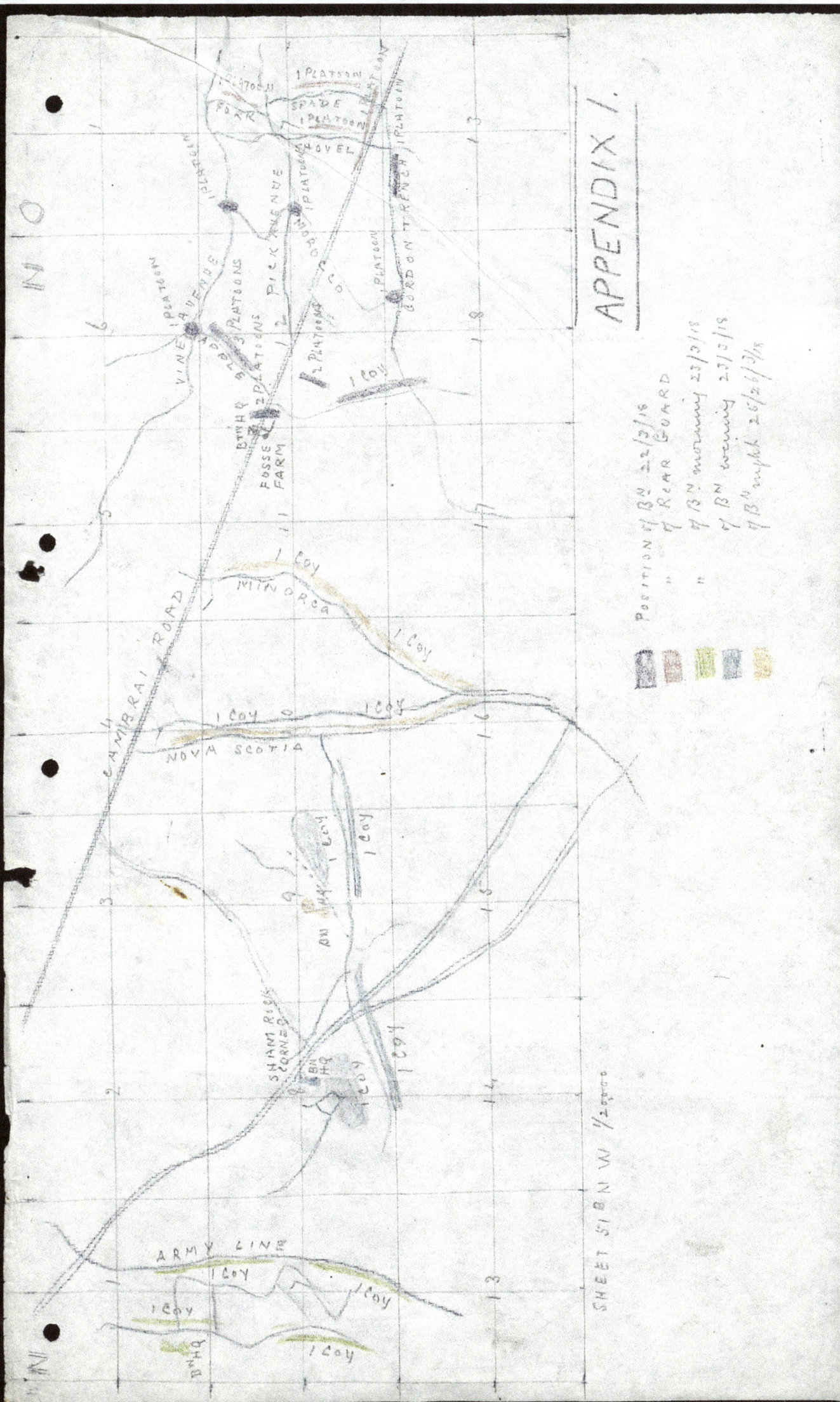

Copy Memo:- 2/Lt S.E. Smith A Coy 6' Cam'Drs
to Lt-Col A Macfie 7 Camerons

Our Left Flank is in the air as the enemy has advanced almost as far as Fench Chapel X Roads on the N side of CAMBRAI Rd. We have thrown back a protecting flank but in the event of another attack by enemy could you give instructions

(Signed) S.E. Smith
2/Lt
6' Cams

10.30 am.

APPENDIX 3.

Evidence of 10495 L/Sgt A McInnes

At 2.45 am 28/3/18 I went on duty along with 2/Lt Denholm. At that time it was quite quiet. We patrolled from the Right to the left of the Company front. By the time we got to the Left of the Coy the enemy had opened his barrage with gas shells on the front line. We waited at the extreme left of the Coy for fully half an hour and then we patrolled the whole Coy area to the Right. We then waited at the right of the Coy for about 20 minutes and started to go to the left again. By this time a heavy barrage opened again on the front line and also apparently on the back areas. We went to the Coy H Qrs which were in the centre of the Coy area to get advice from Capt Ireland. We then went right along to the Cambrai Road and saw that every one was standing to. This would be a considerable time after 4 am. We then came back and patrolled the right half of the Company and kept patrolling it until the enemy came over.

At about 5.15 am the enemy put down

2

down a very heavy T.M Barrage on the company front, more especially on the left. At this time we saw parties of the enemy jumping from shell hole to shell hole advancing from Tossee Tsom and we put up the S.O.S. We at once opened rapid fire. Shortly afterwards we saw the enemy advancing on the whole front. They were about 200 yards from where I was but were very near C.y H&no + I then put up the second S.O.S. Mr Sentolin was then killed. I then took charge of the right half coy which at that time consisted of about a dozen men and kept up rapid fire until I saw the enemy coming through about the centre of the coy. I could not see further to the left on account of the smoke of the barrage.

When the enemy were right on top of me we commenced to retire and kept up covering fire to allow the left of B coy to retire.

I saw nobody surrender. It was impossible for any one on the left of the Cambrai Road ~~and~~ to see what was going on

3

on the Right of the Road both on account of the dense smoke caused by the barrage and on account of the formation of the ground. I believe that practically everyone in D Coy was either killed or wounded before the enemy came across.

S/Sgt MacInnes, A.

"Evidence of 40234 Pte. A McIntosh
17766 Pte. J. Donaldson
203192 Pte. A. McDonald

We were on the Right Post of D Coy. During the first barrage which was very heavy on the front line more especially on the left of D Coy we took cover. The barrage slackened and went on to the Brown line and we came up into the trench and held our post. The barrage then came back on the front line heavier than ever. On instructions of S/Lt DENHOLM the post to which we belonged moved along two traverses to the Right to avoid the main force of the barrage. None of the other posts of D Coy with the exception of our one moved to the Right. The barrage lulled a little and we got on to the fire steps and we saw the enemy about 100 yards immediately in front of us. They were nearer to our trenches on the left. At that time an enemy aeroplane came over and apparently spotted the men in the front line as immediately he again put down a very heavy barrage on the front line. We kept up rapid fire on/ ↓ more especially on the left on the enemy and we distinctly heard rapid fire on both our left and our right. The next thing we saw was the enemy behind our front line and some of D Coy being forced up the trench from left to right. Then the line started to retire some men firing while the others got back.

We saw no men surrender and feel sure they would not surrender. We are sure that the large majority of those of D Coy who moved to the Right were killed during the retiral.

Pte A MacIntosh
J Donaldson
A McDonald

P. O. BOX 885.

THE MASONIC CLUB,
ALEXANDRIA, EGYPT

6. 1. 21.

Lt Col. J. Stewart. D.S.O.
9. Rowland Gardens.
London. S.W. 7.

Dear Sir,

I have read with great interest, & much pleasure, in the Overseas Daily Mail, that you are engaged in compiling the history of the 15th (Scottish) Division.

The map which I enclose herewith shows the exact position held by us on the Scarpe from the battle of Arras (April, 1917?) until the Boche push in March 1918. In addition, this particular map also illustrates one of the most exceptional stationary positions which

3.

will show you the distance we had to traverse "No man's land" in full view of the Germans on the other side of the bridge. Similarly they vacated their post at daybreak & so confident were they in being unmolested that I have seen them leave & enter with rifles slung. The opposing sentries gave one the impression that a coughing competition was being held all night, owing to the prevelence of "flu" at that time. (Decr 1917).

I do not know if subsequent personal careers are of any interest to you but during my period of recuperation, after being incapacitated when with the 15ᵗ Div., I was given a "soft job" as Ship's Adjᵗ on the famous "Leinster" torpedoed in the Irish Sea on 10ᵗʰ Octr, 1918.

I enclose herewith a cutting

4.

from the "Glasgow Herald" of 23rd Jany, 1919. relating to that event & may mention that in addition to the Royal Humane Society's highest award, in the following King's Birthday Honours I was awarded the M.B.E. (Military Division.)

I shall look forward with keen interest to the publication of the glorious work done by & recorded in the "History of the 15th (Scottish) Division & I am sure it will be a volume treasured in many ~~the~~ homes in all parts of the world.

Yours faithfully,
H. L. Parker.
late 7th Cameron Highlanders.
15th Division.

2.

existed, due entirely to "accident of battle". Here you have on one side our trenches well behind the German trenches on the other side and vice versa.

Reference 19. D. 8.0.9.6.

The above gave rise to this very curious position. At the bridge indicated by the reference we held a post — I think it must have been the remains of a café judging by the number of plates we found in the cellar —— and on the other side of the bridge the Germans also held a post "down a hole", — a distance of perhaps 15 yds. Acting on similar lines, the posts were changed every 24 hours. It was a remarkable case of "live and let live". About 8. P.m. (when it was my turn on duty) I'd take down a Corporal & three or four men & bring the others back. Reference to the map

EXTRACT FROM A PAPER. (DATE AND PAPER UNKNOWN.)

SCOTTISH GALLANTRY.

At its first metting for the year, held yesterday, the committee of the Royal Humane Society, under the presidency of Admiral C.D. Morant, made the following awards:-

Silver medal to Captain H.L. PARKER, Cameron Highlanders, for his heroic gallantry on the occasion of the torpedoing of the s.s. Leinster in the Irish Channel on October 10th. When thrown into the water Captain Parker, whose left arm is practically paralysed as the result of action in France, went to the help of a lady who could not swim, and succeeded in supporting her until they were picked up by a boat form the destroyer Mallard, after being in the water for one and three-quarter hours.

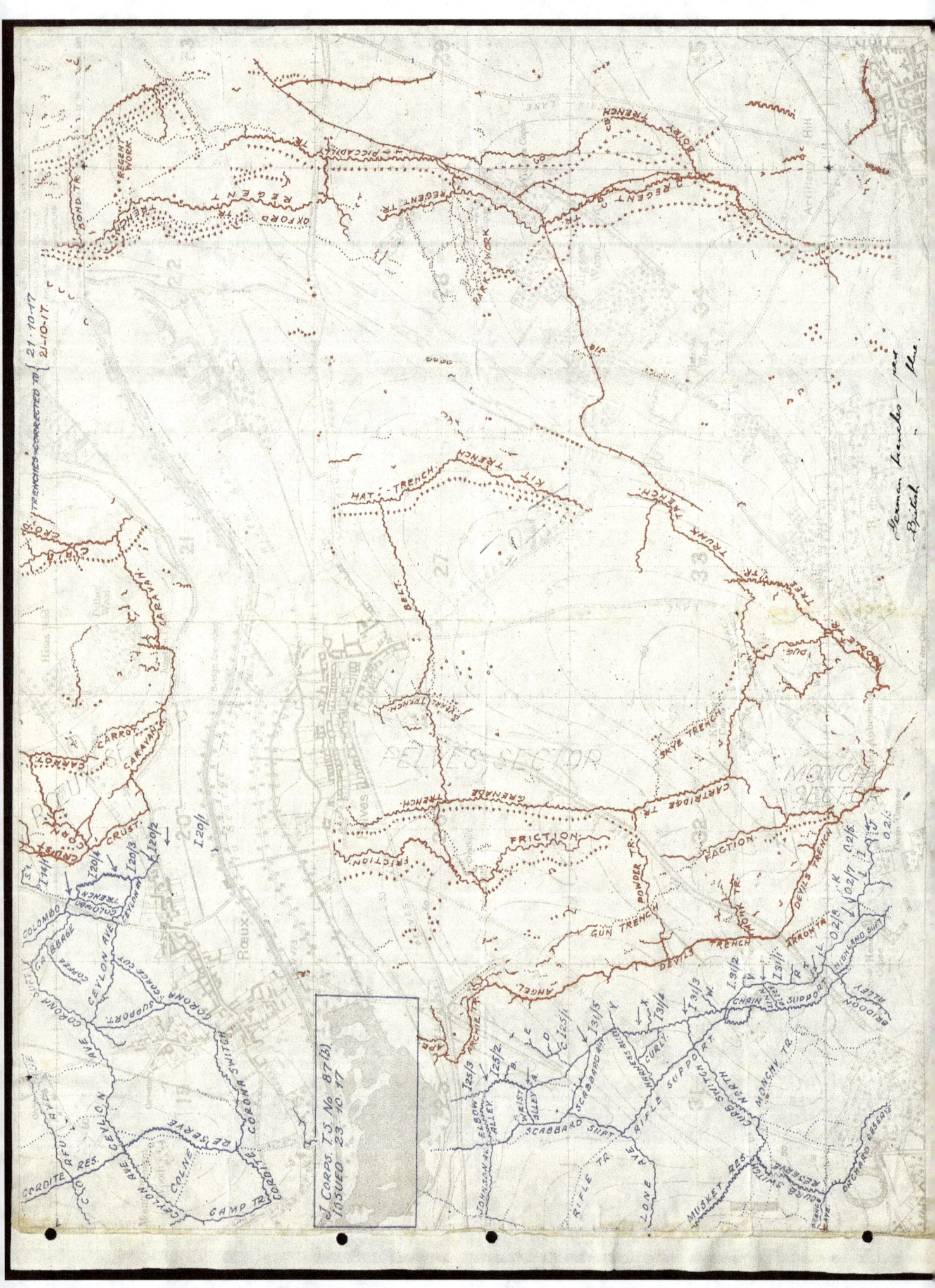

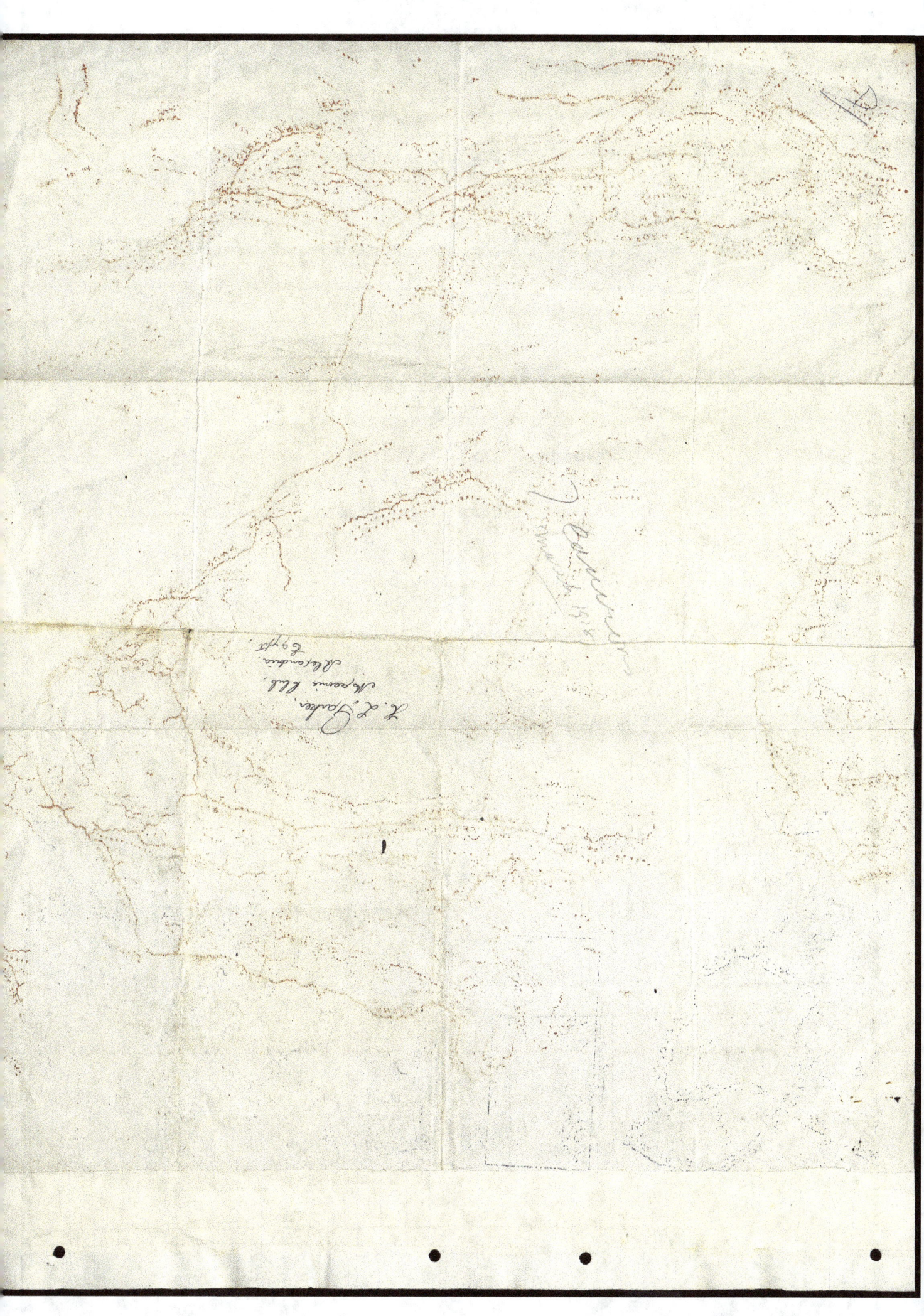

15th Div.
44th Bde.

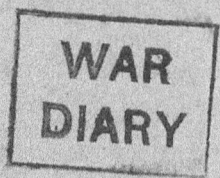

7th BATTALION

THE CAMERON HIGHLANDERS

APRIL 1918

~~Attached.~~

~~Report on Operations 22nd-29th April.~~

Vol 34

Ms B.(2).

Q31

CONFIDENTIAL

7TH (S) BN CAMERON HIGHLANDERS

War Diary

PAGES: 268 — to — 272

From 1st April 1918 to 30th April 1918

WAR DIARY
INTELLIGENCE SUMMARY

Army Form C. 2118.

Place	Date	Hour	Summary of Events and Information	Remarks and references to Appendices
ARRAS	1/4/18		Page No. 268. In connection with the fighting in which the Batt. took part towards the end of March last in the defence of ARRAS the following letters were received:— From G.O.C. 15th Division - dated 29 March 1918. "My Dear Colonel. A hurried line to tell you that while I feel most deeply your heavy losses I cannot sufficiently express to you my humble thanks for the gallantry and devotion shown by your Battalion yesterday under your leadership. If you have a moment let me know any details I know. I cannot but send on you or needless to say I would. I may say that the CORPS COMMANDER says the division then, it is hoped saved ARRAS and I know held the 7th Cameron Highrs bore the hardest brunt of the fight. Yours sincy H.F. Reed. (signed) From G.O.C. 44th Infantry Brigade dated 30/3/1918. My dear Colonel. I ask you and for and to thank you and all ranks under your command for the grand work during the last two months which culminates in the gallant fight put up by your Battalion on the 28th and I consider that it was entirely due to this fight that the 15th Division was practically saved from destruction, or at any rate an ignominious retirement. I should like you to convey to all ranks in your Battalion my sincerest sympathy with them in their losses, and the many friends they have left behind in the great struggle. The Divisional Commander to-day, in expressing his thanks for the work of the 44th Brigade, in all sincerity told me that our work has saved ARRAS. Yours very sincerely (signed) Edward Williams Brigadier General Commanding 44th Infantry Brigade. To Lt. Col. N. MacLeod D.S.O 7th Cameron Highrs. The 44th Infantry Brigade relieved the 45th Brigade. The 7th Cameron Highrs having so reduced in numbers had 1 Coy of the 9th Gordon Highrs attached and occupied the old Trenches in rear of the intermediate Army Line, just H.9.c at G.35.D.15.90. Norman MacLeod Lt Col	
IN RESERVE IN THE TRENCHES	2/4/18			

Army Form C. 2118.

WAR DIARY
or
INTELLIGENCE SUMMARY.
(Erase heading not required.)

Instructions regarding War Diaries and Intelligence Summaries are contained in F.S. Regs., Part II and the Staff Manual respectively. Title pages will be prepared in manuscript.

Page N° 269

Place	Date 1918	Hour	Summary of Events and Information	Remarks and references to Appendices
IN THE TRENCHES ARRAS.	3/4/18		The Coy of 9th Gordon High[rs] attached to the Batt[n]. occupied the 8/10th Gordon High[rs] on putting the intermediate Army line in a state of defence.—	
	4/4/18 to 8/4/18		The Divisional Boundaries were re-adjusted on the night of 3/4 April in conjunction with the 1st Canadian Division. The 7th Cameron High[rs] did not move but the Coy. of 9th Gordons attached to the Batt[n]. moved to 1st Canadian Army Line from G 36 d 1.9. to G 36 b 85.75. and to trenches in rear of Two and to dugouts in Bailleul.— 2nd Lt. N. MACLEOD was transferred to ENGLAND on the 23-3-18 (sick) and struck off strength; 9 O.R. evacuated & struck off strength.—	
ARRAS.	8/4/18		The 44th Infantry Brigade while relieved the 45th Infantry Brigade on the night of the 4/5th April; A+C. Coys. 7th Cameron High[rs] being relieved by A+C. Coys. 13th Royal Scots. "B+D" Coys[ly] 13 +D Coys 13th Royal Scots. On relief the Batt[n]. proceeded to Billets in PETIT PLACE, ARRAS. While in Divisional reserve work parties were furnished nightly.—	
IN THE TRENCHES ARRAS.	9/4/18 to 13/4/18	6 P.M.	The 44th Infantry Brigade relieved the 45th Infantry Brigade on the night of the 8/9th April. The 7th Cameron High[rs] were in reserve and relieved the 13th Royal Scots. B+D Coys. occupied the kennel & Coy. H.Q[rs]. near Batt. H.Q.; A+C. Coy. occupied the large dugout in the old German line at M.5.6.3.7. 10 O.R. evacuated and struck off strength. A draft of 22 O.R. arrived on the 6th arrived on the strength. A draft of 5 O.R. arrived on the 9th April.— 5 O.R. proceeded to the base on the 10th April as unfit for further service in the line. 1 O.R[?] off strength.— 2/Captain J.D.W. McCRACKEN was wounded in action on the 6th April.	
ARRAS.	13/14 April		The 7th Inf. Brigade were relieved by the 45th Inf. Brigade on the night of the 13/14 April. The 7th Cameron High[rs] were relieved by the 6th Cameron High[rs]. Each double Company of the 7th Cameron High[rs] were relieved by one Coy. of the 6th Cameron High[rs]. On relief the Batt[n]. proceeded by Companies to PETIT PLACE, ARRAS. While the Brigade was in Divisional Reserve in ARRAS work parties were furnished nightly by the Batt[n]: 9 O.R. were evacuated and struck off strength. 3 O.R. died of wounds on the 28 + 29th March. 4/M officers arrived by draft on the 6th April and taken on the strength of the Batt[n]. Capt[n] T. ORR, M.C. Capt[n] J. FINDLAY, M.C. Major C.C. GRIEVE was evacuated to ENGLAND sick on the 30-3-18 and struck off strength R.— The Commanding Officers lectured to A.B.C.+D Coys. in ARRAS. 7 O.R. wounded in Action on 10 + 12 April.— 3 O.R. evacuated and struck off strength.—	
	15-4-18			

Norman Munro [?]
Lt Col

Army Form C. 2118.

WAR DIARY
or
INTELLIGENCE SUMMARY.
(Erase heading not required.)

Page No. 270.

Place	Date	Hour	Summary of Events and Information	Remarks and references to Appendices
ARRAS.	17/4/18		Capt. J. FRASER, was invalided to ENGLAND on 1/4/18 and struck off strength. — I.O.R. arrived drafts retaken on strength. — 259 O.R. arrived by draft on the 13th inst. and were taken on strength.	
	18/4/18	9 p.m.	The 7th Cameron High[rs] relieved the 8/10th Gordon High[rs] on the rt. Division of the 18th April. Order of March was as follows: 'B' Coy, 'C' Coy, 'D' Coy, A Coy. nights. By platoons at 1 minute interval. — Route. — PORTE-DE-FER. Entrance to ST. SAUVER TUNNEL.	
IN THE TRENCHES.	20/21/4/18	8 p.m.	The 44th Infantry Brigade relieved the 143rd Inf[y]. Brigade in the line on the night of 20/21st April. The 7th Cameron High[rs] relieved the 6th Cameron High[rs] in Supports and were disposed as follows:— A Coy. 7th Cameron High[rs] relieved 'A' Coy. 6th Cameron High[rs] in LONDON AVENUE and INVERNESS TERRACE (H.25.d.) 'B' do. do. 'D' do. do. in BLANGY front and support lines from near PELVES LANE 'C' do. do. 'B' do. do. in BLANGY front and support lines (H.31.C.N.W.) and GAMBRA ROAD INCLUSIVE. 'D' Coy 7th Cameron High[rs] relieved 'B' Coy. 6th Cameron High[rs] in TALBOT RESERVE (H.31.C.N.W.) 1 platoon ST PATRICKS R[D]. (H 31a Central). 1 platoon r. Coy H.99	
	22/4/18		'D' Coy 7th Cameron High[rs] relieved 'B' Coy. 6th Cameron High[rs] in BLANGY front and support lines S. of CAMBRA, ROAD. On this date a warning order was received stating that whilst in the Line the 44th Brigade was to be prepared, if necessary, to be relieved by the support Brigade, 56th Division at short notice. —	
Bn. H.Q.	23/24/4/18		The 44th Inf[y]. Brigade was relieved by the 167th Brigade on the nights of the 23/24th April. The 7th Cameron High[rs] was relieved by the 8th MIDDLESEX REG[T]. A Coy. 7th Cameron High[rs] was relieved by 'A' Coy 8th MIDDLESEX REG[T]. On relief platoons proceeded independently via STATION BOULEVARD. 'B' Coy. do. do. 'C' Coy. do. CARNOT & the ROAD FORK in the 'C' Coy. do. do. 'B' do. do. FAUBOURG D'AMIENS at point- 'D' Coy. do. do. 'D' do. do. G.25.b.6.3. Thus the Bn. formed up and proceeded by Coys at 200 yards interval to BERNEVILLE VIA DAINVILLE and WARLUS. A portion of the Batt[n]. were conveyed in Motor waggons.	
BERNEVILLE.	24/4/18		IN CAMP cleaning up and inspections by Company officers. The Commanding officer arrived on this date and was taken on the strength. — A draft of 157 other ranks arrived by draft on this date and was taken on strength. L[t]. N.B. SIM. M.C. arrived by draft in the evening. —	

Norman Macfarlane Lt Col

WAR DIARY
or
INTELLIGENCE SUMMARY.
(Erase heading not required.)

Army Form C. 2118.

Place	Date	Hour	Summary of Events and Information	Remarks and references to Appendices
BERNEVILLE	25/4/18	7.20AM	Page No. 2711. The 44th Infantry Brigade moved by Bus on this date to CAMBLAIN-CHATELAIN and AUCHEL. The Brigade embarked on the WARLUS - AGNES LES DUISANS Road. The transport moved separately. AUCHEL was reached about 10'c. and companies marched to Billets. The Commander of the XVII Corps visited the Brigade at the Embussing point on the departure of the Brigade leaving this Corps, and the following communication was received by the G.O.C. 15th (SCOTTISH) Division. "I wish to express to you and to all ranks in the Division my great regret at your departure from the XVII Corps. We have been associated for many months, and I had hoped that we might have seen this battle through together. "That however is not to be, and I can only hope that the fortune o/s war may some day bring us together again. "The Division has a great reputation and may well be proud of it. I know that the honour of Scotland is safe in its keeping, and that those now serving will prove themselves worthy of those gallant men who have won glory for the Division in the past. "I wish you all good luck and success from the bottom of my heart. sd/ Charles Fergusson, Lieut. General. Commanding XVII. Corps.	
AUCHEL Ditto	26/4/18 27/4/18		The day was devoted to cleaning and Kit inspections. Company Training and Training of specialists under instructions. — 13 OR. arrived by draft on the 23 + 26 April and were taken on strength. — 9 OR. struck off strength; 31 other ranks previously reported missing, now reported. The 4/m officers arrived by draft on the 25/4/18 and were taken on strength:— Lt. S. McD. SHAW. Lt. E.F.B. CAMERON. " J.A. SINCLAIR. 2Lt. A.H. EDMISTON. " G. WEDDERSPOON. 2Lt. F.H. MACBETH. No.S/18231 Pte. J. WICKERS A.Coy.R " STEWART. 2Lt. N.J.N. WILSON. P. of W. on 28th March. " D. WISHART. 2Lt. J.P. CRAN. and R/9697 Pte A. MACDONALD 'B' Coy previously reported as " R.C. HAMILTON 2Lt. A KING. P. of W. 28.3.18 escaped and joined this our lines on 23-4-18. — 3 OR arrived by /6 on 21/4/18 and taken on strength.	
DITTO DITTO	28.4.18 29.4.18		Church Parades. Company Training with Specialists under instructors. The following awards have been made:— Lieut E.J.G. GIBB Military Cross. 2Lt. J. McMURRAY Do 2Lt. P. AUSTIN Do R/9708 Sgt (A/c.S.M.) T. YATES. DISTINGUISHED CONDUCT MEDAL. S/14297 4/Sgt. A. SIMPSON. M.M. MILITARY MEDAL. S/10495 L/Sergt. A. McINNES. S/10064 Sergt. R. GRIERSON. S/17913 C.S.M. AB.993 T. WRIGHT. S/17962 L/c. G. LOGAN. S/14322 Pte. S. HILL.	

Vivian Murphy Lt Col

Army Form C. 2118.

WAR DIARY
or
INTELLIGENCE SUMMARY.
(Erase heading not required.)

Place	Date	Hour	Summary of Events and Information	Remarks and references to Appendices
			Page No. 272.	
AUCHEL	30/4/18		Company training and Rifle practice on the range. Specialists under instructors — 4 other ranks struck by lightning on 13 & 14 April. 14 other ranks arrived by draft on 14 April and were taken on strength. 85 other ranks arrived by draft on 19 April and were taken on strength. 2 Lt. W.F. GRIEVE previously reported as wounded and missing 28/3/18. now reported P. of W. unwounded 28/3/18. Wounded 2 Lt. On 17 Cunnington.	

7th Bn Cameron Highlanders

MAY - Aug 1918

WO 35

Q 32

War Diary
of
7th (Service) Battalion Cameron Highlanders
Pages 273 to 275
From 1st May 1918 to 31st May 1918

Confidential

Army Form C. 2118.

WAR DIARY
or
INTELLIGENCE SUMMARY.

(Erase heading not required.)

Page No 273

Place	Date	Hour	Summary of Events and Information	Remarks and references to Appendices
AUCHEL.	1/5/18	10.30 a.m.	The Battalion paraded and marched to the Brigade parade at RAMBERT where ribbons were presented by M.G.O.C. 15th Division to Officers, N.C.O.s and men of the Brigade who gained medals during the recent operations. The Brigade Commander in a short address to the Brigade thanked all ranks for their work and also him in the attack on ARRAS. In the afternoon Rifle practice was carried out on RAMBERT RANGE. 2/Lt D.M.B. WHITE returned from 44th T.M.B.; 2/Lt J. HOGG arrived by draft on this date & was taken on strength. 17 O.R. arrived by draft and was taken on strength; 12 O.R. evacuated and struck off strength.	
Do. No.	2/5/18		The following is a copy of a communication received from the Brigadier General commanding the 44th Highland Brigade. From Brig.-Genl. Commanding 44th Highland Brigade. To O.C. 7/5 Bn. Cameron Hydrs.— I wish to thank you and all ranks of your battalion for the excellent behaviour and smart appearance of the Battalion the whole time we have been in billets in AUCHEL. I think it will be very gratifying to you to know that the Divisional Commander during the muster yesterday told me that he considered the 44th Brigade the best command in FRANCE, and that the new Army Commander (General BYNG) of the 75 Cameron Hydrs. never been anywhere or eleven men in any billage during the war than the 75 Cameron Hydrs. I think I would like you to notify all ranks of the Division Commanders high appreciation of their successful efforts to keep up the credit of the 44th Highland Brigade. (signed) Edward Hilliam. Brigadier General. Commanding 44th Infantry Brigade.	
Do.	3/5/18		2nd May. 1918. Company training on Battn. Parade Ground and specialists under instructors. Rifle practice was carried out at RAMBERT RANGE. Firing practice with Rifle grenades was carried out at 25 bombing ground. 10 O.R. evacuated and struck off strength. — 3.5.18. 1 O.R. died of wounds 30.4.18 — 2/Lt D.M.B. WHITE and 30.R. ranks wounded in action (accidental) — 3.5.18. now reported "wounded and P.O.W. 28.3.18." 3.O.R. previously reported as "missing unknown 28.3.18." now reported to the date to the XVII Corps area.	
Do.	4/5/18	8.30 a.m.	The 44th Infantry Brigade moved on this date to CALONNE-RICOUART and entrained and proceeded by rail to The 7/5 Cameron Hydrs proceeded by route march to Y"HUTS, ETRUN. ACQ where the Battn. detrained and proceeded by route march to Y"HUTS, ETRUN.	
Y HUTS ETRUN.	5/5/18		Church Parades. — 7 O.R. evacuated and struck off strength. P.O.N. 22.3.18. Escaped and came this over lines on the 4-5-18. — Reported P. of W. S/23969 Pte A. Wood }battalion } 447th T.M.B. /43228 " E. TULLOCH /35744 " M. McPHERSON	

W.Macleod Lt. Col.

Army Form C. 2118.

WAR DIARY
or
INTELLIGENCE SUMMARY.
(Erase heading not required.)

Instructions regarding War Diaries and Intelligence Summaries are contained in F.S. Regs., Part II. and the Staff Manual respectively. Title pages will be prepared in manuscript.

Page N°. 274.

Place	Date	Hour	Summary of Events and Information	Remarks and references to Appendices
Y HUTS ETRUN.	6/5/18	4 P.M.	The 44th Infantry Brigade moved to the support area on this date. The 7th Cameron High'rs were disposed as follows:— H.Q. & 2 Pl. PORTSMOUTH CAMP, G.3.b.9.2.; B & C Coys. COLLINGWOOD CAMP G.3.b.6.6.; CINEMA HUT G.2.b.6.3.; A Coy. TRAFALGAR CAMP G.3.d.7.4. Conferences attended by the Coy. O.C's at Bn. H.Q. at 200 yds interval on ARRAS-LENS ROAD; ARRAS RD.; ROND POINT, ST. CATHERINE.	
SUPPORT AREA ARRAS-LENS R⁰	8/5/18 9/5/18		3 O.R. Reinforcements arrived. In the following order:— The 7th Cameron High'rs relieved. 4 O.R. arrived by draft and taken on strength. 2 O.R. previously reported wounded, relieved.	
DITTO.	10/5/18		2ⁿᵈ Lt. J.G. TELFORD was on 29/4/18 evacuated to ENGLAND sick; is now officially reported P. of W. P. of W. 28/3/18 now confirmed. 5/15632 Pte. A. RUSSELL B Coy. reported prisoner since 28/3/18, escaped and came through our lines on 8/5/18; 1 O.R. previously reported wounded, relieved. 1 O.R. struck off strength.	
IN THE TRENCHES.	10/11/5/18	6 P.M.	The 44th Infantry Bde. relieved the 46th Inf. Bde. in the Right Section on night of 10/11 May. The 7th Cameron High'rs relieved the 10th Scottish Rifles in the Left and Sections. Companies of the 7th Cameron High'rs relieved in the Companies of the 10th Scottish Rifles.— Platoons moved up in file at 100 yds intervals via arden A.C. H.99.B.D. — L'ABBAYETTE — CAM VALLEY. by the following route, COLLINGWOOD CAMP, Road Junction G.9.C.7.1. — ST. NICHOLAS — OIL FACTORY — ST. LAURENT BLANGY	
DITTO	11/5/18		2 O.R. struck off strength; 5 O.R. arrived by draft and taken on strength. Barn H.Q. and R. Aid Post at M.16.d.1.8. 1 O.R. evacuated by draft and taken on strength.	
DITTO	12/5/18		S/8231 Pte J. VICKERS. A Coy awarded the Military Medal for an act of gallantry in the field.—	
DITTO	13/14/5/18		5 O.R. evacuated and struck off strength. The Battalion side stepped on the 13/14 May, taking over area held by 6th Cameron High'rs as far back as H.17.b.35.60. — The dispositions of Battalion after move was as follows:— A Coy in front line from pivoted Coy H.9.B. H.17.d.0.2.(inclusive) to H.17.b.35.60. with three platoons. The front platoon (reserve) with A Coy (M) AVENUE from H.16.a.60.60. to H.17.c.10.70. — B Coy as at present with C Coy in present C Coy H.Q's at H.16.a.5.2. C Coy in front line from H.17.d.10.60. to H.23.a.30.90 with 3 Platoons. The 4th Platoon (reserve) in a cellar at H.17.c.45.35. D Coy in Brigade trench as far north as H.16.b.70.60 with H.Q's at H.9.9 PIDDING trench at present occupied by C Coy. 6th Cameron H⁰. Of A Coy 7th Cameron H⁰ took over posts 1,2,3,4 & 6 from C Coy. 6th Cameron H⁰. N⁰ 5 post is a Liaison post. —	
	14/5/18		1 O.R. wounded in action on the 12/5/18	

Munro L. Lee

Army Form C. 2118.

WAR DIARY
or
INTELLIGENCE SUMMARY.
(Erase heading not required.)

Page N° 275.

Place	Date	Hour	Summary of Events and Information	Remarks and references to Appendices
IN THE TRENCHES.	14/5/18		An inter Company relief was carried on the night of 14/15 May. "A" Coy was relieved by "D" Coy. 12 O.R. joined Battn. from Divisional camp. 10 O.R. arrived by draft as 1st Divisional wing on 14.5.18 and taken on Strength. Capt Geo. J.S. LUMSDEN, M.C. proceeded on 14/5/18 to UNITED KINGDOM for Instructors Course at ALDERSHOT. Struck off strength. 24 O.R. joined the Battn. from Divisional wing. 1 O.R. arrived by draft at Divisional camp & taken on Strength.	
	17/5/18		2 O.R. wounded in action on 14 and 16th May respectively. 10 other ranks arrived by draft as 1st Divisional wing on 13th May and are taken on Strength.	
IN SUPPORT AREA.— STIRLING CAMP.	17/18/5/18		The 7th Cameron High[rs] was relieved by the 8/10th Gordon High[rs] in the Left section of the Bde. front on the night of 17/18 May. On relief the Battn. took over accommodation in STIRLING Camp vacated by 8/10th GORDON H[r]S and became Support Batt[n]. C.G. CAMERONS were relieved by C Coy. GORDONS. RIGHT FRONT. All relief Coys marched to Baggage Area and were disposed as follows:— "D" Coy. " " "A" Coy. " LEFT FRONT A Coy High — STIRLING CAMP. "B" Coy. " " "B" Coy. " RIGHT SUPPORT. B Coy Cam. VALLEY; D Coy in "A" Coy. " " "D" Coy. " LEFT SUPPORT. Cellars + old Gun pits ATHIES. 6 other ranks evacuated and struck off strength. 1 O.R. died of wounds 16.5.18. 3 other ranks struck off strength. 2 O.R. arrived by draft at 15th D.R.C. on 16.5.18 and taken on Strength.	
	19/5/18		2 O.R. arrived by draft at 15th D.R.C. coming 16.5.18 and taken on Strength. Pte. O.R. wounded in action on 17-5-18. 4 O.R. evacuated & Struck off strength. 2 O.R. struck off strength.	
DITTO.	20/5/18		5/13776 Pte A. GALLACHER and 5/22799 Pte J. NIGHT escaped from the GERMAN INTERNMENT CAMP & came through to British lines on 20 May, 1918. 2 O.R. reported on this date & taken on Strength.	
DITTO.	24/25/5/18	10.30 pm	The 47th Cdn[?] S[?] Bge was relieved by the 45th Cdn Regt. on the night of 24/25 May. The 7th Cameron High[rs] were relieved by 13th Royal Scots. On Completion of relief Companies proceeded to Peloton at 100" interval to ROCLINCOURT AREA and proceeded via Route— ST LAURENT-BLANGY; ST NICHOLAS; ST CATHERINE. ARRAS-LENS ROAD.— Disposition B. & C.— COLLINGWOOD CAMP.— A Coy. TRAFALGAR CAMP — D Coy Guinea Hut, Batt[n] H.Q[rs] PORTSMOUTH CAMP.	
BRIGADE IN DIVISIONAL RESERVE.	25/5/18 to 31/5/18		The Battn. whilst in reserve carried out a programme of training pertaining Scouts reviews and Musketry practice and Rifle Bombing, Mr Family of Lewis Gunners. Lieut S.A. LUEN and Lieut C.R.G. SCOTT arrived by draft on 25.5.18. 13 other ranks struck off strength. 2 other ranks taken on strength & attd. to Bn's wounded. 20 other ranks taken on strength. 1 O.R. reported from Tour of duty as Home on 24.5.18.— Lieut A.B.S. LEGATE Reported from Tour of duty as home on 23.5.18.—	

Murdoch Little

HONOURS AWARDED TO THE 7th BATTALION QUEENS OWN CAMERON HIGHLANDERS

C.M.G.

LT. Colonel J. W. Sandilands D.S.O.

D.S.O.

Major T. L. Cunningham
Major Norman MacLeod
a/Capt. J. A. Symon

M.C.

2nd Lieut. R. R. Anderson
Lieut. P. Austin
2nd Lieut. W. Black
2nd Lieut. J. T. Bockless
Capt. A. C. Baterman, R.A. M.C.
Lieut. J. Findlay
2nd Lieut. J. W. Graham
Lieut. E. J. C. Gibb
2nd Lieut. H. B. Goudie
2nd Lieut. R. Jardine
a/Capt. J. L. C. Jenkins
S/13232 C. S. M. A. Kidd
Capt. G. J. S. Lumsden
2nd Lieut. G. R. Morton
2nd Lieut. W. L. Muir-Kay
2nd Lieut. J. Miller
2nd Lieut. J. H. Mauchlin
2nd Lieut. J. McMurray
Lieut. I. J. McDonald
2nd Lieut A. R. Macdonald
2nd Lieut. T. Orr
2nd Lieut. R. B. Purdon
Captain W. G. S. Stuart
2nd Lieut N. S. Sim
2nd Lieut. R. W. B. Semple

D.C.M.

S/13635 C.S.M. C. Davie
Sgt. J. Drysdale
3074 C.S.M. P. Fleming
S/13537 L/Sgt. W. C. Lamb
S/15857 a/C.S.M. J. Little
S/14241 C.S.M. J. McGill
Sgt. J. Montgomerie
S/12647 a/B.S.M. A. Scott
S/13840 L/Sgt. H. Winning
9708 a/C.S.M. T. Yates

M.M. with Bar

6765 Sgt. A. Macdonald
S/14147 Sgt. M. Morrison
S/15565 Pte. J. MacLeod
S/14297 Sgt. A. Simpson

M.M.

40965 Pte. J. Allan
R/5563 a/C.S.M. D. Anderson
S/359184 L/Cpl. J. Anderson

.2.

M. M. Continued

S/17792 Pte. J. Boyle
S/18090 Pte. R. Bell
S/18578 Pte. A. Craig
18323 A/C.Q.M.S. R. Cameron
8900 Cpl. A. Donegan
15513 Cpl. W. Fulton
S/141016 Pte. H. Finlay
S/43231 L/Cpl. J. Forsyth
S/16816 L/Cpl. R. Gardner
S/14684 Sgt. R. Grierson
S/23439 Pte. T. Govern
S/20039 Pte. J. Healy
S/14322 Pte. S. Hill
S/14002 Pte. W. Johnston
18641 L/Cpl. J. Kelly
22946 L/Cpl. J. Keiller
200334 A/Sgt. M. R. King
17962 L/Cpl. C. Logan
S/16957 L/Cpl. J. MacDougall
S/16536 Sgt. D. H. McGilp
S/13888 L/Cpl. J. McGowan
14069 Sgt. G. McLean
15565 Pte. J. MacLeod
25532 Sgt. D. Maxwell
14147 Sgt. M. Morrison
10501 A/Sgt. T. Morgan
S/1039 L/Sgt. W. Mackay
S/12095 A/Sgt. A. McInnes
S/13686 L/Cpl. W. McMillan
S/16086 Pte. T. McLellan
200204 L/Cpl. J. Nicolson
S/16973 Cpl. W. Ramage
9808 Cpl. T. Rowett
26863 L/Cpl. W. Ross
23246 Pte. J. Rose
S/13024 A/L/Sgt. G. S. Sutherland
S/12824 Sgt. R. F. J. Small
14032 L/Cpl. J. Shumacker
S/200542 L/Cpl. J. Stoddart
S/18170 Cpl. J. Spiers
E/9039 Pte. J. Spence
R/8983 L/Sgt L. Smith
S/14297 Cpl. A. Simpson
S/16738 Pte. W. Train
S/21669 L/Cpl. E. Thomson
22930 Cpl. W. Taylor
16391 Pte. J. Tulloch
S/18231 Pte. J. Vickers
S/122993 Sgt. T. Wright
14140 L/Cpl. R. Young

Meritorious Service Medal

16824 A/Sgt. R. Burton

Royal Humane Society Parchment for Saving Comrades Life from Drowning

S/23888 Pte J.H. Ritchie

Mentioned in Dispatches

Lieut. R. R. Anderson
13184 L/Cpl. A. Bell
5651 C.S.M. J. Cranston

Mentioned in Dispatches

Captain A. R. Chapman
Major P. McF. Cram
Lieut. G. J. S. Lumsden
S/13901 Cpl. P. Macdonald
S/15814 L/Cpl. J. McCallum
S/13008 Pte. A. E. Morgan
Captain K. Macrae
S/14241 Sgt. J. S. McGill
Major Norman MacLeod
 13241 Pte. W. Macintosh
Lieut. Colonel Norman MacLeod
2nd Lieut. J. Mackenzie
Lieut. J. H. Mauchlin
Lieut. J. D. W. McCracken
Captain A. Ogilvie
 13866 Pte. J. Oliphant
 16137 L/Cpl. J. O'Rourke
Lieut. J. S. Robertson
Lieut. Colonel Sandilands D.S.O.
Lieut. W. G. S. Stuart
Lieut. J. A. Symon
 15620 Cpl. T. Torrance
S/13603 Q.M.S. T. F. Watson
 13264 R. Q.M.S. J. Wilson

Belgium Croix de Guerre

S/16824 A/Sgt. R. Burton
R/ 3871 R. S. M.   W. Vase
S/13264 R.Q.M.S.   J.P.W. Wilson

TRAINING CADRE
39TH DIVISION
118TH INFY BDE

7TH BN. Q.O. CAMERON HDRS
JUN - AUG 1918

16

T.C/39   J.6 36   118/39

G 33

Confidential

War Diary
—of—
7th Battalion The Queen's Own Cameron Highlanders Training Staff

From 1/6/18   To 30/6/18

Pages 276 - 280 (both inclusive)

Went to 116 Bn 39 Rn
10-8-18

Army Form C. 2118.

WAR DIARY
or
INTELLIGENCE SUMMARY.

(Erase heading not required.)

Page No. 276.

Place	Date	Hour	Summary of Events and Information	Remarks and references to Appendices
PORTSMOUTH CAMP NEAR ROCLINCOURT.	1-6-18		The Commanding Officer delivered Lectures to the Companies prior to going into the line and the programme of the day was devoted to cleaning Camp and preparing for the line.	Operation Order No. 129
	1/2 /6/18	8 P.M.	The 44th Bn. Bge. relieved the 46th Bn. Bge. in the line on the night of the 1/2 June. 1918. The 7 CAMERON HIGH'RS relieved the 105th Bn. SCOTTISH RIFLES as 6½ Bn FRONT BATT. Companies of the Camerons relieved similar Companies of the Scottish Rifles. Companies marched off in the order C', A', B', D', HQ. by platoons at 100 yards interval. Head of Column passed junction of CHANTECLER ROAD and ROCLINCOURT ROAD at G.5C.6.4. at 9.10 P.M. Route was by 'B' Track to junction with ROCLINCOURT and CHANTECLER – PLANK ROAD. RENDEZVOUS for Guides – junction of PLANK ROAD and GAVRELLE ROAD H.8 Central.	
	6/7/18		The 4/5th ROYAL HIGH'RS relieved the 7th CAMERON HR'S on the night of 6/7 JUNE. On relief the 7th Camerons withdrew to PETITE PLACE, ARRAS. 'B' & 'D' Coys at RUE DES TROIS VISAGES. (Billets vacated by 4/5 ROYAL SCOTS.) 'C' Coy H'Qrs. proceeded to junction of PLANK ROAD and GAVRELLE ROAD at 9.30 P.M. to await incoming Platts. The order of relief was as follows:– 'C' Coy. 4/5 ROYAL H'R'S relieved 'C' Coy 7 CAMERON HR'S. 'A' Coy. 'B' Coy. 'D' Coy. 'A' Coy. Completion of relief was notified to Bn. HQ. by wire using code word "LAST". 29 MR.C.	
			LT. R. MACFADYEN joined Bn. Wing on 15.5.18 and taken on strength of the Bn. D. of R. struck off strength. The following Casualties occurred during the last tour of the Trenches:– KILLED – 2 O.R. DIED OF WOUNDS 2 O.R. WOUNDED 'K' CAPT R.B. PURDON, M.C. LT. G. WEDDERSPOON. (AT DUTY). 16 Other Ranks. LT. N.S. SIM, M.C.	
ARRAS.	10/6/18		The 7th Bn. CAMERON HIGH'RS was on this date amalgamated with the 6th Bn. Cameron High'rs and a Battalion Training Staff formed from both Bn'ns to continue a nucleus of the 7th Bn. The Training Staff detailed from the 7th Bn. proceeded to join the 39th Catre Division to provide a Training Staff for units of the U.S.A. Army. All transport of the 6th & 7th Batt'ns. surplus to the establishment of the 6th Bn. and the Bn. Training Staff proceeded to the Base. The following officers and other ranks from the 7th Bn. proceeded on the 10th inst. with the Bath. Training Staff:– LT. A.B.S. LEGATE. E. GEORGE WEDDERSPOON. L. & Q.M. J. AITKENHEAD. and 41 other ranks. The Transport of Bath. Training Staff proceeded to BARLIN on same date.	

Army Form C. 2118.

WAR DIARY
or
INTELLIGENCE SUMMARY.
(Erase heading not required.)

Instructions regarding War Diaries and Intelligence Summaries are contained in F.S. Regs., Part II. and the Staff Manual respectively. Title pages will be prepared in manuscript.

Page No. 277.

Place	Date	Hour	Summary of Events and Information	Remarks and references to Appendices
ARRAS	10/6/18		All vehicles, equipment and personnel & Transport surplus to establishment of 1 Batt., plus the establishment of the Training Staff Batt. proceeded on this date to COQ, near LE TOQUET under Lt. J.H. MACHLIN, M.C. with 20 other ranks. The following Officers and other ranks were absorbed in the 6th Bn Cameron High'rs:— Lt Col. N. MACLEOD. D.S.O. & Command. Lt S. McD. SHAW. 2Lt P.F. PRENTICE. and 383 other ranks. Major R. McFCRAM. 2nd in Command. Lt D. STEWART. Lt A. BANKS. Capt T. ORR. M.C. Lt D. WISHART. 2Lt H.T. MACBETH. Lt J.R. PARK. Lt E.R.B. CAMERON. 2Lt M.T.H. WILSON. Lt R.A.M. MacCROSTIE. Lt R.S.D. POLLOCK. 2Lt A. KING. Lt R.C. HAMILTON. 2Lt R. AUSTIN. 2Lt J. HOGG. Lt E.V.G. GIBB. M.C. 2Lt R.C. MITCHELL. 2Lt J.R. CRAN. The following Numbering Officers and other ranks were transferred to the Base M.(S) Depot:— Capt J. FINDLAY. M.C. Lt S.A. LUEN. and 466 other ranks. Lt E. CAMERON. Lt R. MACFADYEN. Lt J.A. SINCLAIR. 2Lt W.A. BAYNES. Lt C.R.G. SCOTT. 2Lt G.S. GREIG. 2Lt. A.H. EDMISTON.	

7th Bn. Q.O. Cameron Highrs. Training Staff. JUNE 1918.

Army Form C. 2118.

WAR DIARY
or
INTELLIGENCE SUMMARY.
(Erase heading not required.)

Hour, Date, Place		Summary of Events and Information	Remarks and references to Appendices
June 19		Page No 298	
LENS 11. 4/100.000. MAROEUIL. LENS 3 I 5.9.	10th.	Formed into a Cadre Battalion for the purposes of Training American Bn. Established to Officers old 60 o.Rs. One designation being 7th. Bn. Q.O. Cameron Highrs. Training Staff, 118th. Infantry Brigade, 39th. Division. B.E.F. Entrained at MAROEUIL at 10a.m.	Nil.
HAZEBROUCK. 5A. 1/100.000.		+ proceeded to BARLIN. LENS. I.H.H.S. by light railway. Railed to line in BARLIN before entraining for AUDRUICQ. HAZEBROUCK 2A 90.52. Weather fine. Casualties nil.	
	11th.	Spent night in train. Arrived AUDRUICQ at 4.15 p.m. and marched to NORTKERQUE. HAZEBROUCK. 2A 30.52. arriving about 6 p.m. where we billeted for the night. Weather fine. Casualties nil.	Nil.
CALAIS 13. 1/100.000	12th.	Left NORTKERQUE at 9 a.m. and marched to RODELINGHEM. CALAIS 13 2.F. 15.02. arriving about 11 a.m. Every body busy cleaning and settling into billets. Weather fine. Casualties nil.	App. 1. Nil.
	13th.	Cleaning equipment & getting billets &c. into proper condition. Making sundry necessities for billets. Weather fine. Casualties nil.	Nil.
	14th.	Instructors under Specialist Officers for refresher classes. Physical training for half an hour. Weather fine. Casualties nil.	Nil.
	15th.	Instructors under Specialist Officers. Physical training. Church parade. Men own bathing. Americans Bn. undergoing training. Weather fine. Casualties nil.	Nil.

Army Form C. 2118.

WAR DIARY
INTELLIGENCE SUMMARY.   JUNE 1918.

(Erase heading not required.)

Hour, Date, Place	Summary of Events and Information	Remarks and references to Appendices
CALAIS 13. 1/100.000 June 18.	Page No 279	
Ref. Map RODELINGHEM 16th.	Lecture by Capt. Christian T.C. to Instructors on Training of American troops. Weather fine. Casualties to book 1.	R/Nil.
17th.	Left RODELINGHEM for CAMP at CALAIS. 13. 3.F. 96.75. arriving at 10am. Erecting bell tents and marquee. Camp necessaries on arrival of work. Affiliated to 3rd. Bn. 119th. Regiment. A.E.F. C.O. and Adj. visit C.O. of American Bn. re training on following day; weather fine. Casualties nil.	App. 2. R/Nil.
3.F.96.75. 18th.	Officers & Instructors parade at 9am with American Bn. & proceed to Training Area. Training hours 9am – 11.30am and 1.30pm. to 4.30pm. Weather fine. Casualties nil.	R/Nil.
19th.	Do. Weather, little rain morning. Casualties nil.	R/Nil.
20th.	Weather, wet evening. Officers & Instructors lecturing & talking to Americans in billets. Casualties nil.	R/Nil.
21st.	Officers & Instructors supervising training on Training Area. Lt. Col. L. Anderson. M.C., late C.O. of 6th. Bn. Q.O. Cameron Highrs. reports as C.O. of this Staff. C.O. visits C.O. of American Bn. re training reorganisation. Weather fine but windy. Casualties nil.	R/Nil.

WAR DIARY / INTELLIGENCE SUMMARY

Army Form C. 2118.

JUNE. 1918.

Place	Date	Hour	Summary of Events and Information	Remarks and references to Appendices
Rel. Trops. CALAIS. 13. 1/100,000.			Page No 280	
	22nd.		Officers' Instruction out on a Recce. Scheme with Americans from 9 a.m. to 1.30 p.m. Half day. Weather very windy but dry. Casualties nil.	Rller.
3.F.86.7.S.	23rd.		C.O. and Capt. Christison up the line reconnoitering WINNEZEELE LINE of defence behind the American Regimental wood held in event of an enemy attack on 2nd Army front. Our men at Baths in LICQUES. Weather windy but fine. Casualties from Hospital 1 O.R.	Rller.
	24th.		Weather very wet. Not much training in consequence. Casualties nil.	Rller.
	25th.		Gas Demonstration by P.G.O. to 3 Coys. all forenoon. One Coy. on ranges in afternoon. 1 Coy. on Outpost Scheme, others usual training. Weather fine. Casualties nil.	Rller.
	26th.		Training i.e. Tactical Schemes (Coys.), Entrance digging Range. Specialists under Specialist Officers. Lt. A.K. Macdonald rejoined from leave to U.S. Weather fine. Casualties nil.	Rller.
	27th.		Training i.e. Range, Assault Course, Tactical Schemes, Specialists under Specialist Officers. Lecture by C.O. to Officers + N.C.Os. of 3/119th. Regt. U.S.A. Weather fine. Casualties nil.	Rller.
	28th.		Training i.e. Trench digging, Wiring, Range, Assault Course, Tactical Schemes and Specialist training. Weather fine. Casualties nil.	Rller.
	29th.		Training i.e. Route march, transport + cookers out. Weather fine. Our Sign. Officer, Lt. A.K. Macdonald left us to go to join the 119th. Regt. U.S.A. Casualties nil.	Rller.
	30th.		Instruction + men at Baths at LICQUES. Football match against 119th. A. & S. H. Training Staff, result 2 goals each. Weather excellent. Casualties nil.	Rller.

Operation Order No 1 by
Captain A.F.P. Christison M.C.
Commanding 7th Cameron Highrs

SECRET   Tuesday 11th June 1918

Routine for Tomorrow

Reveille   6.30 am
Breakfast   7.30 am

1. The Battalion will move from NORTKERQUE to RODELINGHEM tomorrow 12th June.

2. Packs will be stacked on G.S. Wagon at Billet No 9 at 7 am.
The ~~Billet~~ Mess Cart will be at Billet No 88 at 8.45 am.

3. Officers valises will be stacked in the Square by 8.30 am

4. COMS Pollock will report to Capt McDONALD at 8.30 am in the Square, with a bicycle to go on ahead to look after Billets.

App. 1

Operation Orders Page 2

5. Battalion will parade in the Square ready to march off at 8.50 am. Dress – Battle Order with Balmoral.

6. Transport will be ready to move off in rear of Battalion

R.W. Marshall Lieutenant and Adjutant
7th Cameron Highlanders

11th June 1918

Distribution:-

C O
Q M
Corpl Milne Transport
C S M Keith
War Diary

Operation Order No 2 by Capt. A.F.P. Christison M.C.
Commanding 7th Cameron Highlanders Training Battalion

Secret.   Sunday 16th June 1918.

1. The 7th Cameron Highlanders Training Battalion will proceed to YEUSE on Monday 17th June 1918.

2. The Battalion will parade in front of the Q.M. Stores, ready to move off at 10 a.m.

3. Dress. - Full Marching Order.

4. Route. - Via LANDRETHUM.

5. Billeting Party. L.Q.M.S's. Pollock and Semple will report to Q.M at Q.M Stores at 8.30. a.m. with bicycles.

6. All Battalion Stores and Officers' Valises will be stacked outside Q.M. Stores at 8.30. a.m.

7. Mess carts will report to Officers Mess at 9.30 a.m.

8. Transport will move in rear of Battalion.

                    Signed N.R. Marshall. Lieut & A/Adjutant
                    7th Cameron Highlanders Training Battalion

DISTRIBUTION:- C.O.
               Q.M.
               R.S.M.
               CPL. MILNE
               WAR DIARY
               FILE

7th Camerons H/S. S.S. - 2/2/7 - 5/8/18

118th Infantry Brigade
―――――――――――

Herewith War Diary of
this Battalion for month ended 31/7/18
Please acknowledge receipt hereon.

R.R. Marshall Lt. & A/Adj. for Lieutenant Colonel
Commanding 7th Cameron Highdrs
Training Staff

WR 37

Q 34

War Diary

of

The Battn The Queens Own Cameron Highlanders
Training Staff

From 1st July 1918   To 31st July 1918

Confidential

WAR DIARY

INTELLIGENCE SUMMARY

(Erase heading not required.)

Army Form C. 2118.

JULY 1918.

Place	Date	Hour	Summary of Events and Information	Remarks and references to Appendices
Ref. MAP. CALAIS S.A. VEUSE 3 F/14.30.	1st.		Training. General Gushing inspects 119th. Regt. at training Bn. on Parade grounds till 1 p.m. waiting for General. Inspection lasted about 10 mins. Orders for Col. Anderson M.C. and Capt. Christian M.C. to proceed with 3/119th. Regt. A.E.F. to forward areas on 2nd. inst. Weather fine. Casualties nil.	Nil.
	2nd.		American Division leaves area. Lt. Col. Anderson M.C. + Capt. Christian M.C. go with 3/119th. Regt., leaving about 9.30 a.m. We move our Camp from wood down to a field in VEUSE village, Officers going into Billets. Weather fine. Casualties Nil.	Nil.
	3rd.		Arranging new Camp + Building necessary Camp requisites. Salvaging + collecting stores left behind by Americans. Weather fine. Casualties Nil.	Nil.
	4th.		Rifle + Ammunition Inspection. Cleaning up Transport Lines vacated by Americans. Weather fine. Casualties Nil.	Nil.
	5th.		Physical Training + Fatigues. C.O. + Capt. Christian M.C. return from 3/119th. Regt. A.E.F. Casualties Nil. Weather fine. about 10 p.m.	Nil.
	6th.		Lt. Legal left at 1 p.m. to join 3/119th. Regt. A.E.F. as Liaison officer + 5 Sgt. Instructors left us to be attached temporarily to 116th. British Inf. Bde. Weather fine.	Nil.
	7th.		Baths at LICQUES. Weather fine.	Nil.
	8th. to 15th.		No Americans to train. Physical Training + Fatigues. Instructors told classes lectures games thereselves. Three Instructors away on Courses. Weather good. Casualties nil. Col. Anderson goes on three weeks Special Leave from 12th. July to 2nd. August 1918.	Nil.
	16th. & 17th.		Four Officers + two N.C.Os. out on a Skeleton Divisional Tactical Scheme. Allotted on LICQUES. CALAIS S.A. 3.F.21.42. night of 16th/17th. Continuing Scheme on 17th. Returned to billets at VEUSE at 3.30 pm. Little rain on 17th. Casualties Nil.	Nil.

2449 Wt. W14957/M90 750,000 1/16 J.B.C. & A. Forms/C.2118/12.

WAR DIARY
INTELLIGENCE SUMMARY

JULY 1918

Army Form C. 2118.

(Erase heading not required.)

Instructions regarding War Diaries and Intelligence Summaries are contained in F.S. Regs., Part II. and the Staff Manual respectively. Title Pages will be prepared in manuscript.

Place	Date	Hour	Summary of Events and Information	Remarks and references to Appendices
Reg. Inf. CALAIS. S.A.	18th		No Answers. Physical Training. Classes & Lectures. Instructors to bring turns at giving Lectures. Lt. Legale returns from 3/119 R. Regt. A.E.F. an 18th. Heavy thunder storms every day. Casualties nil.	Rain
YEUSE 3.F.74.80.	21st			Rain
	22nd		Officers under L.G.O. for instruction on L.Gun. N.C.Os. on map reading. Very wet day. Casualties nil	Rain
	23rd		Officers under L.G.O. N.C.Os. organised into platoons and under L.G.O. for instruction on Tactical handling of L.Gun. Weather fine.	Rain
	24th		Officers & O.Rs. on range. Firing practices at 400 & 600 yards. Weather fine. Casualties nil.	Rain
	25th		Day spent packing up & cleaning Camp preparatory to moving to Billets in LISTERGAUX tomorrow. Weather fine. Casualties nil	Rain
HATEBROUCK 1/40000 LISTERGAUX 2A.7.3.	26th		Left YEUSE for billets in LISTERGAUX by march route. Arr. settled in new billets by 2pm. Weather wet. Casualties nil.	APP 1 Nicer Rain
	27th		Nothing doing. Very wet day. Casualties nil	Rain
	28th		Left LISTERGAUX at 3.30 pm for VII Corps Reinforcement Camp WATTEN by march route to entraining point. Two trains took us and move off. Weather fine. Casualties nil	APP 2 Rain

2449 Wt. W14957/M90 750,000 1/16 J.B.C. & A. Forms/C.2118/12.

WAR DIARY

INTELLIGENCE SUMMARY JULY 1918.

Army Form C. 2118.

Place	Date	Hour	Summary of Events and Information	Remarks and references to Appendices
Ref. Map. HAZEBROUCK 1/100000 WATTEN 2.C.58.00.	29th		WATTEN. Instructions received for us to take over 823 O/Rs. and about 20 Officers from the Scottish Depot, CALAIS, leaving by train and arriving WATTEN Station on 30th. inst. where we would join train & take over command of then organised them into a battalion & proceed with them & detrain at ARNEKE where we would receive further orders. Weather fine. Casualties Nil.	Ritten.
	30th.		Left WATTEN at 12.30 p.m. arriving ARNEKE Station about 4 p.m. Men had to meal in fields adjoining station then marched to Billets which were very scattered & none too good. Bn in billets about 8.30 p.m. Bn. made up of Black Watch, Seaforths, Gordons. Stopped 350 O/Rs at CASSEL Station to join A. & S. H. who also had charge of a Bn. of reinforcements. Our Bn. are reinforcements for 51st Division under gun command for work on back areas of 2nd Army Front. The Bn. to be called XIXth Corps Reinforcement Bn. & only to be used as such & under direct orders from D.A.G. 3rd Echelon. Weather fine. Casualties Nil.	APP. 3 Rain
ARNEKE 3. E. 90. 99.	31st		Left ARNEKE and marched via CASSEL to a Staging Camp in ST. ELOY Area, HAZEBROUCK Map. 3. H. 30.85. Rested in route in field between CASSEL and STEENVOORDE for 3 hrs. where men had their midday meal. Arrived Camp about 6.30 p.m. where we had to use tents. Weather very hot. Slight shelling as we passed through STEENVOORDE. Two other ranks slightly wounded.	APP 4. Rain.

OPERATION ORDER No. 3. BY CAPTAIN A. F. P. CHRISTISON M.C.
Commanding 7TH BATTALION THE QUEEN'S OWN CAMERON
HIGHLANDERS TRAINING STAFF.

SECRET   THURSDAY, 25th July, 1918.

Ref.   HAZEBROUCK 5.a.

1. - The 7th Cameron Highlanders Training Staff will move to Billets in LISTERGAUY tomorrow, 26th July, 1918.

2. - The Battalion will parade in full marching order and ready to move off outside CHATEAU at 9.50 a.m.
   Transport will move in rear of Battalion.

3. - ROUTE.   Battalion will pass starting point ROAD JUNCTION 3.a.10.98, at 10 a.m.; thence by ARTRES - NORDAUSQUES ROAD - NIEILES LEBARDES - 2.a.40.24. - 2.a.83.28.

4. - All stores will be stacked at Quartermasters Stores by 8 a.m.   Blankets, rolled in bundles of ten, will be stacked at the same place by 8.30 a.m.
   Officers' Valises will be stacked outside CHATEAU by 9 a.m.
   The Mess Cart will report at Officers' Mess at 9 a.m. for Mess Kit.

5. - A Billeting party consisting of the Lieutenant Quartermaster and two C.Q.M.S's will report to Orderly Room at 8.30 a.m.

6. - Billets &c will be thoroughly cleaned before leaving. All latrines &c will be filled in.
   The Commanding Officer will inspect Camp at 9 a.m.

7. - The G.O.C., 39th Division will inspect the Battalion whilst on the march. Strict march discipline will be maintained.

                                                Captain,
7th Bn., The Queen's Own Cameron Highlanders Training
                    Staff.

Distribution.-

        O.C.
        Q.M.
         R.S.M.
        Cpl W. Milne.
        War Diary
        File.

SECRET   THURSDAY, 25th July, 1918.

APP. 7

SECRET.

OPERATION ORDER NO. 4 BY CAPTAIN A.F.P. CHRISTISON, M.C.,
COMMANDING 7TH. BATTALION QUEEN'S OWN CAMERON HIGHLANDERS
BATTALION TRAINING STAFF.
----

1. The Battalion will march to VII Corps Reinforcement Camp, WATTEN, today, 28th. July, 1918.

2. The Battalion will parade in full marching order in front of Orderly Room at 3.15 p.m.

3. Blankets, Officers' Valises and Orderly Room boxes will be stacked at Quartermaster's Stores at 2.30 p.m.

4. Mess Cart will be at Officers' Mess at 3 p.m.

5. The Quartermaster will detail 2 O.R. to remain in charge of surplus stores, one of whom will report location of store to Brigade. They will be rationed by Brigade Headquarters from 30th. July inclusive.

6. Rations for 29th. inst. will be carried on G.S. wagon.

7. Billets must be left thoroughly clean. The C.O. will inspect billets at 3 p.m.

R.H. Marshall. Lieutenant and A/Adjutant,
7th. Queen's Own Cameron Highlanders Bn. Training Staff.

Field, 28/7/18.

Distribution.
  C.O.
  Officers Mess.
  Q.M.
  R.S.M.
  File.
  War Diary.

APP. 3

SECRET.

OPERATION ORDER NO. 5 BY CAPTAIN A.F.P. CHRISTISON, M.C.,
COMMANDING 7TH. BATTALION QUEEN'S OWN CAMERON HIGHLANDERS
BATTALION TRAINING STAFF.
----

1. The Battalion will entrain at WATTEN at 12 noon on 30th. July and will detrain at ARNEKE.

2. The Battalion will parade at VII Corps Reinforcement Camp in full marching order at 11.30 a.m.

3. Officers' Valises will be stacked outside billets at 10 a.m.

4. The Mess Cart will collect Officers' Valises and convey them to Transport Lines.

5. The Mess Cart will be at Officers' Mess at 11.30 a.m.

6. The Transport will move to ARNEKE by march route under the Quartermaster.

7. Rations for 30th. inst. will be carried on the man. Rations for 31st. inst. will be carried on G.S. wagon. Rations for 1st. August and onwards will be drawn from Supply Officer, XIX Corps.

8. A Billeting Party consisting of the Signalling Officer and C.Q.M.S's Pollock and Semple will leave WATTEN at 8.30 a.m. and report to Area Commandant, ARNEKE, to take over billets for Battalion.

R.M. Marshall.
Lieutenant & A/Adjutant,
7th. Queen's Own Cameron Highanders Bn. Training Staff.

Field, 29/7/18.

Distribution.

C.O.
Officers Mess.
Q.M.
R.S.M.
File.
War Diary.

App. 4

OPERATION ORDER NO. 6 BY CAPTAIN A.F.P. CHRISTISON, M.C.,
COMMANDING XIX CORPS REINFORCEMENT BATTALION.
----

1. The Battalion will march from ARNEKE to a Staging Camp in the ST. ELOY area.

2. Companies will parade in Field beside Transport Lines at 10 a.m.   DRESS:- Full Marching Order.

3. Officers' Valises, Orderly Room Boxes, Camp Kettles, etc. will be stacked outside X by 9 a.m. where they will be picked up by the Transport and conveyed to Transport Field.

    X Billets

4. C.Q.M.S. Pollock will report to the Signalling Officer on Parade Ground at 10 a.m. with a cycle to go on ahead and take over camp.

Distribution:-
    C.O.
    O.C., "A" Coy.
    O.C., "B" "
    O.C. "C" "
    O.C., "D" "
    Q.M.
    File.
    War Diary.

                                R.R. Marshall
                                Lieutenant &A/Adjutant,
                                19th. Corps Reinforcement Battalion.

Field, 30/7/18.

SECRET & CONFIDENTIAL.

D.A.G., 3rd Echelon,
  G. H. Q.

      Herewith War Diary of 7th Bn. Cameron Highlanders for the period 1.8.18. - 14.8.18., the Battalion having been disbanded from the latter date.

      Kindly acknowledge receipt to this office.

22nd August, 1918.

                                Major-General.
                       Commanding 39th Division.

WR 38
39
40

Cursed

Q 35

War Diary
— of —
7th Bn Cameron Highlanders Training Staff
from 1/8/18 to 14/8/18

7th Cameron Highrs on XIX Corps Reinforcement Bn.

Army Form C. 2118.

Instructions regarding War Diaries and Intelligence
Summaries are contained in F. S. Regs., Part II.
and the Staff Manual respectively. Title pages
will be prepared in manuscript.

WAR DIARY
INTELLIGENCE SUMMARY.

(Erase heading not required.)

AUGUST 1918

Place	Date	Hour	Summary of Events and Information	Remarks and references to Appendices
Ref map Sheet 27 K 24.a.3b.5.0.	1st.	1/40,000	Busy striking Camp & preparing to move forward. "A & D" Coys under Capt. E.L. M'Hardy left Camp in ST. ELOY area at 1 p.m. marched to L.33.c. area where they billeted in barns and old farmhouses. H.Q. "B" & "C" Coys left same Camp at 4 p.m. marched to Sheet 28. G.24.c.6.6. arriving at 10 p.m., not being enough accommodation here. "B" Coy. were billeted in an old Chinese Camp about 2 miles behind. Accommodation for H.Q. & "C" Coy. was roughly awful. Rations & Officers valises arrived at H.Q. about 2.30 a.m.	APP. 1. Rhr.
Sheet 28 G.24.c.6.6.	2nd.		Weather very hot. Quiet night, no shelling in our area. Very misty morning. Men busy trying to improve barns & billets. Very wet in afternoon, not one of the barns or shelters could keep out rain. Capt. Christison complained to 6th Division H.Q. and arrangements were made for us to move back to Chinese Camp.	Rhr.
Sheet 27 1/40,000 L.33.c.	2nd		In evening Bn. H.Q. & "C" Coy. moved back to Chinese Camp beside "B" Coy.	
Sheet 28 G.14.A.05.70	3rd.		Move complete about midnight. Quiet day. Weather very wet.	
Sheet 28 G.14.A.05.70 & L.33.c.	3rd		Quiet night. Slight shelling. Morning spent in cleaning up Camp and trying to make it habitable. Camp in a filthy mess. Working parties from Div. "A & D." In afternoon & at night on WESTOUTRE-GOED MOET MILL LNE. "A & D."	Rhr.

WAR DIARY

INTELLIGENCE SUMMARY. AUGUST 1918.

(Erase heading not required.)

Army Form C. 2118.

Place	Date	Hour	Summary of Events and Information	Remarks and references to Appendices
Sht 28 Ypres. G.16.A.05.70. & Sht 27. L.33.c.	3rd.		Coys. working on their own under B/Os. Bivouacs B. & C. Coys. under 6th Bivouac. Slight shelling of back areas during day. Weather fine.	Wlr.
	4th.		Quiet night. Little shelling. Small working parties by day, remainder working at night. Lt. Col. F. Anderson M.C. returns from leave to U.K. Weather fine.	Wlr.
			Little shelling round about during day. C.O. at Corps re Lithuanos Camp & arrangements made for one Coy. to move the following day.	
	5th		Shelling of back areas at night. Small working parties by day. Orders received for nearly all reinforcements to join 51st Division. Night working parties cancelled & arrangements made for draft parly to leave on 6th usual.	Wlr.
	6th.		Shelling of back areas by day. Weather fine. Shelling of back areas at night, one or two very near camp, no casualties. 310 ORs conducted by 6 Officers left for 51st Div. from B. & C. Coys. "A" & "D" Coys. paid. Heavy shelling of back areas during day. Weather very wet.	APP. 2 Wlr.
	7th.		Little shelling at night. 348 ORs conducted by 6 Officers left for 51st Div. from "A" & "D" Coys. Remainder of reinforcements cadre and Cadre Bn.	APP. 3 Wlr.

WAR DIARY

INTELLIGENCE SUMMARY. AUGUST 1915.

Army Form C. 2118.

Instructions regarding War Diaries and Intelligence Summaries are contained in F.S. Regs., Part II. and the Staff Manual respectively. Title pages will be prepared in manuscript.

Place	Date	Hour	Summary of Events and Information	Remarks and references to Appendices
Ref. map				
HAZEBROUCK 1/100.000	7th.		Entrain at REMY SIDING on light railway at 4.30 p.m. for LA CLOCHE arriving ESQUELBECQ Station about 8.15 p.m. Marching to billets in LA CLOCHE. Bn. in billets by 9.30 p.m. Weather fine.	Rhr.
HAZEBROUCK 1/20000 LA CLOCHE	8th.		Today spent in cleaning up, building necessary camp requisites. Men paid out. Orders arrive at night for remainder of reinforcements to 2.E. 90.59. proceed forthwith to join 5/106. Bn. Weather fine.	Rhr.
	9th.		Arrangements made for remainder of reinforcements to leave on 10th. Orders come in that 4/th. Cameron Highrs. have been placed at disposal of D.A.G. for reinforcements. Weather fine.	Rhr.
	10th.		The 4 Officers at 6th. Div. Reception Camp + 41 O.Rs. from no leave for 5/106. APP. to Bn. as reinforcements. All reinforcements now away, only 4th. Cameron Rhrs. Highrs. left. Weather very hot.	APP. to Rhr.
	11th.		Sunday. Very hot day. Men cleaning equipment.	Rhr.
	12th.		Orders arrive for us to return to 39th. Division and billets in LISTERGAUX. Weather very hot.	Rhr.
			Men busy cleaning up + preparing for move.	Rhr.

WAR DIARY

INTELLIGENCE SUMMARY. AUGUST 1918.

Army Form C. 2118.

(Erase heading not required.)

Instructions regarding War Diaries and Intelligence Summaries are contained in F. S. Regs., Part II. and the Staff Manual respectively. Title pages will be prepared in manuscript.

Place	Date	Hour	Summary of Events and Information	Remarks and references to Appendices
Ref. Map.				
HAZEBROUCK 1/100,000	13th.	8.30 a.m.	Leave LACLOCHE billets and march to ESQUELBECQ Station and entrain at 8.30 a.m. for AUDRUICQ. Transport by march route. Entrain at AUDRUICQ	APP. 5.
LISTERGAUX			for LISTERGAUX arriving about mid day. Same billets as we were in before.	RWm
2.A. 70.31.		1.30 p.m.	Receive orders at 1.30 p.m. that the 7th. Cameron Highrs. to be broken up & all officers Oks. to be sent as reinforcements to 6th. Bn. Lt. Col. Y. Anderson, M.C. receives orders to take over command of 8th. Seaforth Highrs. Busy arranging to hand in Ordnance Stores & to hand over Transport. Weather fine.	APP. 6
	14th.	11.30 a.m.	March from LISTERGAUX to AUDRUICQ and entrain at 11.30 a.m. for 15th. go straight on to ROUEN via ETAPLES. Adjutant & Orderly Room Sgt. go straight on to ROUEN BASE to wind up & check words.	RWm

RW Randall Major for Lt. Col.
Commanding 7th. Cameron Highrs.

Field
18.8.18.

www.ingramcontent.com/pod-product-compliance
Lightning Source LLC
Chambersburg PA
CBHW080825010526
44111CB00015B/2609